Ecology

ADVANCED
BIOLOGY

Ecology

ADVANCED
BIOLOGY
READERS

Peter
Chenn

**JOHN
MURRAY**

Other titles in this series:
Microorganisms & Biotechnology   0 7195 7509 5

First published in 1999
by John Murray (Publishers) Ltd
50 Albemarle Street
London W1X 4BD

Layouts by Janet McCallum
Illustrations by Mike Humphries
Cover design by John Townson, Creation

Typeset in 11.5/13pt Goudy by Wearset, Boldon, Tyne and Wear
Printed and bound in Great Britain by Alden Press, Osney Mead, Oxford

A catalogue entry for this title is available from the British Library

ISBN 0 7195 7510 9

Contents

Introduction

Ecology is the branch of biology that makes a formal study of relationships between organisms and their environment. It has grown from what was virtually an unheard of science before the 1960s to a commonly used household word. It is an interdisciplinary science that tries to establish patterns in the balance of nature and predict how the biological systems that control nature are likely to be affected by change.

Ecology begins by defining the fundamental concepts and builds up to the broader picture through chapters on energy flow, biogeochemical cycles, factors affecting distribution, ecological interactions as well as communities and succession, before looking at human influences and conservation. The final chapter provides guidance on the practical aspects of ecology.

Ecology is aimed at A level students of mixed ability. To the A level student taking the Ecology unit/option, this book is intended to be enjoyable to read, as well as being informative, interesting, concise and up-to-date. There are data interpretation questions from recent examinations at the end of each chapter.

Advanced Biology Readers is a new series written to support a range of A level Biology options that extend the coverage in traditional textbooks. Ecology is the latest addition to this series by Peter Chenn, which includes *Microorganisms and Biotechnology*.

Acknowledgements

I owe my greatest debt to the numerous ecologists and researchers who have contributed to the *New Scientist, Scientific American* and *Biological Sciences Review*; without their work this book would not have been possible. My thanks to Sally Morgan for writing Chapter 9. I am also indebted to Chris Clegg, co-author of *Advanced Biology: Principles and Applications*, for reading the manuscript and for his very useful suggestions during the preparation of this book. I would also like to express my thanks to the entire team at John Murray, especially Katie Mackenzie Stuart (Science Publisher) for her guidance, encouragement and patience and, not least, my family.

Exam questions

Exam questions have been reproduced with kind permission from the following examination boards:
Associated Examining Board (AEB)
London Examinations, a division of Edexcel Foundation (formerly ULEAC)
Northern Examinations Assessment Board (NEAB)
Oxford and Cambridge Schools Examination Board (OCSEB)
University of Cambridge Local Examinations Syndicate (UCLES)
University of Oxford Delegacy of Local Examinations (UODLE)

Source acknowledgements

The following are sources from which artwork and data has been adapted:

Figure 3.2, p.23 Robert A. Berner & Antonio C. Lasaga 'Modelling the geochemical carbon cycle' *Scientific American* (March 1989) page 56
Figure 5.11, p.84 Eugene P. Odum *Ecology* (1963) Figure 6-4, page 99 (Holt, Rinehart & Winston, New York)
Figure 5.13, p.88 E.J. Hatfield *An Introduction to Biology* (1963) Figure 45 page 148 (Oxford University Press, Oxford)
Figure 7.10, p.127 John Lee 'Acid rain' *Biological Sciences Review* (September 1988) page 15
Figure 9.1, p.185 Gareth Williams *Techniques in Fieldwork and Ecology* (1987) Figures 2.3–2.5 page 12 (Bell & Hyman, London)
Figure 9.2, p.187 Gareth Williams *Techniques in Fieldwork and Ecology* (1987) Figures 2.13 page 16 (Bell & Hyman, London)
Figure 9.3, p.188 Gareth Williams *Techniques in Fieldwork and Ecology* (1987) Figures 3.22 page 50 (Bell & Hyman, London)
Figure 9.4, p.191 Gareth Williams *Techniques in Fieldwork and Ecology* (1987) Figures 2.31 page 28 (Bell & Hyman, London)
Figure 9.5, p.191 Gareth Williams *Techniques in Fieldwork and Ecology* (1987) Figures 2.32 page 28 (Bell & Hyman, London)
Figure 9.7, p.192 Gareth Williams *Techniques in Fieldwork and Ecology* (1987) Figures 4.22 page 66 (Bell & Hyman, London)

Figure 9.8, p.192 Gareth Williams *Techniques in Fieldwork and Ecology* (1987) Figures 4.24 page 66 (Bell & Hyman, London)
p.202 Data for worked example from the Field Studies Council
p.203 Data for worked example from the Field Studies Council

Photo credits

Thanks are due to the following for permission to reproduce copyright photographs:

Cover Mark Martin/Planet Earth Pictures; **p.2** *t* Astrid & Hanns-Frieder Michler/ Science Photo Library, *b* Richard Herrmann/Oxford Scientific Films; **p.3** Vanessa Miles/Environmental Images; **p.5** Harold Taylor ABIPP/Oxford Scientific Films; **p.8** Claude Nuridsany & Marie Perennon/Science Photo Library; **p.29** Jean-Loup Charmet/Science Photo Library; **p.31** Dr Jeremy Burgess/Science Photo Library; **p.34** Mike Magnuson/Tony Stone Images; **p.43** Science Service; **p.49** Heather Angel/Biofotos; **p.51** *t* David Thompson/Oxford Scientific Films, *b* Paul van Gaalen/Bruce Coleman; **p.57** Mark Edwards/Still Pictures; **p.61** Heather Angel/ Biofotos; **p.66** B & C Alexander/NHPA; **p.69** G.I. Bernard/Oxford Scientific Films; **p.72** Sinclair Stammers/Science Photo Library; **p.75** E & D Hosking/FLPA; **p.77** Holt Studios International; **p.79** Paul Kay/Oxford Scientific Films; **p.80** UNEP/ Benard/Topham; **p.82** Mark Hamblin/Oxford Scientific Films; **p.89** Sinclair Stammers/Science Photo Library; **p.90** London Scientific Films/Oxford Scientific Films; **p.95** Staffan Widstrand/Bruce Coleman; **p.96** Heather Angel/Biofotos; **p.99** Martin Withers/FLPA; **p.100** *all* © Dr O.L. Gilbert; **p.103** Steven Meyers/Ardea; **p.105** *l* Roger Tidman/FLPA, *r* Gerald Cubitt/Bruce Coleman; **p.106** M. Kavanagh/ Survival Anglia/Oxford Scientific Films; **p.108** François Gohier/Ardea; **p.109** A. Greensmith/Ardea; **p.110** *t* John Murray/Bruce Coleman, *b* Charles & Sandra Hood/Bruce Coleman; **p.115** Brian Rogers/Biofotos; **p.117** Tony Morrison/South American Pictures; **p.119** Jean-Paul Ferrero/Ardea; **p.120** Mark Edwards/Still Pictures; **p.121** Mark Edwards/Still Pictures; **p.123** J.C. Allen/FLPA; **p.124** Toby Adamson/Environmental Images; **p.126** David Hoffman/Still Pictures; **p.129** *t* OSOA/Science Photo Library, *b* Mark Edwards/Still Pictures; **p.132** Mark Edwards/Still Pictures; **p.133** F. Polking/FLPA; **p.136** Mark Wagner/Tony Stone Images; **p.137** Nello Giambi/Tony Stone Images; **p.138** © Greenpeace/Morgan; **p.139** Dr Roy Clark & Mervyn De Calcinagoff/Science Photo Library; **p.140** George Morbiot/Still Pictures; **p.142** John Lancalosi/Bruce Coleman; **p.144** D. Burrows/Liaison/Gamma/Frank Spooner Pictures; **p.146** Dr Jeremy Burgess/ Science Photo Library; **p.149** John Edwards/Tony Stone Images; **p.151** SIPA/Rex Features; **p.153** Thomas Raupach/Still Pictures; **p.154** Matthew McVay/Tony Stone Images; **p.155** John Frost Historical Newspaper Service; **p.158** John Giles/PA News Photo Library; **p.164** Paul Chesley/Tony Stone Images; **p.165** *t* Barry Peake/Rex Features, *b* © Steve Forrest/Guzelian; **p.166** Edward Parker/Still Pictures; **p.167** Ted Wood/Tony Stone Images; **p.168** Irene R. Lengui/Environmental Images; **p.171** Peter Scoones/Planet Earth Pictures; **p.173** *t* Richard Packwood/Oxford Scientific Films, *b* Rex Features; **p.174** Jagdeep Rajput/Planet Earth Pictures;

p.176 Michael Major/Holt Studios; **p.177** Gerald Cubitt/Bruce Coleman; **p.178** © Dylan Garcia; **p.179** UPEN/Supakit Tiyawatchalapong/Topham; **p.181** Vanessa Miles/Environmental Images; **p.191** Robin Redfern/Oxford Scientific Films.

(t = top, b = bottom, r = right, l = left)

The publishers have made every effort to contact copyright holders. If any have been inadvertently overlooked they will make the necessary arrangements at the earliest opportunity.

Ecology and its fundamental concepts

Ecology is the study of living organisms in relation to their environment. The term **ecology** was coined by a German zoologist named Ernst Haeckel in 1866 from two Greek words, *oikos* meaning 'dwelling place' or 'house' and *logos* meaning 'study'. Haeckel used it to refer to the web of interrelationships that link organisms with their environment.

   Ecology is an interdisciplinary science. Besides observations and experimentation, ecologists may bring together data from a variety of sources for analysis and integration with a view to predicting and comprehending the balance of nature. Given that every sexually reproducing individual in a population is genetically unique and that every observable response is a result of interactions between many variables, the task is indeed daunting. Unlike the natural historian, who tends to make careful records of small differences between organisms, ecologists adopt what is known as a *holistic approach* by emphasising the overall picture and minimising species-specific details. In some respects, ecology is comparable to economics. In economics, although individuals manage their own finances in accordance with their own personal needs, the economist may be called upon to pronounce on future trends in the economy of the nation as a whole. Similarly, in ecology, ecologists may be required to make broad predictions on how biological systems that control nature are likely to be affected by environmental changes.

Some fundamental concepts in ecology

In their search for patterns in the balance of nature and in trying to explain the causal processes that underlie them, ecologists use a number of concepts such as **environment, habitat, niche, community, biosphere, ecosystem** and so on. Most people have some idea of their meaning but it is probably useful to start by defining exactly what they mean.

Environment

Environment means surroundings. An organism's immediate environment is the physical and chemical conditions that impinge on its external surface. However, organisms are not affected only by their immediate surroundings but also by events or conditions beyond the area of immediate contact with their body surface. For example, a wall may cast its shadow over a seedling and thus affect its growth. Similarly, a lion within striking distance of a deer will undoubtedly affect the smaller animal's behaviour. When ecologists speak about the environment, they are therefore referring to the sum total of the external factors or influences that directly or indirectly affect the life of an individual or community.

Habitat

Another commonly used ecological term is **habitat**. It refers to the characteristic physical locality in which specified organisms live. For example, the habitat of sand crabs is a sandy seashore because that is where sand crabs can typically be found.

Unlike the concept of the environment, which is essentially abstract and which extends outwards, without any boundary, as a three-dimensional space with the organism at its centre, habitats have real existence with a definite geographical locality and a definite boundary. Common examples of habitats include a pond, a rock pool, a woodland, a meadow, and so on.

Microhabitat

Different species of organisms tend to distribute themselves in accordance with their specialist needs. In a forest habitat, for example, caterpillars will be found inhabiting the canopy of trees. Certain insect larvae will be found living in the crevices beneath the bark of living tree trunks while other types can be found beneath rotting logs on the forest floor. The term **microhabitat** is used to refer to subdivisions of a habitat such as tree canopy, leaf-litter zone, rotting logs, water holes, and so on. In general, different groups of organisms occupy different types of microhabitats.

Figure 1.1 The cracks in the bark of the tree provide a moist microhabitat for these woodlice

Niche

Most dictionaries define a **niche** as a place which is specially adapted for its occupant. Ecologists use the term **niche** to refer to the way of life of an organism in its natural surroundings. It is a description of *where* and *how* an organism lives, what factors affect it and how it affects other members of the community. It is an important concept because it defines the precise conditions a species needs for survival.

Consider, for example, horses, cows, bison and giraffes. All are herbivores, but the first three occupy fairly similar niches in their natural habitats and would compete with one another if put together on the same grassland habitat. Cows and giraffes, on the other hand, occupy somewhat different niches because one is a grazer and the other is a browser.

Figure 1.2 The niche of a shark is that of 'top' predator in this marine ecosystem

An ecological niche is, in other words, primarily a description of an organism's feeding behaviour or functional role in the ecosystem. For example, in a marine ecosystem, the niche of a shark is that of 'top' aquatic predator. The 'top predator' niche on the plains of Africa is filled by lions. Similarly, there is a niche in any ecosystem for scavengers which, in coral reefs, is filled by crabs because they are the ones that will eat up scraps of food. On land, the scavenger niche is filled by vultures, among others.

Where an organism lives can also play a key role in determining the type of niche it occupies. Tawny owls and kestrels, for example, are both birds of prey but tawny owls feed on mice and shrews in oak woodland habitats and do not compete with kestrels, which occupy a similar niche on open grasslands.

Species

A **species** may be defined as any group of organisms, sharing a large number of common features, which are capable of interbreeding but not with members of other similarly defined groups.

Population

A **population** consists of a group of organisms of the same species living in a definite area within a limited framework of time. The members of a population normally interbreed except in rare cases where they reproduce only asexually. The boundaries of a population are often indistinct, in which case, for study purposes, an arbitrary decision is made with respect to its boundaries.

Community

An **ecological community** consists of all the organisms living within a defined area or habitat and which, in various ways, affect one another. Each ecological community is made up of two or more populations. A forest community, for example, comprises different types of green plants – dominant trees, shrubs, non-woody herbaceous plants, various climbers and creepers and a variety of animals. The plants provide food, shelter and shade for the herbivorous animals such as squirrels, caterpillars, plant bugs, stick insects, grasshoppers, and so on. The herbivores are preyed upon by various carnivores such as hawks, snakes, lizards. A community will also have its share of parasites, scavengers and saprophytes. In general, communities that consist of an abundance of plant life will also support an abundance of animal

Figure 1.3 An ecological community consists of all the organisms living within a defined area

life and communities comprising a rich diversity of plant species will support a rich diversity of animal species.

Ecologists can usually predict the species content of a community from the dominant vegetation of the community. For example, if the dominant vegetation consists of a stand of red mangroves, one can be fairly certain that the habitat will be populated by fiddler crabs, mud-skippers and a variety of gastropod molluscs. Such predictability justifies the practice of naming communities after their dominant vegetation (e.g. oak forest).

Biome

Communities that extend over large geographical areas are known as **biomes**. The more important biomes of the world include:

1 **tropical rain forests** – these cover the low-lying regions near the equator and are described in detail in Chapter 6
2 **temperate deciduous forests** – these comprise trees that shed their leaves during winter. They occupy vast areas of North America, western Europe and eastern Asia where the climate is fairly moderate, with some snow during winter
3 **boreal or coniferous forests** – these occupy a broad belt across North America and Euroasia where the winters are relatively severe. Conifers are typically conical in shape with leaves that are small and stiff. They do not shed their leaves in winter and are said to be evergreen
4 **tundra** – this is a broad, treeless belt sandwiched between the polar ice caps and the great boreal forests where the soil is frozen for much of the year and the growing season is too short for trees. The vegetation of the tundra consists mostly of small or dwarfed, mat-like grasses and sedges
5 **temperate grasslands** – these include the prairies and plains of North America, the steppes of Euroasia, the pampas of Argentina and the veld of South Africa. The dominant vegetation consists of various types of grasses, legumes and members of the Compositae family (e.g. sunflower).

Aquatic biomes

Besides the terrestrial biomes, there are a number of aquatic biomes. These may be broadly subdivided into two groups – **freshwater** and **marine**. The freshwater biomes include **lentic** communities of lakes and ponds and the **lotic** communities that are characteristic of running water (e.g. streams). The marine biomes include the **shoreline** communities of sandy and rocky shores, **coral reefs** (described in detail in Chapter 6), **marshes** and the **bentic** communities that live on the seabed.

Biosphere

The **biosphere** is the thin outer shell of the Earth which is inhabited by living organisms. It includes the entire global community of living organisms and the physical and chemical environment in which they live. It is the largest and most nearly self-sustaining unit known to humans. Ecologists view the biosphere as divided into smaller subunits called ecosystems.

Ecosystem

An **ecosystem** is a stable unit of nature consisting of a community of organisms interacting with one another and with their physical and chemical environment. Examples of ecosystems include a pond, a lake, a forest, a grassland, a seashore. A forest ecosystem, for example, consists not just of a stand of trees but a complex of abiotic (non-living) and biotic (living) components such as the soil, air, water, minerals, the climate, bacteria, fungi, herbaceous plants, insects, reptiles, birds and so on.

A close examination of an ecosystem reveals that it is made up of five main components. These are the:

1 **abiotic component** – the inorganic substances involved in mineral cycling as well as the climatic regime such as temperature, rainfall, light intensity, wind and other environmental factors
2 **producers** – mainly the green plants
3 **consumers** – the herbivores, carnivores and omnivores
4 **agents of decay** – bacteria of decay, fungi and a variety of invertebrate animals
5 **organic compounds** – these form a link between the biotic (living) and the abiotic (non-living) sectors of the ecosystem.

Figure 1.4 The abiotic, organic and living components of an ecosystem are often inexorably intermixed and intertwined as in this forest habitat

The various components of the ecosystem are inexorably intermixed and intertwined, having evolved together over billions of years. The oxygen in the air, for example, which the animals need for respiration, is derived from the splitting of water molecules during photosynthesis by green plants. Similarly, the organic molecules that make up the body of the animals are derived from organic compounds originally elaborated by the plants from inorganic raw materials present in the abiotic component of the ecosystem. The dynamics of energy flow through the ecosystem associated with the need for food is described in Chapter 2.

Questions

1 Distinguish between the following:
   a habitat and niche
   b population and community
   c ecosystem and biosphere.
2 What do you understand by the term **ecosystem**? Illustrate your answer by reference to a *named* habitat.

Examination question

1 a State what is meant by the word *ecology*. (1)
  b The following terms are often used by ecologists. Provide a brief explanation of the meaning of each:
    i) population (2)
    ii) community (2)
    iii) ecosystem (2)
    iv) niche. (1)

(total = 8)

O & C, June 1996

The flow of energy through ecosystems

2

The essence of life is activity. To carry out the many and varied activities of life, all organisms need a supply of energy. The energy that sustains life is the energy of sunlight trapped by photosynthetic organisms (mainly green plants) and converted into chemical energy in organic food molecules.

Producers

Plants, algae and a few types of bacteria are the only organisms capable of trapping the energy of sunlight for conversion into the chemical energy of organic food molecules. Ecologists refer to them collectively as **producers** because they provide food not only for themselves but for virtually all other organisms.

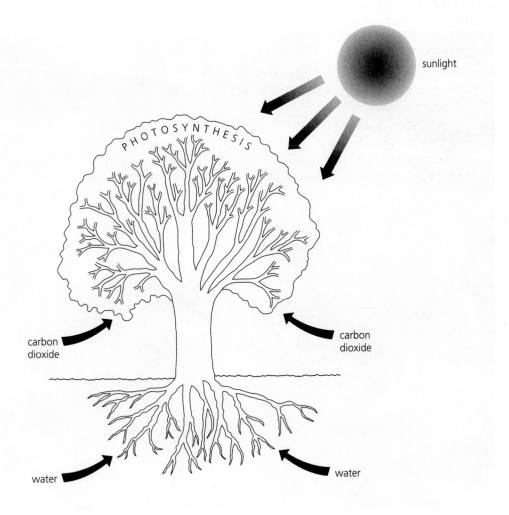

Figure 2.1 Producers make their own organic food molecules by photosynthesis

Consumers

Unlike plants, animals cannot capture solar energy for conversion into a form which they can use. To meet their energy and most of their material requirements, animals must eat plants or other organisms that ate plants. The term **consumer** is used to refer to organisms that must meet their energy requirements by ingesting other organisms or organic matter derived ultimately from plants.

Among the consumers, there are those that feed directly on plant tissues. These are known as **primary**, or **first order consumers** or **herbivores**. Examples include grasshoppers, caterpillars, bees, snails and deer. Carnivores that feed on herbivores are known as **secondary** or **second order consumers**. Examples include ladybird beetles, centipedes, frogs, starlings and shrews. By feeding on herbivores, these secondary consumers are making use of energy originally stored in organic molecules synthesised by plants. **Tertiary** or **third order consumers** are large carnivores that feed on smaller carnivores. Examples include snakes, hawks, monitor lizards, foxes and sharks.

Figure 2.2 Large carnivores, such as the lizard shown above, feed on smaller carnivores

Decomposers

When an organism dies, its body soon decomposes, unless it is immediately consumed by scavengers. The term **decomposer** is used to refer to organisms, mainly bacteria and fungi, that obtain their energy by breaking down dead organic matter. Decomposers play a very useful role in promoting the leaching of minerals by rain and water from dead tissues and the re-use of these minerals by plants.

Decomposers, in the form of bacterial and fungal spores, are found nearly everywhere. They are often present on the surface of organisms even before they die. They feed on sugars and amino acids that diffuse out of the dead cells and are usually the first colonisers of a dead body. These early colonisers lack the enzymes for breaking down organic compounds which are more resistant to digestive breakdown such as cellulose, lignin, suberin and cutin.

Fungi are generally better adapted than bacteria for breaking down plant matter. Their thread-like hyphae are ideally suited for penetrating into dead tissues. Many fungi also possess enzymes for breaking down cellulose and other structurally complex molecules. Bacteria, on the other hand, thrive in environments lacking oxygen such as within the gut of animals and among the detritus at the bottom of ponds and lakes. They are also important agents of decomposition in places where animal activities are likely to break up fungal hyphae.

Microbivores

The term **microbivore** is used to refer to minute invertebrate animals that feed by ingesting bacteria, fungi and other microorganisms. Common examples include nematode worms, rotifers and free-living unicellular organisms such as *Amoeba* and *Paramecium*. Microbivores feed on living organisms and are not agents of decomposition. They are closely associated with the detrital compartment of ecosystems and are the main predators of the decomposers. They play an important role in preventing aerobic bacterial populations from growing too rapidly and depleting the dissolved oxygen content of their watery surroundings.

Detritivores

The term **detritivore** is used to refer to a variety of invertebrate animals that feed by ingesting bits of dead plant and animal matter, thus promoting decomposition by shredding organic matter so that the surface area for enzyme activity increases. Common examples include earthworms, termites, mites, springtails, blowfly larvae and millipedes. Vast numbers and a rich variety of detritivores occur in temperate, terrestrial ecosystems where the soil is moist and rich in organic matter. There are generally fewer detritivores in the hot, drier terrestrial ecosystems of the tropics because the higher temperature allows a faster rate of decomposition of organic matter by bacteria and fungi.

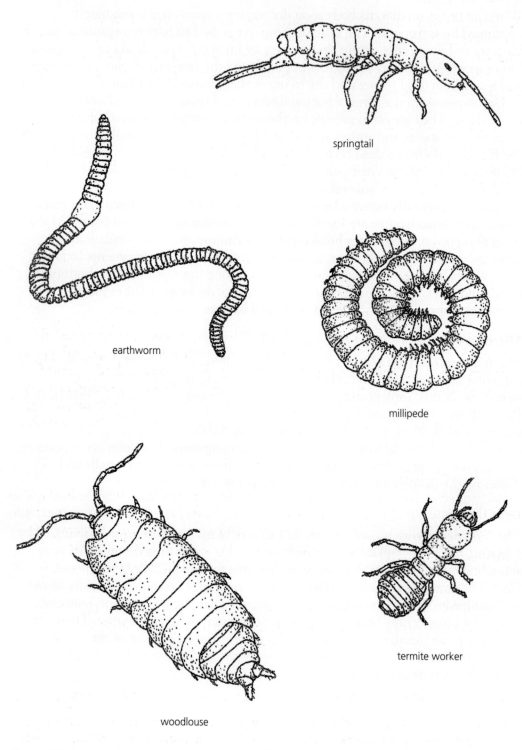

springtail

earthworm

millipede

woodlouse

termite worker

Figure 2.3 Some common examples of detritivores (not drawn to the same size)

Food chains

Each time food is consumed, energy and materials are transferred from the food to the feeder. A **food chain** consists of a series of organisms through which energy and materials are passed as each organism provides food for the next organism in the sequence. Two basic types of food chains are recognised. These are (i) grazing and (ii) detrital food chains.

Grazing food chains

In a grazing (or herbivore) food chain, the primary consumer feeds on the living tissues of plants (or on plant sap) and energy is transferred from living plants to grazing animals and then to carnivores. For example:

1 grass ⟶ rabbit ⟶ fox
2 foliage leaves ⟶ caterpillar ⟶ starling ⟶ hawk
3 nectar ⟶ butterfly ⟶ flycatcher ⟶ kite
4 phytoplankton ⟶ zooplankton ⟶ minnow ⟶ pike

or, *in general,*

$$\text{plant} \longrightarrow \text{herbivore} \longrightarrow \text{carnivore}_1 \longrightarrow \text{carnivore}_2$$

Grazing animals consume on average about 15% of the available plant tissues in terrestrial ecosystems. The rest of the plant matter, such as leaves, twigs, and so on, together with faecal matter, nitrogenous excretory wastes and the dead bodies of animals, falls to the ground to enter detrital food chains. In aquatic ecosystems, on the other hand, due to the water buoyancy, plants do not require tough supporting tissues and the bulk of the plant matter is efficiently consumed by herbivores with little left over for the detritivores.

Detrital food chains

Dead organic matter is a source of food for a variety of organisms that live in the soil or in the detritus at the bottom of ponds or lakes. Examples of organisms that exploit this source of energy in forest ecosystems include bacteria, fungi, mites, springtails, termites, woodlice, various insect larvae, earthworms and millipedes. These detrivores are in turn eaten by carnivores. Examples of decomposer/detrital food chains include:

1 dead rat ⟶ blowfly maggot ⟶ ground beetle ⟶ frog ⟶ viper
2 dead leaves ⟶ earthworm ⟶ toad ⟶ grass snake ⟶ eagle
3 dung ⟶ dung beetle ⟶ guinea fowl ⟶ civet

or, *in general,*

dead organic matter ⟶ invertebrate detritivore ⟶ carnivore_1 ⟶ carnivore_2

Many detritivores do not feed exclusively on dead organic matter. Some, for example nematodes, feed on dead organic matter as well as the living roots of plants. Others feed opportunistically on whatever food is available.

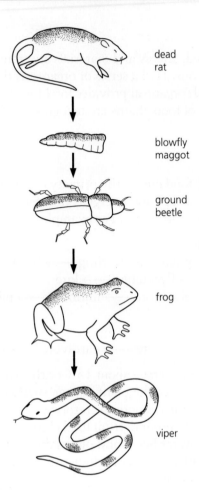

dead
rat

blowfly
maggot

ground
beetle

frog

viper

Figure 2.4 A food chain

Food webs

Within any single ecosystem, there are usually many different types of plants and several types of herbivores and carnivores. Most herbivores can utilise more than one type of plant as a food source and most carnivores can vary their diet and exploit an alternative prey should their main food source become scarce. Some organisms will, therefore, appear in more than one food chain. To complicate matters further, some organisms may be primary consumers in one food chain and secondary consumers in another. The feeding relationships in any one ecosystem are in fact much more intricate than just a series of separate food chains. There are in reality many cross linkages between food chains. It would, therefore, be more appropriate to think of an organism as a part of a complex **food web** rather than as a link in a single straight chain. An example of a food web comprising several interlinked food chains for a freshwater pond ecosystem is illustrated in Figure 2.5.

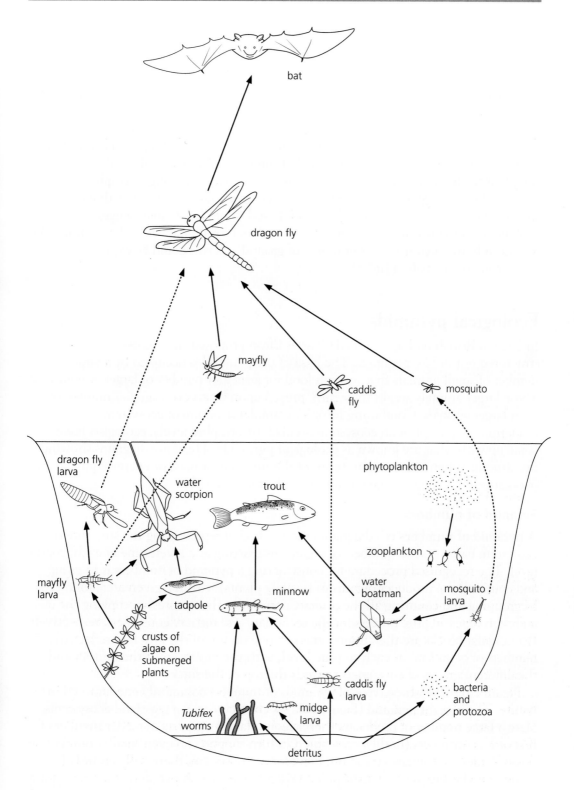

Figure 2.5 A food web for a freshwater pond ecosystem

Trophic levels

An American named Raymond Linderman, who died of liver disease at the age of 26, wrote in a paper published after his death in 1942 that ecosystems could be understood by tracing the flow of energy through them. In Linderman's view, plants, regardless of species, could be put in one group called **trophic** (or **feeding**) **level 1** because their energy has been transferred once, namely from the Sun to the plant. All types of herbivores comprise another group called **trophic level 2** because their energy has been transferred twice, namely from the Sun to the plant and again from the plant to the herbivore. Carnivores that eat herbivores belong to **trophic level 3** because their energy has been transferred three times. Large carnivores that eat smaller carnivores belong to **trophic level 4**, and so on. Linderman suggested that ecologists could measure the energy content of each trophic level by determining the weight of living organisms per unit area of ground and this could be expressed in units of energy (usually $kJ\,m^{-2}$).

Ecological pyramids

In 1927, a British biologist named Charles Elton proposed that ecosystems are structured not unlike pyramids. The base of the pyramid is occupied by a large number of small animals that serve as food for a smaller number of larger animals. These larger animals are, in their turn, preyed upon by an even smaller number of even larger animals. Combining Elton's pyramidal structure of ecosystems with Linderman's concept of an ecosystem divided into trophic levels, ecologists have come up with what are known as **ecological pyramids**. These are diagrams showing the structure of an ecosystem in terms of the numbers or mass or energy equivalents of organisms existing in a given time at each trophic level.

Pyramid of numbers

A **pyramid of numbers** is a diagrammatic method of representing the structure of an ecosystem based on the numbers of organisms existing at a given time at each trophic level. The recognised procedure for constructing a pyramid of numbers is to group and count all the producer organisms (usually plants) within a given area, followed by grouping and counting all the primary consumers (herbivores) occupying the area and then repeating the process for the secondary and tertiary consumers, respectively. Rectangular blocks are then drawn, stacked one on top of the other, to reflect the numbers of organisms at each trophic level, with the producers at the bottom and the different grades of consumers towards the top of the stack.

Figure 2.6 shows three types of pyramids of numbers commonly encountered in nature. The upright pyramid (Figure 2.6a) is characteristic of grassland ecosystems. Here a large number of producers (herbaceous plants) supports a smaller number of first order consumers (herbivores) which in turn supports an even smaller number of second order consumers, and so on. For a forest ecosystem, there will certainly be many more herbivores (e.g. caterpillars) than large trees. A pyramid of numbers for a forest ecosystem (Figure 2.6b) will have a narrow base, but it will otherwise have a normal pyramidal shape. The third type, which is the inverted pyramid of numbers (Figure 2.6c), is characteristic of parasitic food chains. It is typically encountered when an investigation is carried out on a plantation of fruit trees (hosts) that are infested with leaf-eating caterpillars (parasites) that are themselves parasitised by, for example, mites (hyperparasites).

The main drawback with these pyramids of numbers is that no allowance is made for differences in size between individual organisms. Producers ranging in size from microscopic algae to giant Californian redwood trees are all dealt with in terms of numbers of individuals present. This severely limits the usefulness of pyramids of numbers. They are, however, relatively easy to construct.

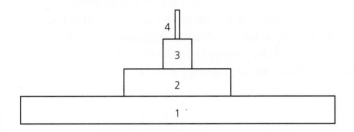

4 = top carnivores, e.g. fox

3 = carnivores, e.g. pheasant

2 = herbivores, e.g. grasshopper

1 = producers, e.g. grass

a Terrestrial grassland ecosystems

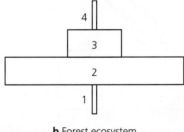

4 = top carnivores, e.g. hawk

3 = carnivores, e.g. blackbird

2 = herbivores, e.g. caterpillar

1 = producers, e.g. oak tree

b Forest ecosystem

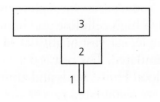

3 = hyperparasites, e.g. mites

2 = parasites/pests, e.g. caterpillars

1 = producers, e.g. apple tree

c Inverted pyramid, e.g. apple orchard

Figure 2.6 Three types of pyramid of numbers

Pyramids of biomass

Pyramids of biomass take into account size differences between organisms because they are based on measurements of the mass of all the living organisms in a given area, sorted out into trophic levels. Biomass measurements are usually expressed as living or dry mass per unit area (e.g. kg per hectare). Parts, such as dead leaves, that have fallen off and are no longer attached to the body of the living organisms are not included in biomass measurements but non-living tissues such as wood are included.

A typical energy transfer efficiency of 10%

Pyramids of biomass are typically upright, with the mass of producers exceeding the mass of herbivores, which in turn exceeds the mass of the carnivores. A useful generalisation that emerges from studies based on pyramids of biomass is that there is an energy transfer efficiency between trophic levels which is typically 10%. What this means is that, on average, only 10% of the energy that enters a trophic level gets passed on to the next level. There are three main reasons for this:

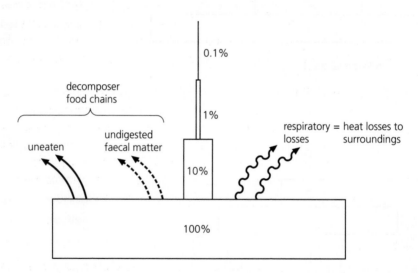

Figure 2.7 Only about 10% of the energy is passed on to the next trophic level

1 Only a portion of the food that is eaten is used for new tissue production. The rest is used for respiratory purposes, for movement and for carrying out the various metabolic reactions essential for sustaining life.
2 Not all the food that is eaten is assimilated. Some passes through as undigested material in the faeces. In general, foods with a high cellulose and lignin content are poorly assimilated. Caterpillars, for example, eat vast quantities of foliage but only about 14% of their ingested food is assimilated. The rest is defecated to serve as food for detritivores living on the forest floor. Fruits, seeds and animal tissues are, in general, relatively easy to digest and are assimilated to a greater extent.
3 Some plants (and animals) escape being eaten by predators by employing various chemical or physical defences against predation. Their dead remains eventually enter detritivore/decomposer food chains.

Why most food chains are fairly short

A consequence of the '10% rule' is that there will rarely be enough residual energy left in a food chain for it to have more than just four or five links. It also explains why in a community of organisms, plants are the most abundant, herbivores are next in order of abundance and why there are relatively few top carnivores such as eagles, lions and killer whales. It also accounts for the fact that the top carnivores must search far and wide for their prey and why no animal specialises in eating them.

The inverted pyramid of biomass

Although pyramids of biomass are usually upright, exceptions do occur. A notable exception is the pyramid of biomass for an open-water ecosystem where the biomass of zooplankton exceeds that of the phytoplankton that they consume. One is naturally led to ask, 'How can this be possible?' The answer lies in the small size and fast turnover rate of the phytoplankton.

A small organism has a larger surface area to volume ratio than a larger organism. Because of their small size, phytoplankton are capable of absorbing nutrients from their surroundings efficiently. This allows them to grow fast and multiply quickly. As soon as one lot of algal cells are eaten by the zooplankton, another lot are produced by cell division to replace them.

The inverted pyramid of biomass arises because pyramids of biomass give a 'snap-shot' view of conditions existing in an ecosystem at a given instant in time. The fact is that there is nothing in biomass measurements which says how fast new materials are being added or, conversely, how rapidly existing materials are being consumed. It is a major omission. For example, two populations with the same biomass measurements could appear to be in the same state and yet be quite different because one could be growing rapidly and the other slowly or even declining.

Pyramids of energy

An obvious way of overcoming the omission would be to construct pyramids based on the rate of inflow of energy to each trophic level. Such pyramids are known as **pyramids of energy**. They are diagrams or charts showing the amount of energy consumed at each trophic level per unit of land or water per unit time (expressed usually in kilojoules per square metre per year). There are not many examples, however, because of difficulties in gathering such data. The pyramid of energy shown in Figure 2.8 is based on data obtained by an ecologist named Howard T. Odum from a study of a river ecosystem in Silver Springs, Florida, USA in 1957.

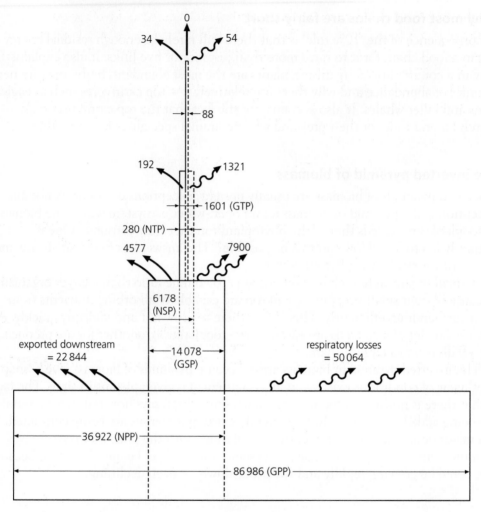

figures are in kJ m⁻² yr⁻¹   G = gross   N = net   PP = primary productivity
SP = secondary productivity   TP = tertiary productivity

Figure 2.8 Pyramid of energy for a river ecosystem at Silver Springs, Florida, USA (based on data obtained from Howard T. Odum)

Odum found that the plants in the river ecosystem were producing organic matter by photosynthesis at the rate of 86 986 kJ m^{-2} yr^{-1}. The term **gross primary productivity (GPP)** is used to refer to the rate of production of organic matter by photosynthesis. Odum's measurements showed that approximately 57% of the GPP (50 064 kJ) was used by the plants for their own respiratory requirements. This portion of the energy was ultimately converted to heat and reradiated to the surroundings and was clearly not available for transfer to the next trophic level. The rest of the GPP was either stored or utilised by the plants for new tissue production and is known as the **net primary productivity (NPP)**. This portion of the captured energy (36 922 kJ) is potentially available for consumption by primary consumers. Odum found that approximately 62% of the NPP (22 844 kJ) became plant debris which was carried downstream to enter detrital or decomposer food chains. Herbivores consumed the remaining 38% (14 078 kJ m^{-2} yr^{-1}). The term **gross secondary productivity (GSP)** is used to refer to the total amount of organic matter assimilated by herbivores from their food.

Odum found that respiratory losses from the herbivores accounted for 56% of the GSP leaving a **net secondary productivity (NSP)** amounting to 6178 kJ m^{-2} yr^{-1}. This gives an efficiency of energy transfer from producers to first order consumers of 17% calculated in the following way:

$$\text{Efficiency of energy transfer} = \text{NSP} \div \text{NPP} \times 100$$
$$= 6178 \div 36\,922 \times 100$$
$$= 17\%$$

Taking the 'typical' energy transfer efficiency as 10%, this is higher than 'typical' but not surprisingly because aquatic plants lack woody tissues and are generally composed of highly digestible materials.

Odum found that 74% of the NSP (4577 kJ m^{-2} yr^{-1}) was carried downstream as dead organic matter to be taken up by the detritivore/decomposer food chains. Second order consumers (carnivores) ate the rest which amounted to 1601 kJ m^{-2} yr^{-1} and which is known as the **gross tertiary productivity (GTP)**. Of this energy, 1321 kJ was used up in carnivore respiration leaving only 280 kJ m^{-2} yr^{-1} as **net tertiary productivity (NTP)**. This is only 4.5% of the NSP.

Efficiency of energy transfer from primary consumer to secondary consumer
$$= \text{NTP} \div \text{NSP} \times 100$$
$$= 280 \div 6178 \times 100$$
$$= 4.5\%$$

It is only roughly 'half-typical' and is characteristic of carnivores that expend a lot of their energy chasing their prey.

Of the 280 kJ m^{-2} yr^{-1} of energy which is potentially available for transfer to tertiary consumers, 192 kJ was exported downriver as dead organic matter. The top carnivores consumed the rest (88 kJ m^{-2} yr^{-1}). Of this energy, 54 kJ was accounted for by respiratory losses and 34 kJ was accounted for by death and decay of the top carnivores, leaving no more energy for transfer to a higher trophic level.

Questions

1 What is a food chain?
2 Give an example of a food chain with at least four links for a *named* ecosystem.
3 Explain why the number of links in a food chain seldom exceeds five or six.
4 Define the term **net primary productivity**.
5 How may the activity of decomposers increase net primary productivity?
6 Write an essay on 'The flow of energy through an ecosystem'.
7 Giving *named* examples, write an account describing a typical food web in a freshwater pond.

Examination questions

1 a The diagram below is a simple representation of a *pyramid of numbers.*

i) What do you understand by this term? (2)

ii) In each of the boxes to the right of the diagram, write the scientific or precise common name of an organism which represents that level of the pyramid in one **named** habitat (name of chosen habitat _____). (3)

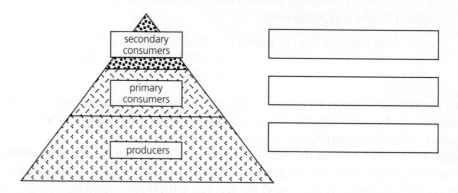

b What do you understand by the term *pyramid of biomass*? (2)

c How does a pyramid of biomass differ from a pyramid of numbers for the same ecosystem? (2)

(total = 9)

UODLE, June 1996

2 The diagram below shows the energy flow for part of a large pond. All values are given in kJ m^{-2} yr^{-1}.

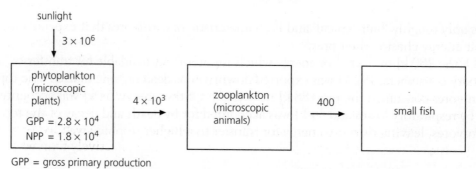

a Name the trophic levels to which each of the following belong:

i) Zooplankton (1)

ii) Small fish (1)

b i) Calculate the percentage energy from sunlight which is fixed as GPP by phytoplankton. Show your working (2)

ii) Suggest *two* reasons why not all of the incident sunlight is utilised in photosynthesis. (2)

(total = 6)

ULEAC, June 1993

Biogeochemical cycles

Whereas energy by its very nature is never recycled but flows through ecosystems in linear pathways and continues to flow because there is an endless supply radiating from the Sun, the nutrients that make up the body of living organisms are driven in circular pathways to be re-used again and again. The very same atoms of carbon, hydrogen, oxygen, nitrogen, sulphur and so on that formed the bodies of organisms long since dead, such as dinosaurs, are still in existence today. Some may even form a part of your body or perhaps the chair you are sitting on now.

The carbon cycle

Take the element carbon for example. It plays a central role in the structure and metabolism of living organisms. It is released into the environment as carbon dioxide by all respiring living organisms. Photosynthetic organisms, mainly green plants, algae and cyanobacteria (blue–green algae), take in carbon dioxide as a raw material for photosynthesis for the production of organic molecules such as sugars. Approximately half of the organic molecules synthesised by plants are used by the plants themselves for respiration and returned to the atmosphere as carbon dioxide. The rest is used for growth to make the stems, leaves, roots and so on. The carbon locked up in plant tissues may then become a part of a food chain when the plant material is eaten by herbivores. The organic compounds assimilated by the animals may then be used as fuel for animal respiration, in which case, the carbon is released as carbon dioxide to the atmosphere.

Plants shed their leaves. Animals excrete and defaecate matter that contains carbon. Plants and animals sooner or later die. Whichever pathway the carbon molecules take, the dead organic matter will next be acted upon by decomposers in the ecosystem, mainly bacteria and fungi. After breakdown by digestive enzymes, the carbon, now in the form of soluble organic molecules, is absorbed into the body of the decomposers and used as fuel for microbial respiration and is thus returned in another circular pathway to the atmosphere as carbon dioxide. These circular pathways by which carbon moves between living organisms and the non-living world of the atmosphere, seas, oceans, fresh water, soil and rocks, collectively form what is known as the **biogeochemical carbon cycle**.

The release of carbon trapped millions of years ago

A carbon atom taking the shortest circular pathway, which is the one involving plant respiration, would probably complete its circuit within minutes. If it took the longest pathway outlined so far, which is the one involving the construction of woody tissues in a tree, followed by decomposition after the tree dies, its journey may take hundreds of years to complete. On a geological time scale, however, that would still be considered a very brief period because there are two other circular pathways requiring millions of years for completion. The first involves the burning of fossil fuels and the second occurs during the weathering of rocks in the **geochemical part** of the carbon cycle.

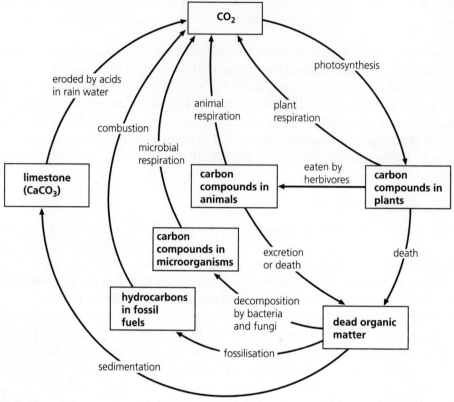

Figure 3.1 The carbon cycle

Fossilisation and the burning of fossil fuels

Coal has its origins in vast forests of trees and other plants that grew in swamps millions of years ago. Buried in mud and under anaerobic conditions, the tightly packed layer of plant matter escaped decomposition and was later subjected to immense pressures transforming the plant matter into coal. Crude oil is believed to have a similar origin except that it is widely thought to be derived from the bodies of marine animals that lived millions of years ago. When fossil fuels are burnt, the carbon is released as carbon dioxide after having been captured for plant tissue construction by photosynthesis many millions of years ago.

The geochemical part of the carbon cycle

There is a natural but much slower analogue to the burning of fossil fuels. It occurs during the chemical weathering of rocks, particularly chalk or limestone and dolomite. These rocks contain calcium and magnesium carbonate. Rain water dissolves atmospheric carbon dioxide to form carbonic acid.

$$H_2O + CO_2 \longrightarrow H_2CO_3$$
$$\text{carbonic acid}$$

The rain falling on carbonate rocks dissolves calcium and magnesium carbonate releasing calcium, magnesium and hydrogen carbonate ions into ground water.

$$CaCO_3 + H_2CO_3 \longrightarrow Ca^{2+} + 2HCO_3^-$$

$$MgCO_3 + H_2CO_3 \longrightarrow Mg^{2+} + 2HCO_3^-$$

The carbonic acid will also attack calcium silicate minerals, such as feldspar, which is common in rocks such as granite and basalt, releasing calcium and hydrogen carbonate ions.

$$CaSiO_3 + 2CO_2 + H_2O \longrightarrow Ca^{2+} + 2HCO_3^- + SiO_2$$

calcium silicate   silicon dioxide

The water containing these ions eventually finds its way, through streams and rivers, into the oceans. Plankton and other marine organisms including corals use the calcium and hydrogen carbonate ions to build skeletons and protective shells composed of calcium carbonate.

$$2HCO_3^- + Ca^{2+} \longrightarrow CaCO_3 + CO_2 + H_2O$$

When these organisms die, they sink to the bottom of the sea where their soft parts decompose, leaving a layer of calcium carbonate sediments on the seabed. Driven by convection currents within the Earth's molten mantle, the sea floor spreads, eventually reaching the margins of the continental shelf where it slides beneath the continental land mass. This process, which is known as **subduction**, may take millions of years to accomplish. It shifts calcium carbonate deposits from the sea floor towards the molten core of the Earth.

Subjected to increasing temperatures and pressures, the calcium carbonate reacts with silicon dioxide (quartz) releasing carbon dioxide and reforming silicate minerals.

$$CaCO_3 + SiO_2 \longrightarrow CaSiO_3 + CO_2$$

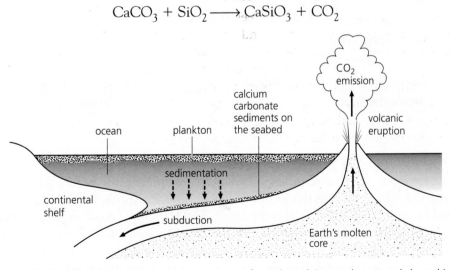

Figure 3.2 Carbon dioxide in volcanic eruptions comes from the calcium carbonate subducted into the Earth's molten core

This process is known as **metamorphism**. The carbon dioxide eventually re-enters the atmosphere primarily by way of volcanic eruptions and also, more subtly, by way of diffusion through the ocean rifts.

During the course of the weathering of carbonate rocks, one molecule of carbon dioxide dissolves in rain water to form one molecule of carbonic acid, which then erodes one molecule of calcium carbonate. When organisms use hydrogen carbonate ions to construct their protective shells, one molecule of carbon dioxide is returned to the atmosphere for each calcium carbonate molecule synthesised by them.

A different picture emerges when one looks closely at the weathering of silicate rocks. Here two molecules of carbon dioxide are removed for the erosion of each molecule of calcium silicate to silicon dioxide. Only one molecule is returned to the atmosphere when hydrogen carbonate ions are used to make calcium carbonate shells. The other molecule gets incorporated into calcium carbonate and finds its way to the bottom of the sea where it may remain trapped for millions of years. Slowly but surely, the weathering of silicate rocks, acting over millions of years, serves as an important sink which reduces carbon dioxide levels in the atmosphere.

Magnitudes of the Earth's various carbon pools

Current estimates are that the atmosphere holds 755 gigatonnes (Gt) of carbon (1 gigatonne = 10^9 tonnes). This amounts to 0.001% of the total mass of carbon in the world. The mass incorporated in living tissues is 560 Gt. By far the largest amount (99.9% of the total) is in sedimentary rocks.

Estimates of carbon masses

Type of carbon pool	Mass of carbon in Gt
All life (plant and animal)	560
Atmospheric carbon dioxide	755
Dead organic matter	1 660
Recoverable fossil fuels	6 500
Dissolved bicarbonates and carbonates	42 000
Sedimentary rocks	75 000 000

Balance sheet for the carbon cycle

Current estimates are that respiration by land plants releases 60 Gt of carbon per year into the atmosphere in the form of carbon dioxide. Another 60 Gt per year is released by animal and microbial respiration. The burning of fossil fuels contributes a further 5.5 Gt per year. Deforestation releases an estimated 1.6 Gt per year and there is another 0.1 Gt per year from volcanic emissions. This adds up to a total of 127.2 Gt of carbon released from the atmosphere per year without taking into account the contributions of the geochemical part of the carbon cycle.

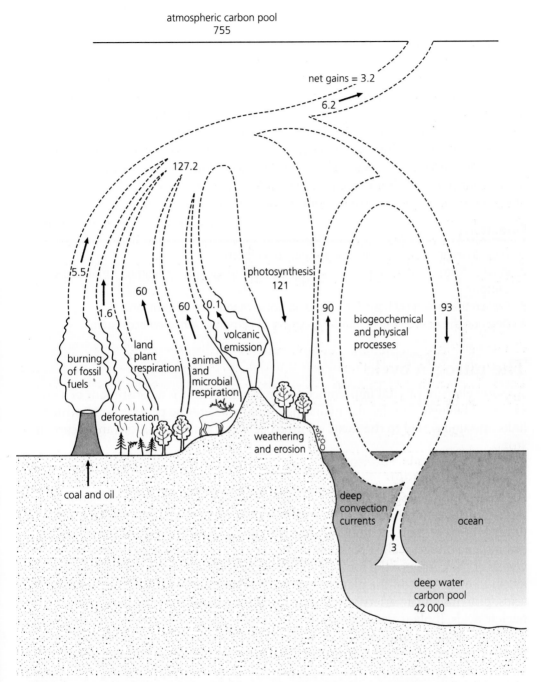

Figure 3.3 Balance sheet for the biogeochemical carbon cycle (figures are in Gt per year)

On the other side of the balance sheet, land plants are estimated to absorb for photosynthesis 121 Gt of carbon per year. Assuming that marine organisms release as much carbon as they absorb, it follows that the mass of carbon added to the atmosphere exceeds the mass absorbed by land plants by 6.2 Gt per year.

It is known with some accuracy that the atmospheric carbon pool is increasing at an annual rate of 3.2 Gt. Presumably the sink for the remaining 3.0 Gt per year must be due to physico-chemical processes such as diffusion into the oceans. The key process here is diffusion of carbon dioxide into seawater around the polar ice caps. About one-half of the dissolved carbon dioxide in these icy waters is drawn by deep convection currents into the deep waters of the oceans. The deep water drifts to other parts of the oceans but never rises to above about 100 metres from the surface because the cold water in these deeper parts is denser. In this way, the cold polar waters play an important role in 'burying' a substantial proportion of the carbon dioxide that dissolves in its icy waters because deep down in the oceans there is insufficient light for photosynthesis. Elsewhere, in the open seas and oceans, diffusion of carbon dioxide in and out of the water is in balance.

Questions

1 Why do living organisms require a supply of carbon?
2 In what form do **a** green plants,　**b** saprobiontic fungi and　**c** animals obtain their carbon?
3 Explain the biological basis for spreading horse manure onto farm land.
4 Describe the flow of energy and the cycling of carbon in a *named* ecosystem.

The nitrogen cycle

Another element of vital importance to life is nitrogen. It is a constituent of a great variety of biological molecules including proteins where the peptide bond, which links one amino acid to the next, is formed between a nitrogen atom and a carbon atom.

Nitrogen assimilation

A convenient place to begin describing the **nitrogen cycle** is with nitrogen in the form of **nitrates** in the soil. Plants absorb nitrates through their roots. After entry through the root hair, the mineral moves from cell to cell through interconnecting cytoplasmic bridges, called plasmodesmata, to reach the cells surrounding the xylem vessels at the centre of the root. From there, the nitrates are transported via the xylem to other parts of the plant where they are **assimilated** and converted to amino acids, proteins and a variety of other nitrogenous organic molecules including nucleic acids. If plant tissues are eaten by animals, the **plant proteins**, which are by far the most important nitrogenous compounds in plant cells, are broken down by digestive enzymes to their constituent amino acids and used as building units to make **animal proteins**.

Ammonification

When plants and animals die, the proteins are broken down to amino acids and then, by a process known as **ammonification**, the amino groups are liberated by conversion to **ammonia**. Filamentous fungi are the main microorganisms responsible for ammonification under aerobic conditions; bacteria of decay, especially *Clostridia*,

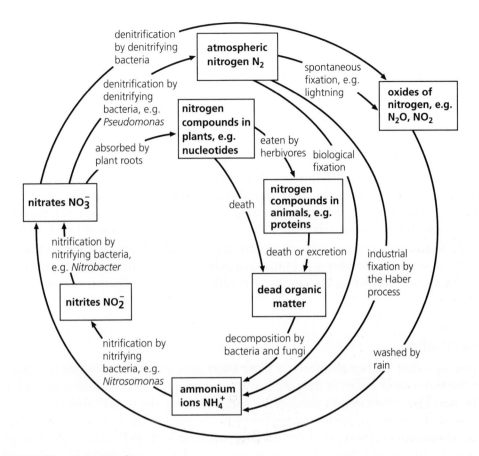

Figure 3.4 The nitrogen cycle

are the effective agents under anaerobic conditions. When animals excrete, the urea in the urine is also converted to ammonia, the decomposition being catalysed by **urease**, an enzyme which remains stable in the soil long after it seeped out of the body of a decomposing organism.

Nitrification

Ammonia is a very soluble gas and it readily accepts protons to become the ammonium ion.

$$NH_3 + H^+ \rightleftharpoons NH_4^+$$

Present in the soil is a type of autotrophic **nitrifying bacteria** which is capable of using the energy released by the oxidation of ammonium ions to nitrites. Under aerobic conditions, these bacteria, which belong to the genus *Nitrosomonas*, convert ammonium ions to **nitrites**, a process known as **nitrification**.

$$\underset{\substack{\text{ammonium} \\ \text{ion}}}{2NH_4^+} + 3O_2 \longrightarrow \underset{\substack{\text{nitrite} \\ \text{ion}}}{2NO_2^-} + 2H_2O + 4H^+$$

These chemosynthetic bacteria use the energy derived from the oxidation of ammonium ions in the same way as plants use light energy to make organic food molecules. Another group of nitrifying bacteria, belonging to the genus *Nitrobacter*, obtain their energy from the oxidation of nitrites to nitrates.

$$2NO_2^- + O_2 \longrightarrow 2NO_3^-$$
$$\text{nitrate ion}$$

Plants can use either ammonium ions or nitrates for synthesising proteins. However, ammonium ions are positively charged and tend to adhere to the surface of clay and humus particles, which are negatively charged. The ammonium ions tend, therefore, to remain at the spot where they are formed until they are converted by nitrifying bacteria to nitrates. Nitrate ions are negatively charged and are repelled by the negative charges on the clay and humus particles. Consequently, nitrate ions tend to move freely with soil water and are more readily available to plant roots for absorption.

Denitrification

Nitrate ions that are not absorbed by plant roots are carried in soil water to drain into the water table beneath the soil or into streams and rivers and then into a lake or the sea. The conditions in the layer of soil just above the water table are anaerobic. These same conditions also exist in the mud at the bottom of ponds and lakes. There are several types of **denitrifying bacteria** such as *Pseudomonas* that are adapted for life in such anaerobic conditions. They have developed what is known as **nitrate (or nitrite) respiration**. These denitrifying bacteria use nitrate (or nitrite) ions as acceptors of electrons for the oxidation of organic food molecules in much the same way as aerobic organisms use oxygen for respiration. During the reaction, the denitrifying bacteria break down nitrates or nitrites, in a process known as **denitrification**, releasing gaseous nitrogen or nitrous oxide.

$$5C_6H_{12}O_6 + 24KNO_3 \longrightarrow 30CO_2 + 18H_2O + 24KOH + 12N_2$$
$$\text{glucose} \quad \text{potassium} \qquad\qquad\qquad\qquad \text{potassium} \quad \text{dinitrogen}$$
$$\text{nitrate} \qquad\qquad\qquad\qquad\qquad \text{hydroxide}$$

$$C_6H_{12}O_6 + 6KNO_3 \longrightarrow 6CO_2 + 3H_2O + 6KOH + 3N_2O$$
$$\text{nitrous}$$
$$\text{oxide}$$

The gases bubble upwards through the wet soil to escape into the atmosphere. Without the activities of these denitrifying bacteria, the entire world's nitrogen would end up in the water table below the soil or in the oceans and remain locked up.

Nitrogen fixation

More than three-quarters of the atmosphere or, to be exact, 79% of dry air consists of nitrogen but in the form of an inert gas called **dinitrogen**, N_2. Neither plants nor animals can make use of this abundant gas for synthesising proteins and the many other nitrogenous compounds that make up the body of living organisms. Only after the nitrogen has been 'fixed', that is, after it has combined with other elements to form nitrogen compounds, is the nitrogen usable by plants for protein synthesis. The fixation of atmospheric nitrogen occurs in three main ways:

1 spontaneous fixation
2 industrial fixation
3 biological fixation.

Spontaneous fixation

Energy is needed to break the triple bond ($N\equiv N$) that binds the two atoms of nitrogen in dinitrogen. Natural phenomena such as lightning, cosmic radiation and meteor trails can provide the energy needed to tear the two nitrogen atoms apart and thus allow oxygen to react with nitrogen to form **nitrogen oxides**. Combustion at high temperatures within the internal combustion engine can also provide the energy needed for the oxidation of nitrogen.

Figure 3.5 During electrical thunderstorms, oxygen reacts with nitrogen to form oxides of nitrogen

In the atmosphere, nitrogen oxides react with hydroxyl radicals, HO, to form nitric acid. (Hydroxyl radicals are formed when a single atom of oxygen derived from ozone reacts with a water molecule.)

$$O_3 \xrightarrow{\text{UV light}} O + O_2$$

ozone   oxygen   oxygen
                     atom   molecule

$$O + H_2O \longrightarrow 2HO$$

hydroxyl
radical

$$NO_2 + HO \longrightarrow HNO_3$$

nitric acid

Rain washes the nitric acid out of the atmosphere on to the soil making nitrate ions once again available for absorption by plant roots. Approximately 15% of the total global nitrogen fixation can be attributed to lightning, combustion and other natural phenomena.

Industrial fixation

In a natural ecosystem, the nitrates taken out of the soil by plants for protein synthesis are returned to the soil when plants and animals die. Their dead remains then decompose to ammonia followed by nitrification into nitrates. In an agricultural system, on the other hand, there is permanent loss of nitrogen from the soil because crops are harvested and plant proteins are exported from the field. Further losses occur owing to soil erosion and leaching of minerals. Land used for agricultural purposes tends therefore to be depleted of nitrogen. The farmer's answer is to apply nitrogen fertilisers.

Most of the nitrogen fertilisers used in today's intensive farming practices are synthesised by the fertiliser industry using a process invented by two Germans, Fritz Haber and Karl Bosch, in 1914. Known as the Haber process, it involves passing hydrogen and nitrogen over a catalyst (usually finely divided iron mixed with alumina) at a temperature of about 500 °C and at a pressure of several hundred atmospheres. The hydrogen reacts with nitrogen to form ammonia.

$$N_2 + 3H_2 \longrightarrow 2NH_3$$

The ammonia may be applied directly on to the land or it may be used as a raw material for the synthesis of urea or ammonium nitrate – two widely used fertilisers. Approximately 25% of the total global nitrogen fixation results from the Haber process.

Biological fixation

Biological fixation by **nitrogen-fixing bacteria** and **cyanobacteria** (formerly known as blue–green algae) accounts for the bulk (60%) of the fixed nitrogen added to the soil. Some of these nitrogen-fixing microorganisms are free living; others form symbiotic associations with plants. The free living nitrogen fixers include certain aerobic soil bacteria of the genus *Azotobacter* and a genus of anaerobic bacteria called *Clostridium*. In aquatic habits, the most important nitrogen fixers are the cyanobacteria. Studies in Japan have shown that the nitrogen-fixing activities of the cyanobacteria can increase the nitrogen in rice paddies by 30% and the rice yield by 20%.

Rhizobium

Undoubtedly, the best known nitrogen fixers are members of a genus of bacteria called *Rhizobium*. Rhizobium species are of widespread occurrence in fertile soils. Free-living rhizobia are, however, incapable of fixing nitrogen. They must first invade the root hairs of leguminous plants, then migrate into the root cortex, multiply and settle in swellings called **root nodules** which are specially made for them by the plant. The bacteria then become larger and rounder as they transform themselves into nitrogen-fixing microbes. In this mutually beneficial relationship – a symbiosis – the plant provides the bacteria with a protected environment and organic food molecules such as carbohydrates, while the bacteria provide in return fixed nitrogen in the form of ammonia, which the plant can readily assimilate.

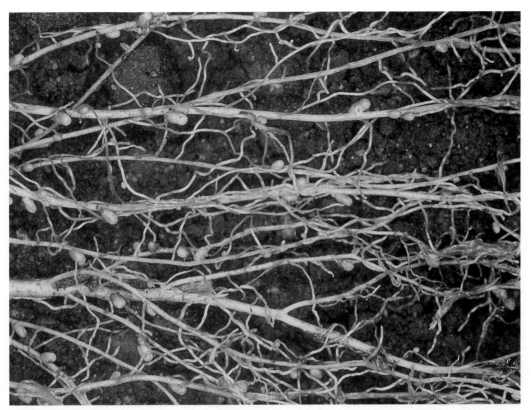

Figure 3.6 Root nodules on the roots of a broad bean plant caused by symbiotic nitrogen-fixing bacteria (*Rhizobium*)

Nitrogenase

The key to biological fixation is an enzyme called **nitrogenase** which all nitrogen fixing microorganisms possess. It in fact consists of two enzymes, one larger than the other. The larger enzyme, which functions by binding nitrogen and probably holding it in just the right position for it to react with hydrogen, has the heavy metal molybdenum as a vital component of its structure. The smaller enzyme catalyses the reactions that produce the energy and reducing power needed to convert nitrogen to ammonia. The overall reaction is summarised below and it shows that 16 molecules of ATP are hydrolysed to ADP (see page 47) for each molecule of dinitrogen fixed as ammonia.

$$\overset{16ATP \qquad\quad 16ADP}{N_2 + 8H^+ + 8e^- \longrightarrow 2NH_3 + H_2}$$

In the Haber process, high temperatures and pressures are needed to cause nitrogen to react with hydrogen to form ammonia whereas, in biological fixation, the same result is achieved at ordinary temperatures and pressures and with only a small expenditure of energy.

A peculiarity of nitrogenase is that both its constituent enzymes are inactivated by exposure to oxygen. To fix nitrogen, the nitrogen-fixing bacteria must therefore protect their nitrogen-fixing enzymes from environmental oxygen. Root nodule bacteria have the ideal shelter for this. They are located in the centre of a capsule-like nodule which acts as an oxygen shield. Only just enough environmental oxygen is allowed to diffuse into the nodule to allow the bacteria within it to produce the ATP needed for nitrogen fixation without damaging their nitrogen-fixing enzymes.

Azotobacter, the free-living nitrogen-fixing bacteria, have evolved a different solution to the problem. Taking advantage of the abundance of organic matter available to them, they use a very high rate of respiration to lower the oxygen concentration of their immediate surroundings. If an abundance of carbohydrate is not available and their respiration rate falls, they use a special protein to protect the nitrogen-fixing enzymes by 'switching them off'.

The cyanobacteria have the added problem of having to deal with the oxygen produced as a waste product of photosynthesis. Filamentous forms of cyanobacteria have solved the problem by confining nitrogen fixation to special cells called **heterocysts** that are rich in nitrogenase. These specialised nitrogen-fixing cells cannot photosynthesise and cannot therefore evolve oxygen.

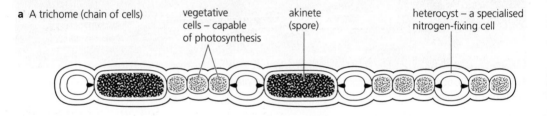

a A trichome (chain of cells)

vegetative cells – capable of photosynthesis

akinete (spore)

heterocyst – a specialised nitrogen-fixing cell

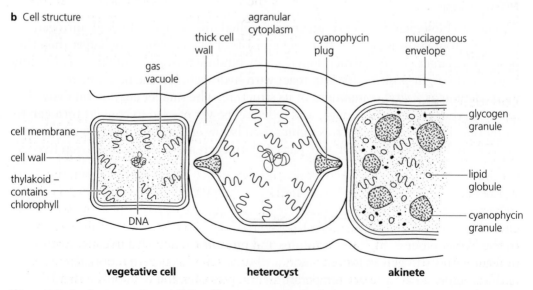

b Cell structure

agranular cytoplasm

thick cell wall

cyanophycin plug

mucilagenous envelope

gas vacuole

cell membrane

cell wall

thylakoid – contains chlorophyll

DNA

glycogen granule

lipid globule

cyanophycin granule

vegetative cell   **heterocyst**   **akinete**

Figure 3.7 *Anabaena*, a nitrogen-fixing, filamentous cyanobacterium

The hydrologic cycle

In its most basic form, the **hydrologic** or **water cycle** may be described as a sequence of natural phenomena in which water in the oceans evaporates in the heat of the Sun, and forms clouds in the atmosphere which deposit rain or snow as the vapour-laden clouds pass over land, the water eventually returning to the oceans by way of rivers and streams. Several processes are involved in the hydrologic cycle, the most important being evaporation, conduction and convection, condensation, precipitation, runoff, interception, infiltration and transpiration.

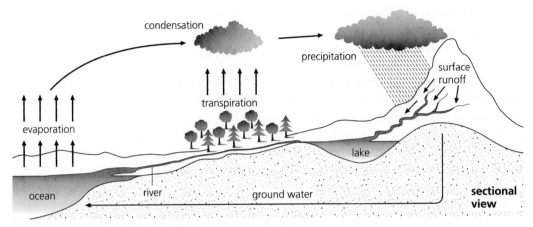

Figure 3.8 The hydrologic (water) cycle

Evaporation

The atmosphere gains water vapour by evaporation not only from the oceans but also from the lakes, rivers, streams, snowfields, glaciers, moist ground and so on. A suitable starting point for a description of the water cycle is with a water molecule near the surface of a body of water. Having acquired a little more energy than the other water molecules in its immediate surroundings, it breaks free through the surface tension of the liquid to become a molecule of water vapour in the air. This process is known as **evaporation**.

Conduction and convection

The air into which the water molecule escapes is in circulation. There are a variety of reasons for this, one of them being the warming effect of the Sun on the land and the ocean, which results in the overlying air being heated up by **conduction** thus causing it to expand. Because the land mass heats up faster than the ocean, the warmer air over the land, having expanded more quickly, is more buoyant and rises, to be replaced by cooler, denser air from the oceans. This transfer of air masses caused by differences in temperature is known as **convection**. It draws air over the oceans towards the land mass during the hot months of summer. This incoming moisture-laden air may be forced upwards by obstacles in its path such as mountains and hills. It may also rise because of the heating effect of the Sun on the ground below.

Condensation

Air expands as it rises because the air pressure above is lower. Now, it is a well known principle of physics that expansion is sustained at the expense of heat. In other words as the air expands, it cools. The cooler the air becomes, the less moisture it can retain as vapour. If the air is cooled sufficiently, the water vapour **condenses** around nuclei such as ice or dust particles to form tiny droplets of liquid water in the air. In large quantities these tiny droplets of liquid water are visible as clouds.

Precipitation

Once condensation around nuclei has begun, the water droplets grow quickly. From about 0.01 mm in diameter to begin with, they can rapidly grow to 0.1 mm in diameter, which is the average size of water droplets in clouds. Gravity has little effect on water droplets that are less than 0.1 mm in diameter, the droplets remaining freely suspended in the atmosphere. If the air continues to cool and the droplets grow to larger than 0.1 mm in diameter, they are then heavy enough to descend under the influence of gravity, falling at the rate of about 1 metre per second when they are 0.2 mm in diameter. Those in heavy tropical showers are often several millimetres across. The term **precipitation** is used to refer to the process by which water, under the influence of gravity, falls from the clouds as rain, snow, hailstones or sleet. Snow consists of feathery or needle-like ice crystals. Snow falls when the vapour in the atmosphere is sufficiently chilled to condense as ice crystals. Hailstones result from strong updraughts of air through thunder clouds. If a water droplet is caught in one of these updraughts that carries it to the top of the thunder cloud, it can freeze to a small ball of ice. As it then falls to the lower parts of the thunder cloud, other water droplets condense and freeze around it. It can then be carried by another updraught and the process is repeated several times, the ice ball accumulating a new layer of ice each time this happens until the ice ball becomes too heavy to be carried upwards and falls as hailstones.

Figure 3.9 When water droplets that form the clouds become too heavy to remain suspended in the air, they will fall under the influence of gravity as rain

Runoff

An estimated 75% of the precipitation falls directly back on to the oceans. The precipitation that falls on land may undergo a variety of fates. Some may fall to the ground only to evaporate immediately and be returned to the atmosphere. If the rainfall is heavy, the tiny spaces between soil particles soon fill up with water and the excess water runs as a thin, barely noticeable sheet of water over the surface of the soil, often taking a heavy load of topsoil with it. This **surface runoff** collects in depressions to form puddles which overflow and merge and are largely responsible for floods and soil erosion. It runs into streams, rivers and eventually into the sea.

Interception and infiltration

If the ground is densely covered with vegetation, the precipitation may be **intercepted** by the leaves and other parts of the plant and evaporated directly from the surfaces of the plants so that only a little reaches the ground. Precipitation of a moderate intensity which lasts for a few days is the type farmers particularly desire because much of it **infiltrates** into the pore spaces between soil particles to serve the useful function of supporting plant and other forms of life.

Transpiration

Plants (and to a lesser extent animals) add a considerable amount of moisture to the atmosphere. After absorbing water through their roots, the water travels up the stem to the leaves where over 99% of the absorbed water is lost by a process of **transpiration** through the leaves. For example, a fully grown oak tree can add more than a third of a cubic metre of water to the atmosphere per average summer's day. A hectare of corn transpires about 33 cubic metres of water on an average summer's day. The term **evapotranspiration** is used to refer to the combined water loss from the Earth's surface due to evaporation and transpiration.

Ground water

Water that infiltrates into the soil trickles slowly downwards to become part of the ground-water supply. There is more freshwater in the ground than in all the world's streams, rivers and lakes combined. Its depth varies because the hard bedrock which acts as an impermeable layer exists at various levels. The topmost level of the ground water is known as the **water table**.

Some of the ground water is drawn upwards by capillarity to serve as a source of water for plants. Some of it comes to the surface at certain points such as springs or seeps where the water table intersects the land. This movement of ground water contributes about 30% by volume of water in rivers taken globally and is responsible for keeping rivers flowing during periods when there is little or no rain. By sinking wells, humans can pump the water up to the surface and thus gain access to this abundant source of freshwater.

Questions

5 Describe how microorganisms contribute to the recycling of the element nitrogen.
6 Draw an annotated diagram to illustrate the part of the nitrogen cycle that is involved in an interchange of nitrogen in soil, in plants and in animals.
7 How do conditions within a root nodule of a leguminous plant help *Rhizobium* fix atmospheric nitrogen?
8 Using the following words, outline the hydrological cycle in no more than four sentences:

   evaporate   condenses   precipitation   runoff   transpiration   cloud formation

Examination question

1 The figure below is a diagram illustrating some of the relationships between plants and animals.

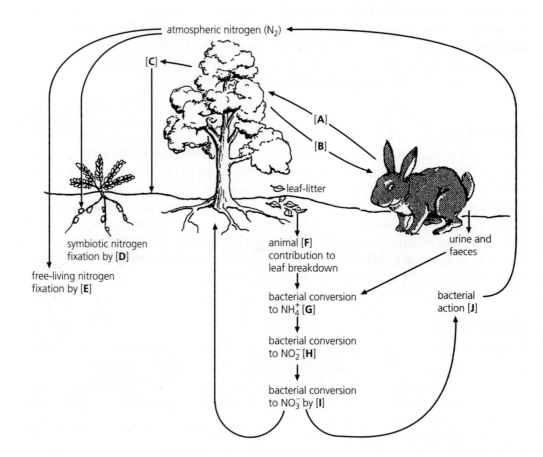

a Give a suitable name to each of the substances **A**, **B** and **C**.   (3)
b Give a suitable name to each of the organisms **D**, **E**, **F** and **I**.   (4)
c Give a suitable name to each of the processes **G**, **H** and **J**.   (3)   (total = 10)

UODLE, June 1986

Physical and chemical factors affecting the distribution of organisms

4

It is a well-known fact that some species are present in certain localities but not in others. For example, the vegetation that constitutes a tropical rain forest is confined to the equatorial regions of the world. The natural habitat of cacti is deserts, and small-leafed, short-stemmed, mat-like sedges are characteristic of the tundra, the region north of the tree line around the Arctic. Closer to home, along the British and Irish coasts, the barnacle *Chthamalus stellatus* occurs higher up the intertidal rocky shore zone whereas another species of barnacle, *Balanus balanoides*, dominates the mid and lower rocky shores. Why?

Ecologists recognise two main types of environmental factors affecting the distribution of organisms. These are **abiotic** and **biotic**.

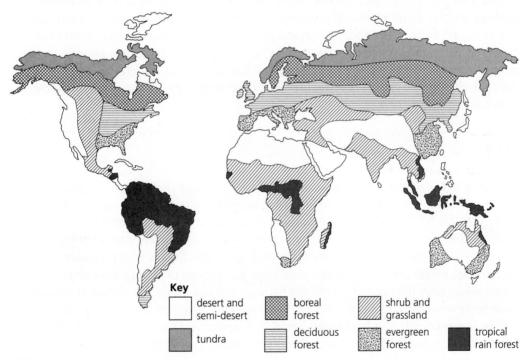

Key

☐ desert and semi-desert	▨ boreal forest	▨ shrub and grassland
▪ tundra	☰ deciduous forest	▨ evergreen forest	■ tropical rain forest

Figure 4.1 Climate has a marked effect on the distribution of plants, as illustrated in this map of the major plant communities of the world

Abiotic factors are physical or chemical in nature and include:

1 **climatic factors** such as temperature, rainfall, light intensity and wind
2 **edaphic factors** such as soil type, pH and salinity
3 **other physical** and **chemical factors** such as water current and oxygen concentration of the water.

The biotic factors are interactions with other organisms such as **competition, predation, parasitism, mutualism, shading** and these will be the subject of Chapter 5.

In general climate and soil conditions determine the distribution of plants whereas the distribution of animals is largely determined by the distribution of their food source.

Climatic factors

The term 'climate' is used to refer to the characteristic pattern of precipitation, humidity, temperature, light and wind conditions for a geographical area. Climate has a marked effect on the distribution of plants because plants cannot move away to avoid unsuitable environmental conditions and eventually die or fail to produce viable offspring if conditions are not suitable.

Water

Liquid water is vital to life. It forms about 90% by weight of the cell. It serves as a medium for the many chemical reactions that are essential to life and as a participant in a number of other chemical reactions. It also serves as a transporter of various dissolved substances within and between cells and helps to maintain a stable body temperature. Water possesses a number of unique properties which makes it particularly suitable for supporting life. All these unique properties stem from the molecular structure of water.

Properties of water

Dipolar nature

Water is a compound of hydrogen and oxygen. The two hydrogen atoms and the oxygen atom in a water molecule are not arranged in a straight line but are set at an angle of 104.5°. The effect of this angular molecular structure is that there is a small net negative charge around the oxygen part of the molecule and a small net positive charge around the hydrogen parts of the molecule. This makes water a **polar (charged) molecule**. When water molecules are in close proximity, they align themselves with the positively charged hydrogen of one molecule attracted towards the negatively charged oxygen of another molecule. This type of intermolecular attraction is known as a **hydrogen bond**. It is a relatively weak bond but its strength is just right to give water the properties that make it so vital to life.

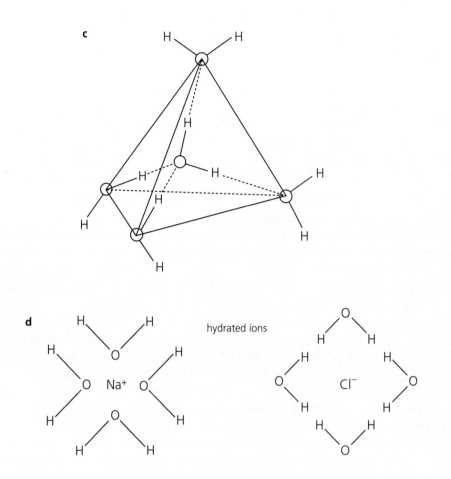

Figure 4.2 a Structure of a water molecule. **b** Hydrogen bonding between two water molecules. **c** Tetrahedral arrangement of hydrogen-bonded water molecules. **d** Arrangement of water molecules and sodium and chloride ions

A liquid at room temperature

Were it not for the hydrogen bonds between water molecules, water would not exist as a liquid at temperatures prevalent on Earth and life as we know it would be impossible. For example, methane, a symmetrical non-polar molecule of similar size to water, boils at −161 °C. Water, on the other hand, boils at 100 °C because it takes a lot more energy to separate the hydrogen-bonded water molecules as compared with the non-polar methane molecules.

Tetrahedral array of molecules in ice (see Figure 4.2c)

When water freezes to form ice, the water molecules align themselves to form a tetrahedral array of hydrogen-bonded molecules. In an ice crystal, each water molecule is attached to all the other neighbouring molecules by hydrogen bonds so that the entire lattice of molecules becomes, in effect, one huge molecule.

Maximum density at 4 °C

When ice melts, the porous three-dimensional structure collapses as some 15% of the hydrogen bonds are broken. The water that forms consists of water molecules that are more compactly packed than in crystalline ice. This explains why water at 0 °C is denser than ice at the same temperature. As the water temperature rises, the increased thermal energy of the water molecules causes more hydrogen bonds to break. The result is that the proportion of water molecules still retaining the porous lattice-like structure decreases, while the amount of the more compactly packed, non-hydrogen-bonded molecules increases. This explains why water becomes denser as its temperature rises from 0 °C. It reaches its maximum density at about 4 °C. Above this temperature, the greater thermal energy forces the water molecules further apart, as water expands and, once again, becomes less dense.

Ice floats and forms an insulating layer

Whereas most crystals are denser than their liquids, ice is exceptional in that it is less dense and floats on water. This fact is of great importance to aquatic life in the colder parts of the world. Imagine what would happen if ice were denser than water. The ice that forms on the surface of, say a lake, would sink to the bottom. More ice would then form and sink to the bottom. This process would continue throughout winter until the lake is frozen solid. Not only would organisms in the lake be killed by being entombed in ice but the lake would remain frozen long after winter, thawing slowly. Likewise the seas and oceans would also be colder and this would in turn affect the Earth's climate. In reality, of course, ice floats and these problems do not arise.

When water at the surface cools in autumn, the denser, colder oxygen-rich water sinks to the bottom, displacing warmer water at the bottom of the lake. The warmer water, which is poor in dissolved oxygen but rich in dissolved minerals, rises to the surface bringing minerals to phytoplankton and surface-living plants. This circulation of water continues until the entire lake is filled with water at 4 °C – the temperature at which water is at its densest. Further cooling does not result in circulation because the colder water is less dense and stays at the surface. Eventually, a layer of ice forms at the surface, insulating the water below from further heat loss.

High capacity for heat

When most substances absorb heat, the added thermal energy may cause the molecules of the substance to vibrate more vigorously (vibrational energy) or it may promote one or more electrons to a higher energy level (electronic energy). Alternatively, the molecules may move more rapidly in relation to one another (motion or translational energy). It is this energy which expresses itself as temperature.

Due to hydrogen bonding between water molecules, much of the heat energy added to water becomes dissipated as movement of the shared hydrogen atoms. Heat causes the hydrogen atoms to vibrate back and forth between the two oxygen atoms to which they are linked. Very little of the added thermal energy appears as translational motion of water molecules. This is why water is such a good absorber of heat and why the temperature of water does not rise as fast as other substances.

Water's **high capacity for heat** keeps the temperature of the cell (which is 90% water) fairly constant. It also serves as a buffer against large temperature fluctuations which would inevitably arise from heat production as a result of the many chemical reactions that occur within the cell. The oceans, seas and lakes absorb a great deal of heat and this helps to keep the temperature on Earth within the range suitable for life. Water vapour in the atmosphere absorbs radiant energy from the Sun and re-emits the heat, thus keeping the Earth's surface warm after sunset.

High latent heat of vaporisation

To change to a gas, the molecules of a liquid must be supplied with sufficient energy to enable them to break loose from the forces that attract them to one another. Due to the large number of hydrogen bonds that bind water molecules together, water requires a lot more thermal energy than other substances to change from a liquid to a gas. Water has what is known in physics as a high latent heat of vaporisation.

When water evaporates from the surface of a body, heat is extracted from the body, cooling it down. Many organisms use cooling by evaporation as a means of preventing themselves from becoming overheated.

A good solvent (see Figure 4.2d)

Another property of water which makes it particularly suitable for supporting life is that it is a very good solvent. It is in fact a better solvent than all the other common liquids because of its marked polarity and its strong tendency to form hydrogen bonds.

For a solute to dissolve in a solvent, three things must happen. Firstly, the attractive forces that bind the solute particles together must be broken. Secondly, the bonds that bind the solvent particles together must also be broken, and thirdly, a form of bonding must occur between the solvent and solute particles. Furthermore, the forces of attraction between the solvent and solute particles must be at least equal to or greater than the sum of the solute-to-solute and solvent-to-solvent attractions. If the cohesive forces that bind the solute particles together or the solvent particles together are too strong, intermingling between solute and solvent particles would not occur and no solution would result.

Consider, for example, sodium chloride and its interactions with water. A dry crystal of sodium chloride consists of an alternating array of positively charged sodium and negatively charged chloride ions. The electrostatic forces of attraction between the two ions are strong. However, when sodium chloride is placed in water, the attraction of the electronegative oxygen end of the water molecule for the positively charged sodium ions, and the similar attraction of the electropositive hydrogens of water for the negatively charged chloride ions are greater than the mutual attraction between the Na^+ and Cl^- ions. The Na^+ and Cl^- ions dissociate to become surrounded by a sphere of regularly arranged water molecules with the oxygen ends adjacent to the Na^+ ion and the hydrogen ends adjacent to the Cl^- ion. Ions that are surrounded by loosely bound water molecules are said to be hydrated.

Substances that are electrically neutral (non-polar), such as oil, are insoluble in water. When shaken with water, they show no tendency to react electrostatically with the water molecules. Instead, the water molecules reform the hydrogen bonds broken by the physical disturbance and push the insoluble material out to form a separate layer outside the watery domain.

Effect of water availability on the distribution of terrestrial organisms

Water availability in association with temperature are the two most important abiotic factors determining the distribution of organisms in terrestrial habitats. In general, where water is plentiful, the vegetation is dense and luxuriant, and where it is in short supply, as in deserts, the vegetation is sparse and composed of relatively short plants. For example, in the tropics, where the average rainfall exceeds 1200 millimetres per annum, the forests are dense and the trees grow 30 to 50 metres in height. On the other hand, in places where rainfall is less than 200 millimetres per annum, the natural vegetation is generally thinly scattered, consisting mostly of plants of short stature, such as grasses.

The distribution of animals depends on the type and richness of the vegetation. Where the vegetation is lush, the accompanying animals are generally numerous and rich in biodiversity, because animals depend ultimately on plants for their food.

Effect of interception

When rain falls, some of it is caught by the leaves and other parts of plants and is evaporated before it reaches the ground. Losses through interception can be as high as 90% of the rainfall for forest communities. The type of vegetation can also be important. In general, interception is greater under coniferous trees as compared with broad-leaved trees. This is partly because the water droplets that form on the needle-like leaves of the coniferous trees are smaller and the air also flows more freely through coniferous trees, thus allowing a faster rate of evaporation to occur.

Adaptations for water conservation

One of the hazards of life on land is the threat of death from dehydration due to water losses by evaporation from the body surface to drier surroundings. To survive, many terrestrial organisms have evolved adaptations for conserving water. An impervious body covering such as the dry leathery or scaly skin of lizards is an example. Confining the moist respiratory surfaces (lungs) within a body cavity is another useful adaptation and so is the production of relatively dry faeces and concentrated urine. Internal fertilisation is yet another adaptation to terrestrial life: gametes shed on to dry land would rapidly dry up if external fertilisation was the only reproductive method available to land animals.

In general, animals such as insects, reptiles, birds and mammals that possess some or all of the adaptations mentioned above, can be found occupying a wide range of terrestrial habitats including hot, arid places such as deserts. Animals such as earthworms, nematodes, woodlice and amphibians that lack effective methods for reducing water losses by evaporation are much more restricted in their distribution and are generally confined to microhabitats where the surrounding air is almost totally saturated with moisture.

Land plants have the added problem of having extensive external body surfaces through which water losses by evaporation can occur. Their external body covering consisting of a waxy cuticle or impervious bark does help to reduce water losses by evaporation to the dry surrounding atmosphere. Land plants nevertheless lose a great deal of water by transpiration through tiny pores in their body surface known as stomata. The land plant's answer to transpiratory losses is an extensive root system which is in direct contact with water in the soil. Provided there is adequate precipitation and there is sufficient water available in the soil, a terrestrial plant can, through its extensive root system, make good all the water it loses in transpiration by absorption through its root hairs.

The actual amount of water available to plants is often determined by a combination of factors especially temperature, wind and type of vegetation. Temperature affects the rate of evapotranspiration and it therefore exerts an indirect effect on the water relations of plants and animals.

In 1937, a Russian botanist named Pavlychenko carefully dug up a cylinder of soil 1.2 m in diameter and 2 m deep in which grew a single 2-year-old crested wheat plant, *Agropyron cristatum*. He then, with the greatest care, washed away the soil a little at a time to ensure that every rootlet was intact. Pavlychenko very carefully measured the entire root system to determine its total length and found that it was 504 km.

In another experiment, a 4-month-old rye grass plant growing in a box 10 × 10 × 13 cm was found to have a total root length of 622 km and this did not include the root hair measurements. The rye grass plant was estimated to have 1.4×10^{10} root hairs giving a total root hair length amounting to a staggering 10 600 km, approximately the distance (as the crow flies) from London to Tokyo.

Figure 4.3 This 2-year-old crested wheat plant had a total root length amounting to 504 kilometres

---

Temperature

There is little doubt that temperature is another major variable which affects the distribution and abundance of organisms. The distribution of the major plant communities of the world is broadly related to the different temperature zones of the world. Broad-leaved deciduous trees, for example, cannot survive temperatures below minus 40 to 50 °C, and where winter temperatures are below about −46 °C, broad-leaved trees give way to pines, firs and other coniferous evergreen trees with needle-like leaves. The influence of temperature on the distribution of plants and animals can be observed when we climb a tropical mountain. The temperature declines the higher we climb and so does the range and abundance of plant and animal species.

The distribution of the holly (*Ilex aquifolium*), an evergreen species, is affected by temperature. It is abundant in western Europe where the winters are mild because of the warming effects of the Gulf Stream, a broad drift of warm ocean currents originating in the Gulf of Mexico. Further east, the holly becomes increasingly rare because the winters there are more severe.

Frost drought

Low temperature can affect the function of roots making them less permeable to water. The term **frost drought** is used to refer to situations where water is present in the soil but not available to plants because the ground temperature is too cold. Evergreen plants in such situations can lose more water by transpiration than by absorption through their roots. The shedding of leaves at the start of the cold season is a useful adaptation because it enables deciduous plants to reduce their water losses by transpiration at a time when ground water is not available because it is frozen.

Frost damage

Many plants are damaged by subzero temperatures because water freezes within the cell denying the cell access to free water molecules for metabolism. Ice crystals may also form within cells and in the intercellular spaces between cells. The crystals are large compared with the cells and their sharp needle-like points can puncture cell membranes causing the cell to leak fluids and die when there is a thaw in weather conditions.

Winter warmth

Some plants like the Scot's lovage (*Ligusticum scoticum*) are adversely affected by a spell of warm weather in winter. The Scot's lovage is a herbaceous perennial which is adapted for life in the cold northern latitudes where solar radiation comes in obliquely and there is consequently a short growing season. It grows rapidly during a spell of warm sunny weather in summer by developing a fast metabolic rate. Its aerial parts then die and the plant survives the winter as a rootstock (underground stem). A warm winter raises the metabolic rate of the plant causing it to use up food meant for an explosive growth rate when summer arrives. Global warming would put such organisms under threat.

Summer cold

Temperature affects the ability of some plants to reproduce themselves. The small-leafed lime tree (*Tilia cordata*), for example, has a natural range in Britain which extends as far north as the Lake District. It flowers in July producing pendulous clusters of small, bowl-shaped, fragrant yellow–white flowers and is commonly grown in parks and along avenues for its handsome appearance.

Laboratory studies show that the critical factor which limits the natural range of this lime tree is the summer temperature. At 20 °C, the pollen tubes have been measured to travel down the style at 100 µm per hour but below this critical temperature, the rate drops to about 40 µm per hour. This in effect means that at temperatures lower than 20 °C, the style withers before the pollen tubes arrive at the ovules to fertilise the ova and so no seeds are formed. The mean July temperature in the Lake District is 19 °C.

More biodiversity where it is sometimes hot, sometimes cold

A surprising recent discovery based on a vast quantity of data collected from ecologists from all over the world is that warm regions with large fluctuations of seasonal temperature, such as the Hoh River Valley in Olympic National Park in Washington State, USA, have a greater variety of species living in them than regions with a more equable temperature. It suggests that the rich and varied forms of life within the tropical rain forests evolved in spite of the uniform conditions and not because of them.

Sexual reproduction in flowering plants

For flowering plants to reproduce sexually, the pollen grains produced by the male sex organs known as anthers, must be transferred to the stigma, a female organ in the flower. This process is known as **pollination**. After pollination, the male gametes which are within the pollen grain must then fertilise the egg cell located within the immature seeds known as ovules. Before fertilisation can occur, however, the pollen grain on the stigma must germinate, and produce a pollen tube that carries the male gametes down the stalk-like female organ called the style towards the ovule.
Fertilisation occurs after arrival of the pollen tube at the ovule. The tip of the pollen tube bursts, releasing the male gametes one of which fuses with the egg cell to form a single cell called the zygote, which is the start of a new individual. Seeds do not usually form if fertilisation does not occur.

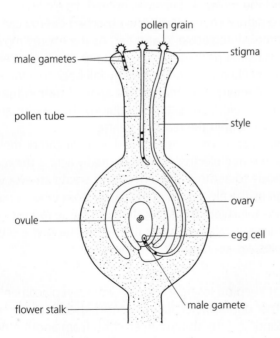

Figure 4.4 Sexual reproduction in flowering plants

Light

Light affects organisms in three main ways:

1 it is the ultimate source of energy for organisms in an ecosystem
2 the length of day is used as a dependable environmental cue by many plants and animals for setting their daily and seasonal rhythms
3 light enables animals to see and be seen.

Light and photosynthesis

Light is needed for photosynthesis – the process by which plants convert radiant energy into the chemical bond energy of organic food molecules such as glucose. The energy of sunlight is absorbed by the green pigment, **chlorophyll**. The molecules of chlorophyll are embedded within a membrane system called a **thylakoid**. There are stacks of thylakoids within chloroplasts of photosynthesising plant cells.

The light reactions

Light comes in discrete packets called **photons**. Light energy is harvested by 'antenna' chlorophyll molecules which are arranged in groups called **photosynthetic units**. Each photosynthetic unit consists of 50 to 300 chlorophyll molecules. At the hub of each photosynthetic unit is a complex of specialised chlorophyll and carrier molecules that form what is known as the **reaction centre**. There are two types of reaction centres called **photosystem I** and **photosystem II**.

When a photon of light strikes a chlorophyll molecule, the packet of radiant energy is absorbed and the molecule becomes excited. Its electrons jump from a lower energy level to a higher energy level. The absorbed energy can be passed around from one chlorophyll molecule to another. As the energy moves, the electrons of the molecule that gains the package of energy jump to a higher energy level while the electrons of the molecule giving up the energy fall back to a lower energy level. Eventually, the photon of energy is funnelled to a **special pair** in the reaction centre which responds by ejecting electrons extremely quickly. The loss of an electron leaves a positively charged 'hole' within the reaction centre.

Associated with the reaction centre is a special array of carrier molecules that provide a pathway for the free electron to hop excitedly across the reaction centre from one carrier molecule to another. The effect is to create an ever widening **separation of charge** as the electron is pulled away from what is now a positively charged special pair of molecules. This separation of charge represents stored energy for the cell because energy is released when negatively charged electrons and positively charged molecules are brought together.

The splitting of water

The special pair cannot keep on losing electrons without replacement. They pick up an electron from another donor molecule adjacent to them to fill up their positively charged 'hole'. The donor in turn obtains an electron from another donor and so on until ultimately electrons are stripped from a source with an abundance of electrons, namely water. Oxygen is given off as a waste product.

$$2H_2O \longrightarrow 4e^- + 4H^+ + O_2$$

Synthesis of ATP

The negatively charged electrons stripped off from water eventually end up near the outer surface of the thylakoid sac. The protons, which are also products of the water-splitting reactions, form a positively charged pool within the thylakoid sac. This build up, of positively charged protons inside the sac and of negatively charged electrons outside, is a source of potential energy which can be released as heat or fluorescence but which in fact is used to synthesise **ATP** (adenosine triphosphate, an energy-rich substance) and to reduce **NADP** (nicotinamide adenine dinucleotide phosphate) to **NADPH**. (The plant cell uses NADPH to reduce carbon dioxide to carbohydrates.)

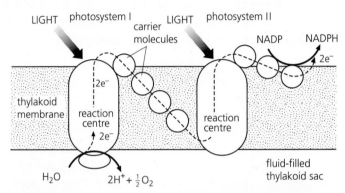

Figure 4.5 A diagram illustrating the stripping of electrons from water and their use for reducing NADP to NADPH

A group of specialised protein molecules known as the **ATP synthetase complex**, which are integral parts of the thylakoid membrane, are capable of harnessing the energy from an outflow of protons for ATP synthesis. The steeper the proton gradient, the stronger the outflow and the greater the potential for ATP synthesis. Since the force for generating ATP is similar to the forces of osmosis, the process is known as **chemiosmosis**.

Reduction of NADP to NADPH

Some of the carrier molecules of the reaction centre are organised to channel electrons to a biochemical pathway that leads to the reduction of NADP to NADPH. Apparently the voltage generated by a single photon of light is insufficient to strip electrons from water to reduce NADP to NADPH. Two photosystems, each absorbing at slightly different wavelengths, are needed to accomplish the task. The two photosystems are coupled together in series in much the same way as we would when we put two dry cells in series in a flashlight to obtain a higher voltage.

The dark reactions

The ATP and NADPH produced during the light reactions are used to drive the reactions that reduce carbon dioxide to carbohydrates. This phase in the process of photosynthesis is known as the **dark reactions** (even though it occurs most frequently when leaves are illuminated) because it does not require the direct participation of light.

The experiments that led to the unravelling of the dark reactions were carried out by a biologist named Melvin Calvin in 1945. Calvin allowed a unicellular alga called *Chlorella* to photosynthesise in carbon dioxide labelled with a radioactive isotope. The isotope was supplied in the form of sodium hydrogen carbonate solution – a substance which on decomposition releases $^{14}CO_2$. After exposure to light for a given length of time, Calvin abruptly killed the algal cells by running them into hot alcohol. This had the effect of promptly stopping the photosynthetic reactions. By progressively shortening the time interval between exposure to $^{14}CO_2$ and the killing of the cells, he was able to determine the sequence of intermediate products of carbon dioxide fixation. An extract of the killed cells was obtained and their constituents were separated by chromatography. The radioactive substances were then identified by using a technique known as autoradiography.

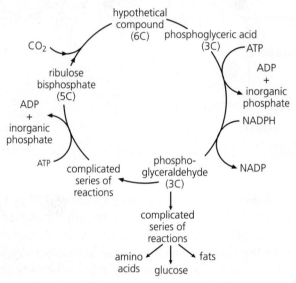

Figure 4.6 The Calvin cycle

The Calvin cycle

Calvin discovered that the dark reactions form a cyclic pathway now known as the Calvin cycle. The first step in the cycle consists of the binding of carbon dioxide to a 5-carbon sugar called **ribulose bisphosphate** (**RuBP**), in the presence of an enzyme called ribulose bisphosphate carboxylase/oxidase (**RUBISCO**). The unstable 6-carbon compound that forms, breaks down to two 3-carbon compounds of **phosphoglyceric acid** (**PGA**). Each PGA molecule is then used in an energy-demanding reaction during which it is phosphorylated by ATP and then reduced by NADPH to form the energy-rich, 3-carbon compound called **phosphoglyceraldehyde** (**PGAL**). A proportion of the PGAL molecules produced in this way are siphoned off for use as building units for synthesis of hexose phosphates, sucrose, starch, fats or amino acids. The rest is used to regenerate RuBP for binding more carbon dioxide molecules that diffuse into the chloroplast from the environment.

Light and distribution of organisms

Green plants occur only in places where there is sufficient light for plant growth. They are, for example, absent in caves. As for animals, their distribution is affected more by whatever influences the distribution of their food source rather than by the presence or absence of light, although, having said that, light does affect the distribution of some animals. Zooplankton, for example, are known to swim towards moderate light and away from intense light.

Some plants function best in bright sunny places. These sun-loving plants are known as **heliophytes**. They have fast metabolic rates that enable them to grow quickly but they also consume a lot of carbohydrates for respiration. To achieve net productivity, they need to receive sufficient light to manufacture enough carbohydrates to compensate for the carbohydrates used up for respiration. This explains why they are also said to be **shade intolerant**. Seedlings of heliophytes die when shaded from direct sunlight often because the weakened, starving plants succumb to attack by fungi.

Plants that are adapted to grow in shady places are known as **shade-tolerant** plants. They have low metabolic rates but they also grow more slowly. The seedlings of shade-tolerant plants are consequently more susceptible to drought because their roots do not grow fast enough to penetrate deeply into the soil. Some dominant sun-loving trees such as oak have shade-tolerant seedlings, a clear adaptation to shading under forest conditions. When a gap appears in the forest due, for example, to the death of a dominant tree, the seedlings develop fast metabolic rates and grow quickly to take advantage of the available light.

In open water, light intensity at the surface and to a depth of a few metres is usually adequate for plant growth. However, near the water's edge there may be shading from overhanging trees. Large quantities of opaque suspended particles such as silt, if present, could also result in light penetration falling off steeply. Similarly, suspended particles in rivers can limit light penetration and consequently impose limits on plant growth even when plenty of mineral nutrients are available. In eutrophic lakes, where there is a dense population of phytoplankton near the surface, light to the deeper parts can be cut off restricting the growth of bottom-living plants to the shallower parts near the water's edge.

Figure 4.7 Many seedlings of forest trees are shade-tolerant

Effect of day length – photoperiodism

Many organisms use the changing length of day or night as a cue for timing their daily or seasonal activities. Unlike ambient temperature, which can fluctuate considerably from day to day, day length offers organisms a highly predictable and reliable measure of the seasons. In many wild plants growing in northern latitudes, the onset of flowering, the cessation of vegetative growth and the start of bud dormancy are all controlled by the length of day. In animals, nest building, breeding cycles, winter plumage and migratory behaviour are initiated by changes in day length. The term **photoperiodism** is used to refer to the responses of organisms to varying day lengths.

Photoperiodism is clearly an important factor in the distribution of plants and animals. It synchronises the breeding times of the members of a population to ensure that the young are born at a time when food will be plentiful. The migratory behaviour of birds to other feeding grounds where food is seasonally abundant, is initiated by day length. The onset of hibernation in small mammals such as hedgehogs is also controlled by day length.

Discovery of photoperiodism

Two American biologists, W.W. Garner and H.A. Allard, discovered photoperiodism in 1920 and gave it its name. They were attempting to use a new mutant variety of tobacco called Maryland Mammoth for cross-breeding purposes. The problem was that the new, rather magnificent variety, would not flower in the summer when planted in the open at a time when other tobacco varieties flowered normally. The plant would only flower when propagated from cuttings and grown in greenhouses and then only in winter. This meant that it could not be used to cross-pollinate the other varieties.

Garner and Allard recognised that the environmental conditions in the greenhouse in winter differed from the conditions that existed outdoors in summer. To try to get the plants to flower in summer, they grew the plants in artificially shortened daylight by transferring the plants into a dark cupboard after the plants had been exposed to the desired number of light hours, corresponding to the number of light hours the plants would have received in the winter greenhouse. To their delight, the Maryland Mammoth plants flowered prolifically in summer. They had clearly discovered a way of getting the plants to flower at will. Garner and Allard also discovered that they could suppress winter flowering by growing the plant in artificially extended daylight by using electric lamps. They could also induce many other plants to flower or to suppress flowering by 'adjusting' the length of day.

Figure 4.8 Earthworms lack eyes but they have light-sensitive cells which enable them to tell light from darkness

Responding to light stimuli

The survival of all organisms depends ultimately on their ability to respond to changes in their environment. An earthworm which is slow in retreating into its burrow at sunrise, for example, is not likely to remain alive for long. Earthworms do not appear to have anything comparable to eyes but nevertheless possess **light-sensitive cells** in their skin which are connected to their nervous system, thus enabling them to distinguish light from darkness.

Many microscopic flagellate algae possess light-sensitive organelles called **eyespots** which enable them to respond to light intensity. Plankton, for example, are known to migrate up and down in lakes and seas in response to light intensity. When the light is too bright for survival, the phytoplankton migrate down to a slightly deeper water which is still illuminated but where photosynthesis can occur without damage. The zooplankton, many of which possess **compound eyes**, migrate with the phytoplankton, their movements being determined by the distribution of their food source.

There are strong selective pressures in favour of the development of good eyesight in animals. A deer, for example, that fails to abandon the food it is eating because it did not see or recognise a stealthily approaching predator, will itself become food for others.

Figure 4.9 Light enables animals to see and be seen

The mammalian eye and how it sees

When we look at something, light reflected from the object enters our eye through a transparent window across the front of the eye called the **cornea**. The light passes through a transparent liquid called the **aqueous humour**, through the **pupil** (a hole in an opaque diaphragm known as the **iris**) and then into the **lens** (a biconvex transparent body). The lens bends the light rays causing them to converge and thus form an upside down image on a light-sensitive layer of cells at the rear of the eye called the **retina**.

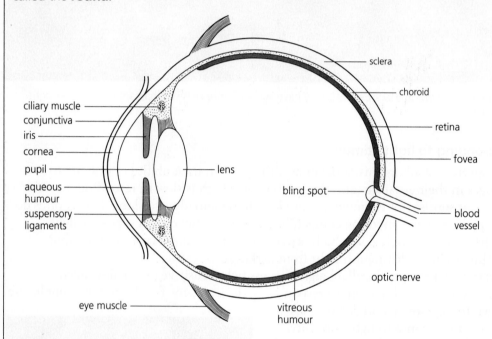

Figure 4.10 Structure of the mammalian eye

The retina is made up of two types of light-sensitive or **photoreceptor cells**. These are known as **rod cells** and **cone cells**. The rods function as photoreceptors in dim light and the cones mediate vision in bright light. Both types are built on the same basic plan.

Structure of rod and cone cells

Each rod or cone cell is divisible into two parts. There is an **inner segment** (which is orientated closer to the lens) and an **outer segment**. The inner segment is structurally like the cell body of a nerve cell or neurone and it contains the nucleus, mitochondria, Golgi bodies and other organelles that sustain the cell. The outer segment contains the light-sensitive apparatus. In rod cells, it is cylindrical in shape and is composed of an orderly pile of **photosensitive membranous discs** within an enveloping **surface membrane**, not unlike a stack of coins within a test-tube. The photosensitive membrane is studded with light-absorbing pigment molecules, which in rod cells consists of a reddish pigment with a protein component called

rhodopsin. The outer segment of the cone cells is similar except that it is cone-shaped (hence its name) and its photosensitive membrane is in the form of a single, elaborately folded sheet which is studded with light-sensitive pigment molecules.

Humans have three kinds of cone cells in their retina: one which strongly absorbs short wavelength (blue) light, another which strongly absorbs middle wavelength (green) light and yet another which strongly absorbs long wavelength (red) light. Humans can see all the different colours of the rainbow using just these three types of cone cells.

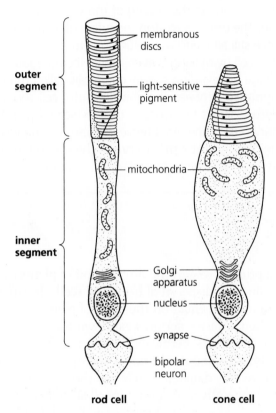

Figure 4.11 Structure of a rod and cone cell of the retina

How rod and cone cells transduce light energy into neural signals

Like nerve cells, the membranes of rod and cone cells are equipped with membrane proteins that function as **sodium–potassium pumps**. Using energy provided by the metabolic activities of the cell, these pumps actively export sodium ions from within the cell and pump in potassium ions. This makes the outside of the cell high in sodium ions and low in potassium ions. The reverse is true within the cell. Because of the higher potassium ion concentration within the cell as compared with the outside, potassium ions tend to diffuse out of the cell, especially through the inner segment of the photoreceptor where the membrane is more permeable to potassium ions.

This loss of positively charged potassium ions causes the inside of the cell to become more electronegative compared with the outside, typically by about 0.1 volts. It is counterbalanced by inflow of sodium ions through the outer segment where the membrane is appreciably permeable to sodium ions. The result is that in darkness, a loop of current known as the **dark current** flows through the photoreceptor cell.

When a photon of light is absorbed by a photosensitive pigment, such as rhodopsin, the pigment molecule changes configuration and its protein component becomes enzymatically active. The activated protein acts catalytically, triggering a series of reactions which result in the closing of the sodium pores in the outer segment's membrane. The effect is to stop the influx of sodium ions (and thus reduce the dark current) while still allowing potassium ions to escape. This hyperpolarises the internal voltage of the cell by making it even more electronegative. The cell responds to the change in voltage by releasing special chemicals called **neurotransmitters** at a junction called a **synapse** between the photoreceptor cell and a nerve cell. The neurotransmitters diffuse across the synaptic cleft (which is a gap between the two cells) to cause the nerve cell to initiate a nerve impulse. The nerve impulse travels via a nerve fibre, passing through the **optic nerve** of the eye to the visual centre of the brain where the nerve impulse is interpreted as a visual signal.

Wind

The wind can exert a primary role in the distribution of plants by assisting in the pollination of flowers and the dispersal of fruits and seeds. It can also, by promoting transpiration, exert an indirect effect on the types of plants growing in a habitat. Strong winds can by their abrasive action wear down the waxy cuticle covering leaves, thus increasing the plants' permeability to water. They can also uproot trees growing on exposed cliff-tops, mountain ridges and open plains. Winds can cause asymmetric growth of trees by damaging buds and shoots on the windward side of the trees. These effects are generally more pronounced at higher altitudes where wind speeds are often greater.

Cold winds can cause plants in mid and high latitudes to die from wind chill by lowering the temperature within cells to below freezing. The ice crystals that form within the cells can rupture cell membranes and cell organelles thus allowing salts and other solutes to seep out of the cells when warmer conditions return.

Dry, powdery soils can also be blown away by the wind making exposed habitats less hospitable for plant growth.

Questions

1 Describe how you would determine what factors affect the distribution, species diversity and abundance of organisms in a *named* habitat.
2 Describe four factors that could affect the distribution and abundance of vegetation growing on north-facing compared with south-facing walls.

Edaphic factors

Derived from the Greek word *edaphos*, which means 'ground', **edaphic factors** refer to the physical, chemical and biological characteristics of soil that affect living organisms.

What is soil?

The soil is formed by the weathering of parent rock and the activities of living organisms that use it as a habitat. It consists of a variable mixture of broken and weathered minerals, both soluble and insoluble, together with water, air, decaying organic matter and myriads of living organisms that use the soil as a habitat. The soil provides water, air and mineral nutrients for plants as well as anchorage for plant roots. The nutrition of plants is therefore dependent on the soil's ability to retain essential mineral nutrients and to make them available to plant roots for absorption.

Mineral solids

The amount and type of mineral solids in soil depend on the parent rock from which they were derived. The mineral solids are classified according to size into clay (less than 0.002 mm), silt (0.02–0.002 mm), fine sand (0.2–0.02 mm), coarse sand (2.0–0.2 mm) and gravel (above 2.0 mm).

The clay fraction

Clay particles are important because they hold water and retain mineral ions. Some clay soils can hold as much as three times their own volume of water, swelling when wet and shrinking when dry. They are, however, prone to becoming waterlogged and deficient in air.

Humus

An important organic constituent of soil is humus. It consists of the decay-resistant remains of plant and animal matter such as lignin, chitin, waxes, fats and some proteinaceous substances. It is jelly-like and dark brown or black in colour and it promotes soil fertility by serving as food for soil microorganisms which in turn break down organic matter and recycle the nutrients needed by plants.

Cation exchange

Clay and humus particles are small in size and carry negative charges on their surfaces. They not only provide large surfaces for water retention but also attract cations (positively charged ions) to their surfaces, thus serving as a reserve source of mineral nutrients for plant roots. These cations are not bound permanently to the clay and humus particles but can be replaced by other ions by a process known as **cation exchange**.

Cation exchange works in the following way. Ions are bound preferentially depending on the strength of their charge. The stronger the electrical charge, the more secure the bonding. In due course, ions with a weaker charge are replaced by those with a stronger charge. If all the ions are present in equal concentrations, sodium ions will be replaced by potassium ions, potassium by magnesium, magnesium by calcium and calcium by hydrogen ions.

Roots and soil organisms are continually releasing carbon dioxide as a product of respiration. The carbon dioxide dissolves in water to form carbonic acid which dissociates into hydrogen ions and hydrogen carbonate ions.

$$CO_2 + H_2O \rightleftharpoons \underset{\text{carbonic acid}}{H_2CO_3} \rightleftharpoons H^+ + HCO_3^-$$

There is, in other words, a continual release of hydrogen ions which act by displacing other cations bound to the clay and humus particles, thus making them available to plant roots for absorption.

Soil type

The structure, depth and nutrient content of the soil are important especially to plants. However, most plants can grow on a wide range of soil types so that soils generally provide only a secondary effect on the distribution of plants and animals. Climatic factors such as rainfall and temperature and the previous history of the land are generally far more important. Nevertheless soils can influence the distribution of plants and consequently of animals in the following ways:

- Depending on the compactness of the soil, the growth and establishment of some types of seedlings may be favoured as compared with others. The constant trampling by humans or wild animals over well-used paths, for example, can affect the types of seedlings that establish themselves on such compacted soils.
- The availability of nutrients could also be a factor in the distribution of plants. Wet soils low in nitrogen, for example, favour the growth of nitrogen-fixing cyanobacteria (formerly known as blue–green algae) over other groups.
- The drainage and water retention qualities of the soil could be a factor. Coniferous forests in the mid latitudes, for example, are usually found growing on well-drained sandy soils of low alkalinity. Oak forests, on the other hand, are typically found growing on richer clayey and sandy soils; beech trees are generally dominant on drier, chalky soils and alders grow best on permanently wet soils.

pH

The pH of the soil can exert an important effect on the distribution and abundance of plants and animals. In general, neutral soils support a greater abundance of plant and animal life than soils which are strongly acid (pH lower than 4) or strongly alkaline (pH higher than 9). Acidity or alkalinity between these extremes may only cause minor direct damage to plants but the indirect effect especially on the availability of soil nutrients can be profound.

- By selectively making ions soluble, acids promote the leaching of vital minerals such as potassium, calcium and magnesium, thus reducing soil fertility.
- They can also act by reducing the population of soil bacteria. This can in turn affect the rate of decomposition of organic matter and consequently, the rate of release of minerals locked up in the tissues of dead organisms.

- By a process known as **cation exchange**, acids can cause the aluminium ion concentration in the soil to rise to toxic levels. Aluminium competes with calcium for binding sites on root cells, thus interfering with calcium ion uptake.
- Plants weakened by mineral deficiency are generally more susceptible to attack by disease-causing microorganisms such as pathogenic fungi.

Alkalis are not commonly the most significant factor restricting the distribution of plants. A yellowing between the leaf veins (a condition known as lime chlorosis) is commonly observed when acid-loving plants, such as *Rhododendron*, grow on calcareous alkaline soils. The condition is caused by a deficiency of iron. Such plants would clearly not be able to compete with plants that can tolerate alkaline conditions and will eventually be eliminated from such habitats.

Acidification of freshwaters

In recent years, fish, especially brown trout, have disappeared from thousands of lakes and rivers in southern Scandinavia. The main cause is believed to be acid rain – precipitation containing sulphuric and nitric acid derived from air pollutants, mainly sulphur dioxide and nitrogen oxides (see Chapter 7). The deaths of fish and shrimps or their inability to reproduce have been linked to surges in acidity in rivers following the melting of snow or heavy autumn rainfall. The acidified lakes and rivers have a low pH, low levels of dissolved calcium and high levels of soluble aluminium leached from the surrounding soil. The acid itself is not the cause of the diminished stocks of fish but poisoning by aluminium ions is widely believed to be the key problem.

All soils contain aluminium but in an insoluble form. Acids dissolve aluminium ores, allowing the aluminium ions to be washed into streams, rivers and lakes. The aluminium affects fish by coagulating mucus on the surfaces of their gills. The fish's ability to take up oxygen is consequently impaired. Fish also lay fewer eggs in acidified waters and the young fish that hatch out are very sensitive and do not survive for long.

Figure 4.12 Trees in the Czech Republic damaged by sulphuric acid in the atmosphere

Salinity

All natural waters, including those that are described as fresh, contain dissolved salts. If a sample of natural water is boiled until all the water has evaporated, white crystals of salts are left behind on the dish. Typically, about a third of the salts consists of common salt or sodium chloride; the rest is a mixture of carbonates, chlorides and sulphates of calcium, magnesium and sodium. These salts are released by a natural process of weathering of rocks which results in both soluble and insoluble particles of rock being carried from uplands to lowlands. The soluble salts are carried down streams, rivers and finally into the sea. Some salts are leached from the surrounding soil.

The term **salinity** refers to the degree of saltiness. It is measured by determining the total dry mass of all the chemical salts in a kilogram of water expressed as a percentage or as parts per thousand. For example, a virgin stream emerging from a mountain watershed may contain as little as 0.005% of dissolved salts whereas open ocean water, through millions of years of salt accumulation, contains on average about 3.5% or 35 parts per thousand of dissolved salts.

Most aqueous environments fall into one of three categories:

1 **freshwater** (salinity less than 0.2 parts per thousand or 0.02%)
2 **marine** (salinity about 35 parts per thousand)
3 **brackish** (formed by the mixing of fresh- and seawater, as in estuaries).

Osmosis

Osmosis is the diffusion of water molecules from a region of their higher concentration to a region of their lower concentration across a partially permeable membrane. It can readily be demonstrated in a school laboratory using a piece of apparatus known as a **simple osmometer** (Figure 4.13). It consists of a special cellulose tubing called Visking tubing, one end of which is tied into a knot to form a bag. The bag is then filled with strong sucrose solution and a glass tube is inserted and secured in place with a thread or length of elastic. The bag is then immersed in a beaker of pure water. Within minutes, the level of solution within the tube can be observed to rise. No such rise is observed in a control experiment with water in place of the strong sucrose solution.

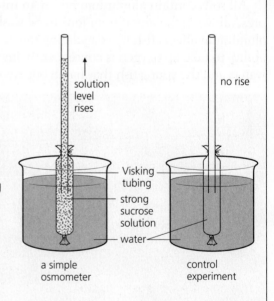

Figure 4.13 A demonstration of osmosis using a simple osmometer

Explanation for osmosis

A special case of diffusion

The traditional explanation for osmosis is to regard it as a special case of diffusion. To understand the traditional explanation, consider the system illustrated in Figure 4.14 which shows a partially permeable membrane standing between pure water on the left of the membrane (side A) and a solution of sucrose on the right of the membrane (side B). The water molecules are small enough to pass through the pores of the membrane but the sucrose molecules, which are too large, cannot pass through.

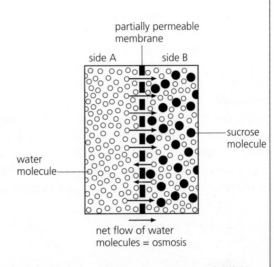

Figure 4.14 Osmosis – a special case of diffusion

At any given moment in time, all the molecules that by random motion bump into the membrane from side A are water molecules, some of which will pass through. At that same instant, from side B some molecules bumping into the membrane are water molecules while others are sucrose molecules. The sucrose molecules cannot pass through because they are too large. Since there are more water molecules striking the membrane from side A than from side B, there is a net movement of water molecules from A to B. It is this net movement of water molecules across the partially permeable membrane which is osmosis.

Mass flow hypothesis

Careful measurements using isotopically labelled water (H_2O^{18}) show that the movement of water by osmosis is far too rapid to be explained in terms of simple diffusion, even if the maximum rate of diffusion is assumed. Current hypotheses concerning osmotic flow are based on the concept of **mass flow** of water driven by energy differences of solutions of different concentrations separated by a partially permeable membrane. The term mass flow is used to refer to bulk flow of materials along a pressure gradient.

According to the mass flow hypothesis, the arrangement of water molecules in pure water is orderly in the sense that every molecular location is occupied by a water molecule. On the other side, the presence of sucrose makes the arrangement disorderly because at any molecular location there may either be a water or a sucrose molecule. The disorderliness lowers the **degree of hydrogen bonding** with the result that the disorderly side possesses less **internal energy** than the orderly side. It is this difference in internal energy which drives the mass flow of water, through the pores of the partially permeable membrane, down the energy gradient, which is osmosis.

Osmoregulation in freshwater species

Freshwater organisms live in a watery medium which is relatively salt free. The dissolved solute concentration of the cell sap and body fluids of these organisms is much higher. There is therefore a strong tendency for freshwater organisms to gain water by osmosis from the dilute water that surrounds them.

Consider, for example, *Amoeba*, a pond-dwelling protozoan (unicellular organism). It is continually taking in water by osmosis through its partially permeable cell membrane. To stop itself from swelling and bursting, it must actively pump out the excess water as fast as the water gets in. This is achieved with a **contractile vacuole**, a spherical sac, which collects the excess water and which from time to time discharges its watery contents to the exterior. This process by which organisms maintain the concentration of their body fluids constant and in equilibrium with their watery surroundings is known as **osmoregulation**.

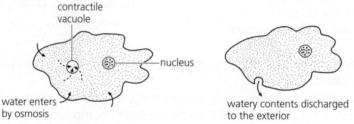

Figure 4.15 Osmoregulation in *Amoeba*

Freshwater fish have a similar osmotic problem. Like *Amoeba*, the osmotic concentration of their body fluids is higher than that of the surrounding freshwater and they are consequently continually taking in water by osmosis through their permeable surfaces, which are mainly their gills and gut lining. Their external body surface, which is covered by scales and a layer of mucus, is relatively impermeable. To get rid of the excess water which threatens to dilute their blood and burst their body cells, freshwater fish have evolved very efficient kidneys that are capable of excreting large quantities of very dilute urine.

A rich assortment of insects live in freshwater habitats such as ponds and lakes. Many spend their entire larval lives in water before metamorphosing into adult flying insects. All insects, including their larval stages, have an external body covering called a hard **exoskeleton** which is impermeable to water. This allows freshwater insects to use excretory apparatus designed for terrestrial life to deal with what is effectively a much reduced water-uptake problem.

Osmoregulation in marine species

Analysis of the blood of marine bony fish shows that their body fluid salt concentration is about a third of that of seawater. The most widely accepted explanation for this is that the ancestors of the bony fish lived in freshwater and that, when they later invaded the sea, they retained their dilute body fluids. Some have challenged this view but there is no convincing mechanism which explains why marine bony fish should have a body fluid salt concentration which is substantially lower than that of the surrounding seawater. Whatever the reason, there is a strong tendency for marine bony fish to lose body water by osmosis to the surrounding seawater and they are consequently living in constant danger of dying of dehydration. To make up for water losses through their gills and gut lining, marine bony fish drink large quantities of seawater. The excess salt which comes with drinking seawater is expelled by secretion through special salt-secreting cells located in their gills.

Cartilaginous fish, such as sharks and rays, have a body salt concentration which is also about a third of the salt concentration of seawater. These fish employ a different strategy to solve their osmotic problems. By accumulating large quantities of urea in their body fluids, cartilaginous fish raise the total osmotic concentration of their body fluids so that it is equal to or slightly above that of the surrounding seawater.

Regulators and non-regulators

Most marine invertebrates such as worms and oysters have body fluid concentrations which are the equivalent of that of seawater. Since the salt concentration of seawater stays always very constant, these animals are rarely exposed to osmotic problems. Problems only arise when marine species invade brackish or freshwater habitats.

The shore crab (*Carcinus* sp.), for example, has body fluids which are in osmotic equilibrium with seawater. To survive in brackish water, the short crab uses special salt-secreting cells in its gills to extract salt from the surrounding water to maintain its body fluid concentration constant. Excess water that enters by osmosis is got rid of by excretion through the crab's excretory organs.

The ancestors of freshwater mussels are widely believed to have moved up estuaries to colonise rivers and lakes. By way of adaptations for survival in freshwater, freshwater molluscs employ two quite different strategies to overcome their osmotic problems. They have evolved very dilute body fluids to minimise the tendency for water to enter through their permeable surfaces and they also have kidneys that can excrete very dilute urine.

Some groups such as the echinoderms (e.g. starfish, brittle stars, sea urchins and sea cucumbers) seem never to have evolved osmoregulatory mechanisms and are consequently confined in their distribution to marine habitats. They are said to be **non-regulators**. Others such as free-living freshwater flatworms (planarians) possess complex, tubular osmoregulatory and excretory organs which are not present in their marine relatives. It is assumed that having evolved such organs as an adaptation to salinity changes, the ancestors of the planarians were thus suitably equipped to move up estuaries to colonise rivers and lakes.

Figure 4.16 There are no freshwater starfish probably because they never evolved osmoregulatory mechanisms

Halophytes

In coastal areas, the combined effect of wind and salt spray can severely limit the growth of plants to just a few types capable of tolerating high levels of salinity. Plants that can live in conditions of excessive salinity are known as **halophytes**.

All plants tolerate some degree of environmental salinity because they require dissolved salts in order to grow. However, most plants cannot tolerate high concentrations of environmental salt because essential water is drawn out of their cells by osmosis leading to cell shrinkage and death by dehydration. To retain water, halophytes must accumulate sufficient salts in their cells to create a positive gradient between themselves and the environment. Their cell sap may have a salt concentration which is five times higher than other plants. Many have succulent stems and leaves containing water storage tissues. Many halophytes also possess special salt-secreting glands or hairs in their leaves.

Water relations of plant cells

Like animal cells, plant cells have a cell membrane which is partially permeable. This property of partial permeability allows the cell to make use of energy differences in the solutions on either side of the cell membrane to force water into or out of the cell. If the fluid outside is more dilute than the cell sap, that is, if the solution outside has a higher concentration of water and a lower concentration of solutes, water will enter the cell by osmosis causing the cell to swell. If, on the other hand, the solution outside is stronger, as for example when a cell is bathed in a molar solution of sodium chloride, water from within the cell will move out into the surrounding solution and the cell will shrink. Such a cell is said to be **plasmolysed** and the process of cell shrinkage due to water loss by osmosis is known as **plasmolysis**. Temporary plasmolysis is not harmful but prolonged plasmolysis leads to the death of the cell as the loss of water inhibits many biochemical processes essential for cell survival.

Water potential, solute potential and pressure potential

Three important terms are used in connection with studies of the forces acting on the movement of water in and out of plant cells. These are **water potential**, **solute potential** and the **pressure potential**.

Water potential

The water potential is a measure of the internal energy of water resulting from the intrinsic properties of the molecules in the system. Since there is no certain way of measuring the internal energy of water, the water potential of pure water at atmospheric pressure is assigned the value of zero. All solutions at atmospheric pressure, by virtue of the fact that they have solutes dissolved in them, have water potential values less than zero, that is, negative values. Cell-to-cell movement of water always occurs from regions of higher (less negative) water potential to regions of lower (more negative) water potential. The internal energy of water is normally expressed in pressure units known as kilopascals (kPa). For example, water moves by osmosis from a cell whose water potential is −300 kPa to an adjacent cell of water potential −500 kPa.

Solute potential

The solute potential is a measure of how much of the internal energy of pure water at atmospheric pressure is lost by the presence of solute molecules. It is, in other words, a measure of the change in water potential due to the presence of added solutes. Since the water potential is zero, values of solute potential are always negative.

The cell sap in a normal vacuolated cell is an aqueous solution containing dissolved sugars, amino acids and various mineral salts. The solute potential of the cell sap of most plant cells ranges in magnitude from about -500 kPa to about -4000 kPa. The prevailing environmental conditions and the intrinsic metabolic activities of the cells affect the solute potential of the plant tissue. Plant tissues taken from plants that have been kept in darkness for a prolonged period of time, for example, generally have lower solute potentials due to depletion of their food reserves compared with plant tissues that have been accumulating sugars, amino acids and mineral salts in their vacuolar cell sap due to photosynthesis.

Pressure potential (turgor pressure)

For plant cells, the solution outside is usually a weak watery solution which is much more dilute than the cell sap. The movement of water is consequently principally from the watery environment outside into the cell, thus enabling the plant to take up water from its surroundings. This will also cause the cells to swell but only a little because the plant cell wall is strong enough to resist stretching. The effect of water entry into a plant cell is, in some ways, not unlike that of pumping air into a rubber tyre. As air enters the tyre, it begins to feel increasingly firm. Similarly, as water enters a cell, the hydrostatic pressure of the cell contents gradually increases and the cell becomes firm or **turgid**. This hydrostatic pressure which is exerted by the swelling protoplast against the cell wall is known as the pressure potential or **turgor pressure**. The pressure potential is a positive pressure with values greater than zero.

Osmosis and turgor

Turgor pressure plays an important role in providing mechanical support for soft plant tissues. By pushing outwards against one another, turgid cells keep the organ firm and enable soft tissues to support themselves without the aid of a rigid skeleton. A well-watered plant seedling, for example, feels firm and stands erect because the cells that make up its stem and leaves are turgid. If plant cells are denied water, as when there is a drought, there is loss of turgor due to evaporation to the dry surroundings. The tissues of such dehydrated plants feel soft and **flaccid**. A plant whose cells are flaccid is said to be **wilted**.

The water potential equation

In a flaccid cell, the protoplast is not exerting any pressure against the cell wall and its pressure potential is therefore zero. When a flaccid cell is immersed in an excess of water, inward movement of water by osmosis occurs and, with continued uptake of water, the pressure potential of the protoplast gradually increases. Subjecting the water in the cell sap to pressure increases the internal energy of its water molecules, thus raising the water potential of the cell sap. Entry of water into the plant cell comes to a halt when the internal energy levels of the solutions inside and outside the cell are equal, or, to put it in another way, when the pressure potential of the sap rises sufficiently to compensate for the difference in water potential between the cell sap and the surrounding water. When dynamic equilibrium is reached, the water potential of the cell sap is zero, exactly the same as the water potential of the surrounding water. If this cell has a solute potential of −1500 kPa, its pressure potential at dynamic equilibrium would have risen to +1500 kPa. This state of dynamic equilibrium is defined by the **water potential equation** as follows:

$$\Psi \quad = \quad \Psi s \quad + \quad \Psi p$$

water potential   solute potential   pressure potential

Therefore,

pressure potential = water potential − solute potential

Consider now what happens when the same flaccid cell with a solute potential of −1500 kPa were to be immersed in an excess of bathing fluid of water potential −600 kPa. At dynamic equilibrium the water potential of the cell sap would be −600 kPa, the same as the bathing fluid. The pressure potential of the sap at dynamic equilibrium can be worked out using the above equation as follows:

$$\Psi \quad = \quad \Psi s \quad + \quad \Psi p$$

water potential   solute potential   pressure potential

Therefore,

pressure potential	=	water potential	−	solute potential
	=	−600 kPa	−	−1500 kPa
	=	−600 kPa	+	1500 kPa
	=	900 kPa		

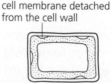

cell membrane detached
from the cell wall

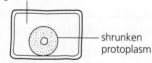

cell chamber filled with
strong salt solution

shrunken
protoplasm

a **turgid cell**
(bathed in water)

incipient plasmolysis (bathed in
a salt solution of the same
concentration as the cell sap)

a **plasmolysed cell** (bathed
in a strong salt solution)

Figure 4.17 Three osmotic states of a plant

Incipient plasmolysis

By varying the solute concentration of the external solution and observing which solution is just strong enough to induce 50% plasmolysis in the cells, biologists can determine the water potential of the cell sap of plant cells. The term **incipient plasmolysis** is used to describe the first signs of plasmolysis. An external solution which can induce it in a cell is taken to have the same water potential as the cell sap because at incipient plasmolysis, the pressure potential of the cell protoplast is zero.

Water movements

It is impossible to separate the effects of the water current and the substratum on the composition of communities in streams. The fact is that where the water is flowing rapidly (over 1.0 m s^{-1}), silt does not settle and the substratum is consequently too rocky for rooted plants to become established. The only types of vegetation found growing in fast-flowing streams are a few types of algae, mosses and liverworts which may become established in crevices between the rocks where the water speed is somewhat reduced. Larger rooted plants are normally found growing further downstream and along the banks where the water is flowing sufficiently slowly to allow some silting to occur. These plants have stems and leaves that are flexible and much dissected or ribbon-like to offer as little resistance to the water current as possible.

The force of the water also tends to wash away all forms of life other than those that are powerful swimmers or capable of finding shelter or that possess well-developed attachment or rooting systems. Plankton, for example, are generally absent in flowing water because they are carried away downstream. Neither would one find free-floating plants such as duckweed (*Lemna* sp.). These plants occur only in ponds and lakes where the water is still or flowing imperceptibly slowly.

One group of animals that can be found in fast-flowing water are the powerful swimming, streamlined fish. Another group consists of animals that exhibit some structural modification that prevents them from being washed away by water current. Planarians (free-living flat worms such as *Polycelis nigra*), for example, have flattened bodies and a slimy adhesive body surface. By living in the 'boundary layer' just above the stony substratum where the water speed is somewhat reduced or in crevices or beneath rocks, they can avoid the full force of the water current and thus escape getting themselves washed off. Freshwater limpets are another good example. They have a conical shell which offers little resistance to the current and a powerful muscular foot which acts like a sucker. Leeches have enlarged suckers, one at the front end and another at the rear end. These are used for attachment and locomotion. Suckers are also a characteristic feature of many small aquatic insects such as the midge larva, *Simulium*. Anchorage can also be achieved with hooks such as those on the rear end of web-spinning caddis fly larvae.

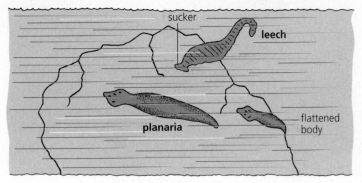

Figure 4.18 Two types of organisms adapted for life in fast-flowing water

Where the water current flows sufficiently slowly to allow fine silt particles to settle, the predominant animals occupying the spaces between stones and gravel change to burrowing forms such as *Tubifex* worms and the so-called 'blood worms' (chironomid fly larvae). Less specialised forms such as the shrimp-like crustacean *Gammarus* are also generally abundant in slow-flowing streams.

Along the seashore, the daily or twice daily ebb and flow of the tides and the crash and swirl of wind-formed waves are dominant factors influencing the types of organisms that inhabit the intertidal zone between land and sea. Many inhabitants of rocky shores possess features that enable them to cling tenaciously to the rocks and thus prevent themselves from being washed off by the pounding action of the waves. Some, such as tube worms and barnacles, live permanently cemented to the rock face. Others such as brown seaweed (e.g. *Fucus serratus* and *F. vesiculosis*) possess strong root-like or disc-shaped extensions of the fronds which anchor the weed firmly to the substratum. Still others, such as shore crabs and shrimp-like amphipods, crawl into cracks in the rocks to avoid the full force of the waves and use claws on their walking legs as anchors to resist detachment.

Some types of shores, for example shingle beaches, support much smaller populations of plant and animal life because the constant grinding action of pebbles thrown against one another by the tides makes such habitats somewhat inhospitable.

Oxygen concentration

Oxygen is needed for aerobic respiration. It is present in abundance in the air and is consequently not normally a resource which poses any limitations on the distribution of air-breathing organisms. However, its solubility in water is quite low – a given

Figure 4.19 Water splashing over rocks as it reaches downstream is generally rich in dissolved oxygen

volume of water contains on average about 30 to 40 times less oxygen than an equal volume of air at atmospheric pressures. This explains why availability of oxygen is often the key limiting factor affecting the distribution of animals in aquatic ecosystems.

Oxygen in the air diffuses into water whenever air and water meet as, for example, at the surface of a lake. Any violent agitation of the water such as when the wind blows to agitate the water surface into ripples, increases the surface area in contact with air, allowing more oxygen to diffuse into the water. This also explains why water splashing over rocks and stones as it rushes downstream is better oxygenated than water that is flowing gently in an estuary. Oxygen is also released by photosynthesising submerged aquatic plants. On a bright sunny day, the water in a weedy pond may contain more oxygen than will readily dissolve in it. The water is then said to be **supersaturated** with oxygen. The dissolved oxygen content may then become depleted during the hours of darkness when only the oxygen-consuming respiratory processes of pond-dwelling animals, microorganisms and plants are active.

Oxygen is less soluble in warm water than in cold water. This fact is important because oxygen consumption by living organisms rises with temperature. There is, on average, a 10% increase in respiratory rates for each 1 °C rise in temperature. These facts may be important in limiting the distribution of upstream species that require plenty of oxygen for respiration.

Some animals such as the nymphs of stone flies and mayflies and the larvae of blackflies are typically upstream species. Conditions downstream may not be suitable for them especially if the water downstream is warmer and less oxygenated. The warmer water would raise the metabolic rates of the animals, thus increasing oxygen demand, at a time when the dissolved oxygen content of the water may be falling.

Water which is rich in decaying organic matter is generally deficient in oxygen. The high levels of organic matter promote rapid growth of bacteria which consume vast quantities of dissolved oxygen. The result is water so deficient in oxygen as to be unable to support any form of animal life except for certain aquatic worms and a few types of insect larvae that possess special adaptations for living in such conditions.

Possession of haemoglobin

One characteristic which is frequently seen in animals adapted for life in poorly oxygenated waters is the possession of a blood pigment such as haemoglobin. It allows animals that possess this pigment to extract oxygen from the water with greater efficiency. The annelid sludge worm, *Tubifex*, commonly found living in soft sediments at the bottom of ponds and lakes and in the mud banks of polluted streams and rivers, is a good example. The segmented worm lives in tubes constructed of mud with much of its posterior end projecting out, beyond the end of the tube. By waving its posterior end rhythmically through the oxygen-deficient water, it creates a current which helps to increase its chances of making contact with whatever little oxygen there is in the water. Another aquatic organism which possesses haemoglobin and which occurs commonly in stagnant or slow-flowing water deficient in oxygen is the reddish, worm-like larva of the dance-gnat, *Chironomus* (known commonly as a blood worm).

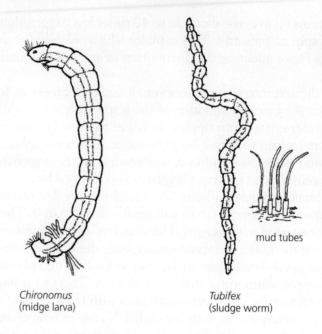

Chironomus
(midge larva)

Tubifex
(sludge worm)

mud tubes

Figure 4.20 Two organisms adapted for life in water deficient in oxygen because they possess haemoglobin

Air breathing

Another useful adaptation for life in poorly oxygenated water is air breathing. There are three main methods:

1 breathing tubes
2 air bubbles
3 lungs.

Breathing tubes

The water scorpion (*Nepa* sp.) and mosquito larvae and pupae are common examples of invertebrate air-breathing aquatic animals that respire through snorkel-like **breathing tubes**. The water scorpion, for example, can often be seen resting head downwards on submerged weeds as it awaits motionless for an unsuspecting prey to pass by. From time to time, it crawls backwards up the vegetation to extrude its breathing tube above the water surface to ventilate its tracheal respiratory system with air.

Air bubbles

Another air-breathing method consists of coming to the surface from time to time to collect a **bubble of air**. With some types, for example, the water boatman (*Notonecta* sp.), the air bubble clings to hairs covering the ventral (or lower) surface of the body. In others, for example the water beetle (*Dytiscus* sp.), the air bubble is carried under the wing covers. Gas exchange occurs between the insect's tracheal system and the

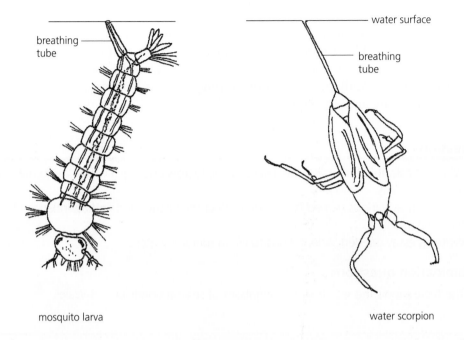

Figure 4.21 Two air-breathing aquatic animals which respire through snorkel-like air tubes

air bubble through breathing holes in the sides of the body known as **spiracles**. The air bubble acts like a **physical gill**. It depends for its function on the fact that it contains nitrogen as well as oxygen. As the oxygen within the air bubble is used up, there comes a point when the oxygen tension within the air bubble falls below that of the surrounding water. When this happens, oxygen from the surrounding water diffuses into the air bubble, thus replenishing the oxygen supply. However, the nitrogen tension within the air bubble is higher than in the surrounding water and nitrogen, therefore, gradually diffuses out of the air bubble causing it to shrink. As the air bubble shrinks, it becomes harder and harder for the insect to obtain enough oxygen. This forces the insect to come to the surface to renew its air bubble.

Figure 4.22 A great diving beetle carrying an air bubble which is shown partly extruded from beneath its wings

Lungs

Some aquatic animals are capable of living in stagnant, deoxygenated water because they possess lungs. The wandering snail (*Limnaea* sp.), for example, possesses a simple lung consisting of a cavity beneath the shell which is lined by tissues that are richly supplied by blood capillaries. From time to time, the snail crawls to the surface of the pond to renew the air in its lungs.

Questions

3 What are **edaphic** factors? Name two edaphic factors and explain how they could affect living organisms.
4 Describe how various *named* factors may affect the distribution and abundance of plankton in a lake.
5 Write an essay entitled 'Adaptations to life in running water'.

Examination questions

1 The table shows the results of investigations of several ponds in mid-Wales.

Pond	pH of pond water	Number of plant species	Number of invertebrate animal species
Mawn Pool	4.4	8	4
Rhulen Hill	4.8	11	5
Llanbadan	5.7	16	9
Mere Pool	6.6	23	19
Beilibedw	8.1	21	14

a Describe the relationship between the pH of these ponds and the numbers of invertebrate animal species.   (1)
b Mere Pool has the greatest species diversity. Use the data to suggest why this is so.   (2)
c Which of these pond ecosystems would you expect to be the least stable? Explain your answer.   (2)   (total = 5)

NEAB, June 1997

2 The willow warbler is a small insect-eating bird. The shaded areas on the map show where willow warblers are found.
a What is the name given to the movement of animals such as the willow warbler from one area to another with changing seasons?   (1)
b i) Suggest and explain at what time of the year you would expect to find willow warblers in Europe.   (1)
   ii) Suggest why it is advantageous to willow warblers to move to Southern Africa for part of the year.   (2)   (total = 4)

NEAB, June 1997

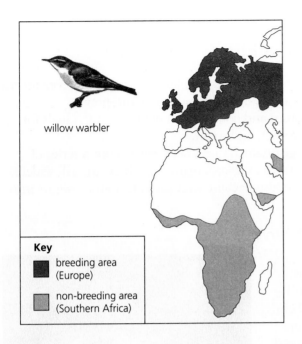

willow warbler

Key

■ breeding area
(Europe)

▨ non-breeding area
(Southern Africa)

Reproduced from *Animal Behaviour*,
McFarland, 1993 by permission of Addison
Wesley Longman Ltd.

3 The figure below shows variations in light intensity, nitrate concentration, numbers of phytoplankton and numbers of zooplankton, in a freshwater lake, over a period of twelve months.

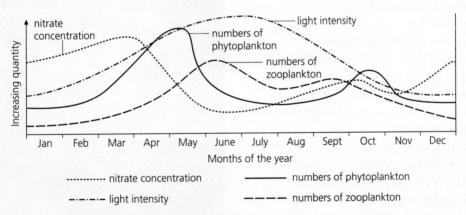

a Using only the data given, suggest possible reasons for:
  i) the increase in numbers of phytoplankton from March to early May. (2)
  ii) the sharp decline in numbers of phytoplankton during mid-May to mid-June. (1)
  iii) the low numbers of phytoplankton in July and August. (1)
b i) Suggest a possible explanation for the second peak in numbers of phytoplankton in October. (1)
  ii) Suggest reasons why this peak is lower than the peak in May. (1)
c State **two** physical factors, other than those given, which might limit the numbers of phytoplankton from mid-November to early February. (2)   (total = 8)

UCLES, June 1986

Ecological interactions

(5)

Biotic factors

The ways in which interactions with other organisms affect an organism or organisms within the area are known as biotic factors. They include predator–prey relationships, parasite–host relationships and competition between individuals for resources such as food, mates, nesting sites, and so on.

In the early 1930s a Russian biologist named G.F. Gause carried out a series of experiments on the growth of populations of microorganisms. These are still widely quoted, not only for their elegance but also because they provide useful insights into how organisms affect one another.

The S-shaped population growth curve

In one of his experiments, Gause introduced a few *Paramecia* – a free-living protozoan (unicellular 'animal') – into a centrifuge tube containing 10 cm^3 of water to which he added a few drops of oatmeal medium. The oatmeal served as food for bacteria which were in turn fed upon by the predatory *Paramecia*. Each day after the start of his experiment, Gause would remove a small sample of the solution with a pipette to count the number of *Paramecia* present. He would then spin the 'animals' to the bottom of the tube, pour away the old water and uneaten food and replace it with an equal quantity of fresh water and oatmeal medium.

In this way, he was able to plot the growth of the population of *Paramecia* against time. Gause obtained an **S-shaped** or **sigmoid growth curve** which showed that the population grew slowly at first, then rapidly, then its growth rate slowed down and, finally, the population stopped growing when maximum size was reached.

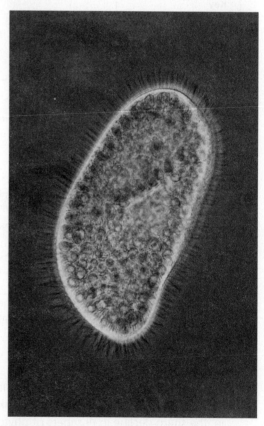

Figure 5.1 *Paramecium bursaria*, a bottom-dwelling ciliate

Exponential growth

It is easy to see why, given an abundance of food and favourable environmental conditions, a few individuals introduced into a new habitat would grow and multiply as fast as their innate capacities would allow them. Each *Paramecium*, in Gause's experiment, would feed, grow and divide to become two cells, the two would then

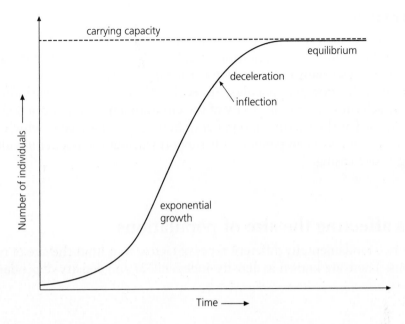

Figure 5.2 S-shaped or sigmoid growth curve of a population of *Paramecia* fed on a steady supply of bacteria

divide to become four cells and so on. This type of population growth in which the population doubles at each generation, from 2 to 4, then 8, 16, 32, 64, 128 and so on is said to be **exponential** or **logarithmic**. A population, growing exponentially in this way, may appear to grow slowly at first even though the rate of change is constant. This is because the numbers of individuals to start with are small. As the numbers increase, from say 128 to 256 and then to 512, the growth curve rises steeply.

Impossibility of sustaining an exponential growth rate

No population can go on increasing at an exponential rate for an indefinite period of time. If this were not so, just a few bacteria multiplying by doubling and redoubling every 20 minutes would increase to a size exceeding the size of planet Earth in less than 48 hours! The fact is that after a period of exponential growth, the habitat becomes crowded with individuals each needing a supply of food and space to live in. By either interfering with one another or competing for limited food supplies, some individuals will inevitably not get enough for growth and reproduction. The result is a decline in the birth rate or an increase in the death rate or both. Population growth slows down and the growth curve shows an inflection as it departs from its steeply rising path and gradually starts to flatten out. During this **deceleration phase**, the birth rate declines although it is still faster than the death rate.

Population growth falls to zero when the birth rate is exactly balanced by the death rate. When this stage is reached, the population is said to be **stable** or in a state of **equilibrium**. During this phase, natural populations may spread to adjacent areas and fluctuate in size often irregularly.

Carrying capacity

A whole variety of factors could act to limit the size of natural populations. These may include availability of food, nesting sites, bad weather, disease and the activity of predators. With so many different factors capable of acting either alone or in concert to limit the growth of populations, ecologists have come up with the term **carrying capacity** to refer to the ability of the environment to support a population. It may be defined as the maximum number of individuals of a species which the resources in a given area can permanently support without the population either increasing or decreasing.

Factors affecting the size of populations

There are two fundamentally different types of factors that limit the size of natural populations. These are known as **density-independent** and **density-dependent** factors.

Density-independent factors

Density-independent factors are environmental factors which reduce the reproduction rate or increase the death rate of organisms independently of population density. An exceptionally harsh winter, for example, can cause many organisms in a population to die. There is, however, no reason to expect that the effects of the cold winter will be any less severe in a sparsely populated area as compared to a densely populated one.

Density-independent factors cause population numbers to fluctuate and they can also determine the level at which a population stabilises. A severe drought, for example, can cause the numbers of aphids to crash by killing off their host plant. The weather is, in this case, acting as a **limiting factor** on the carrying capacity of the environment. It does not act as a regulatory factor (see density-dependent factors, below) but it does affect the available food supply and therefore the carrying capacity of the environment.

Other examples of density-independent factors include floods, deep snow falls, acid rain, fire and so on.

Density-dependent factors

Density-dependent factors are interactions between living organisms that tend to reduce the population when numbers are high and allow the population to increase when numbers are low. All types of biotic interactions including predation, competition, territoriality and disease can limit survival and reproduction and thus act as density-dependent controls on the sizes of populations. These factors regulate populations by constraining population fluctuations, keeping them close to equilibrium. Put another way, they act by preventing populations from growing (or declining) indefinitely.

Predator–prey relationships

Consider for example, how predators act to regulate the size of prey populations. If the prey are numerous, predators should have little difficulty locating and capturing them. With an abundance of food, predator numbers would increase and this would in turn lead to a reduction in the numbers of prey. If the predators take too many prey, they would eliminate their food source, starve and predator numbers would then decline. This would once again lead to a rise in prey numbers and so on. Thus by a density-dependent, negative feedback process, a balance is reached between the numbers of predators and prey.

Obtaining evidence for density-dependent regulation of prey populations by large vertebrate predators is, however, not easy. To keep track of the activities of lions, for example, requires a considerable investment in time. Whatever data there are seem, however, increasingly to suggest that large predators take the sick and the old, which are in any case about to die. They, therefore, act more like impatient scavengers and seem to play only minor roles in determining the size of prey populations.

Figure 5.3 If predators take too many prey, they eliminate their food source – the photo shows a puffin chick with a beakful of sand eels

The hare and the lynx

Perhaps the most widely quoted example of predators allegedly controlling the size of prey populations is the coupled cyclic fluctuations in the populations of the hare and the lynx. Studies based on fur returns recorded by the Hudson Bay Company seemed to suggest that the predatory activities of the lynx kept the population of hares in check. However, it is now known that such an interpretation is misguided. In regions where the lynx has become virtually extinct, hare populations continue to fluctuate as before. Clearly, it was not the lynxes that were controlling the size of hare populations but the other way round! Recent studies suggest that interactions with the plant food are in fact the key factors controlling the size of hare populations. In response to heavy grazing, the plants produced high levels of toxins which made them unpalatable to the hares. The chemicals remain in the plants for 2 to 3 years, which explains why there is a 2½ year delay between the start of the decline in hare numbers and the recovery of their food supply.

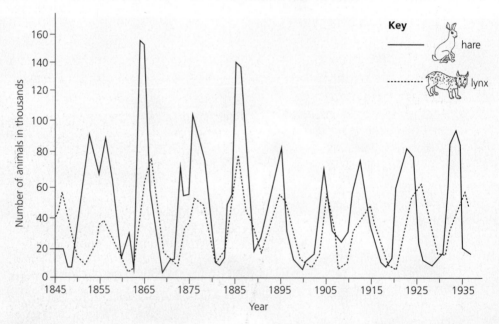

Figure 5.4 Fluctuations in the numbers of hares and lynxes based on fur returns of the Hudson Bay Company

To summarise, resource-regulation rather than predator-regulation appears to be the main ecological factor controlling the size of the hare populations described above.

Whereas there is some doubt as to whether large vertebrate predators do in fact exert effective control over the size of their prey populations, there is no doubt that small predators can and do exert effective and even stringent control over the numbers of their prey. Some of the most spectacular examples of this come from work involving the control of agricultural pests.

Biological control of the cottony-cushion scale

In the 1880s, citrus groves in California became heavily infested with a small, sap-sucking, fluffy insect called the cottony-cushion scale (*Icerya purchasi*). The attack by the cottony-cushion scale on the Californian citrus plants was, in a way, not unexpected. The cottony-cushion scale was known to attack citrus trees in Australia, which was the country from where the Californian plants had in the first place been imported. Australia and California both share fairly similar climates and if the trees could grow well in either country, there seemed no reason why the pests, which were inevitably imported together with the trees, should not also have thrived in their new habitat. What was unexpected, however, was the severity of the attack. Whereas in Australia the citrus trees became only lightly infested with the insect pest, in California, the trees became so heavily parasited that the entire citrus industry was in danger of collapse. The most likely explanation for this was that the scale insects had accompanied the trees from Australia but not their natural enemies. It was reasoned that if the natural enemies of the insect pests could be found and released on to the Californian citrus orchards, the industry might yet be saved from ruin.

A young biologist named Albert Koebele was sent to Australia to look for the natural enemies of the scale insect. He soon discovered that its principal enemy was an attractive, small, predatory ladybird beetle called *Rodolia cardinalis*. The adults as well as the larval stages of the beetle were observed to be carnivorous. Koebele reported that the predatory insects crawled up branches infested with the scale insect and quite literally chewed them up – sap-sucking adults, immature stages, eggs and all.

Koebele sent a consignment of the ladybird beetles to a colleague in California and a total of 129 of them survived the long sea voyage. In the meantime, preparations were made to receive the predatory animals. An orange tree heavily infested with the cottony-cushion scale was covered in a muslin tent. The ladybird beetles together with a few parasitic flies, which were known to attack scale insects, were released into the tent. The parasitic flies did not prove to be particularly effective but the ladybird beetles proceeded to eat the cottony-cushion scale and, within 2 weeks, virtually the whole population of scale insects on the tree had been eaten up.

Figure 5.5 A branch of a citrus tree infested with the cottony-cushion scale (insect)

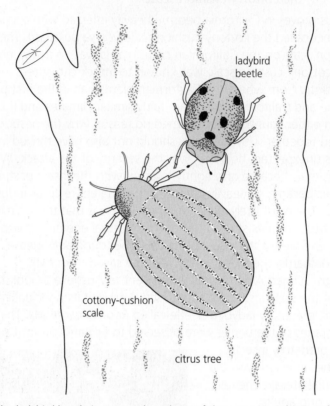

Figure 5.6 The ladybird beetle is a natural predator of the cottony-cushion scale, a sap-sucking, fluffy insect

The beetles were then let out of the tent and they rapidly spread from one citrus orchard to another. Within less than a year, the cottony-cushion scale became no longer an economic threat and by 1890, the citrus trees in California were virtually free of the dreaded pest.

This method of using a natural enemy to combat the spread of a pest is known as **biological control**.

Questions

1 Discuss the ways in which biotic factors, excluding human activity, may affect the size of animal populations.
2 Write an essay entitled 'The interdependence of animals and plants'.
3 What is meant by the term **carrying capacity**? Explain how the population sizes of predators and their prey may be influenced by their interrelationships.

Alien species

Before an alien species is introduced into a new environment, care should be taken to see whether it would attack the target's nearest indigenous relatives or any other organisms of commercial value. This is important because alien species deliberately or accidentally introduced into a foreign environment can quite often wreak a great deal of havoc to crops or natural ecosystems. The case of the Japanese starfish, *Asterias amurensis*, is a fairly typical example.

Japanese starfish lays siege to Tasmania's shellfish industry

Asterias amurensis is normally restricted to the waters of the northern Pacific, around Japan and the Bering Sea near Alaska. In the 1980s it appeared for the first time around the shores of Tasmania in Australia and was most probably brought there as free-swimming larvae in ballast water that was discharged by ships into the port of Hobart to enable the ship to take on cargo on its return journey. The waters of Tasmania, 43° latitude South of the equator, proved as good for the starfish as the waters of Japan 43° latitude North of the equator. Lacking its natural predators, the alien species multiplied and spread from Tasmania northwards. Feeding on the mussel beds along the Australian coastline, the starfish grew and grew until it became a considerable threat to South East Australia's commercially valuable

Figure 5.7 These starfish, feeding on mussel beds, are so numerous because they have no real enemies

shellfish industry. Australian volunteers were recruited to remove by hand tens of thousands of these undesirable invaders without having the slightest impact on the problem. The fact is that *Asterias amurensis* is a very fecund creature and each female starfish can lay millions of eggs into the water to maintain its phenomenal rate of population increase.

Research is still going on to find a solution to the problem. One possibility consists of releasing a ciliate into the Tasmanian waters. This ciliate, *Orchitophyra stellarum*, is a parasite of the starfish and is known to be keeping the Japanese populations of the starfish in check. However, more research needs to be carried out before any such biological control action is taken because there are many other marine organisms in Tasmanian waters which could serve as hosts to the ciliate. At least four genera and seven species of starfish are known to be parasitised by the ciliate.

There are many other examples of alien species that have found themselves released into an environment which is climatically not too unlike the conditions back home but where there is plenty of food and no real enemies. This has allowed them to multiply at a rapid rate and to become a threat to local or indigenous populations.

The alien flatworm

There is, for instance, the alien flatworm, *Artioposthia triangulata*, which was probably brought into Britain in the soil of potted plants imported from New Zealand. It has a mouth which can bite and hold on to a struggling earthworm as it secretes digestive enzymes on to its prey. The flat worm then sucks up the soluble products of digestion and can, in this way, consume an earthworm in about half an hour. Since their first appearance in Northern Ireland about 30 years ago, the alien flatworms have been spreading fast and earthworm populations in infected areas have virtually collapsed. This has undoubtedly led to reduced crop yields in infected areas because earthworms perform the immensely important task of promoting soil fertility.

The latest reports are that the alien flatworms have now spread to Scotland and a few parts of England. They have so far not been detected in Wales.

Losing out to the grey squirrel

Probably the best known alien invader of the English countryside is the North American grey squirrel, *Sciurus carolinensis*. It was introduced into Britain either deliberately or accidentally towards the end of the 19th century. Since then, it has multiplied and become so common that virtually everyone now accepts the endearing creature, with its large appealing eyes and bushy tail, as part of the English countryside. The native red squirrel has sadly been pushed out of much of its own territory and is confined to the Isle of Wight in the south and to forests in Scotland, Ireland and north-east and north-west England.

A number of theories have been put forward to explain why the red squirrels have apparently lost out in competition to the grey squirrels. Probably the most frequently voiced theory is that the grey squirrels, being larger, have edged out the red squirrels in direct competition for food. The scientific evidence, however, points in a different direction. There is evidence that after years of evolution in the deciduous forests of North America, the grey squirrels have evolved the ability to digest chemicals in acorns called polyphenols. Red squirrels, which normally live in coniferous woods, cannot do this and they will consequently only eat acorns with reluctance. Both species can also feed on hazelnuts. However, because grey squirrels have the choice of acorns or hazelnuts, they can put on 20% of their body weight in fat stores over the winter as compared to only 10% for the red squirrels. This extra margin of fat allows the grey squirrels to withstand food shortages much better than the red squirrels and their reproduction rate is consequently less affected by seasonal factors. The result is that the grey squirrels are slowly displacing the red squirrels, not by direct competition for food, but by quite simply out-breeding them.

Figure 5.8 The red squirrel, *Sciurus vulgaris*

Competition

When faced with shortage of a needed resource such as food, predator-free territories, mates, nesting sites, light, dissolved oxygen, mineral salts and so on, individuals will compete with one another or with individuals belonging to other species, for the limited resource. The term **competition** is used to refer to interactions between individuals brought about by the shared need for a limited resource. No competition exists for a resource, such as atmospheric oxygen, which is available in abundance. Neither does competition necessarily imply open conflict. Often threatening behaviour is sufficient.

If one compares two situations, one where competition does not exist because a resource is present in abundance and another where competition does occur, the latter situation is clearly the less favourable because a competitor could even die from lack of a particular resource.

Competition is said to be **intraspecific** if it occurs between individuals of the same species and **interspecific** if it occurs between individuals of different species.

Intraspecific competition

Competition between individuals of the same species plays an important role in regulating the size of the population. Consider for example a population of deer which is limited by its food supply (herbaceous plants). When the deer population is high, its food becomes scarce and some individuals will inevitably not have enough to eat. The death rate rises and the birth rate falls and the result is a decline in population density. At low population densities, the opposite happens. The food-plant becomes more abundant and the population of deer, having more to eat, starts to grow again. In this way, by a negative feedback process, competition for food acts as a density-dependent ecological thermostat keeping the size of the deer population stable and at equilibrium with its environment.

Although many types of interactions can be observed among individuals competing for a limited resource, these can broadly be subdivided into two main types. At the one extreme, there is a type of competition known as **scramble** and at the other there is another type known as **contest**.

Scramble

In scramble, all the competing individuals get some of the resource, with the result that if the population density is high, none of them may have enough for growth and reproduction. A familiar example of this type of competition is seen in flower beds when seedlings are grown too close to one another. Unless the young plants are thinned out, they will all grow weak and spindly and few, if any, flowers will be produced when they mature.

Scramble competition is typical of species that exploit transient food supplies such as carrion or soil minerals. It can produce wild fluctuations in population size with an average population density which is well below the carrying capacity of the habitat.

Contest

In contest competition, an item of resource is contested for until one individual acquires it and the other is left without. Even in very high population density conditions, some individuals will always survive while others will be left with insufficient resources for growth, reproduction or survival. A behaviour pattern known as **territoriality**, in which individuals compete for space, is an example of contest.

Territoriality

This type of behaviour is seen in many types of birds, mammals and some invertebrates during the breeding season. At the start of the breeding season, the male stakes claim to a definite area of the habitat which it then defends against intrusion by rival males of the same species. The defended area of the habitat is known as a **territory**. The boundaries of the territory are established by a variety of signals including singing, bellowing, scent markings or threatening gestures such as the baring of fangs. A male that can successfully hold on to a territory stands a good chance of mating with females that are lured to his territory.

Figure 5.9 The stag announces his possession of the hinds in his territory by pacing purposefully and making a series of coughing roars

Males that are unable to establish a territory will usually not be able to breed. The territory provides the breeding pair with a source of food, nesting sites, a place where copulation can occur undisturbed and an environment where the young can be reared in relative safety.

From an evolutionary point of view, territoriality limits reproduction to the fittest and works in favour of improving the gene pool of the population. By confining reproduction to just a few individuals, it also acts as a density-dependent, self-regulatory system which limits population growth and thus helps to avoid over-exploitation of the food source followed by the sort of 'crash' in population numbers associated with widespread starvation.

Interspecific competition

Interspecific competition occurs when individuals living in the same general area, but belonging to two or more different species, have very similar resource requirements which are in short supply. Mathematical models suggest that two species that compete strongly cannot coexist. The faster growing competitor will eliminate the slower growing competitor and eventually occupy the area completely. This is known as the **principle of competitive exclusion**. Coexistence is possible if competition between species is substantially avoided by the two populations occupying different niches.

Interspecific competition among Paramecia

The Russian biologist, G.F. Gause was one of the first to carry out experiments to determine the outcome of interspecific competition. In 1934, he studied the population growth of three different species of *Paramecium* which he cultured in centrifuge tubes by providing them with controlled amounts of food. Gause found that when the three different species were cultured separately, their population densities increased rapidly and the expected sigmoid curves were obtained. However, when *Paramecium caudatum*, a relatively large, slow-growing species, and *Paramecium aurelia*, a smaller, faster growing species, were cultured together, both species increased rapidly at first but as the culture became crowded, it was *P. caudatum* that succumbed to competition. Its population levelled off and then declined while that of *P. aurelia* continued to increase.

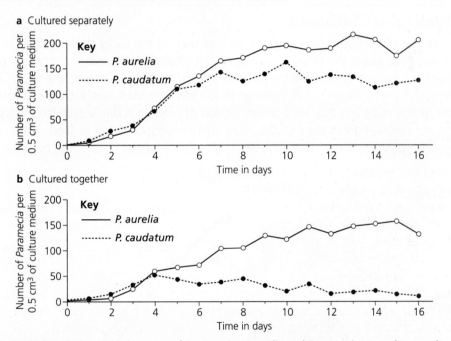

Figure 5.10 Population growth curves of *Paramecium aurelia* and *Paramecium caudatum* cultured separately (a) and cultured together (b) (based on data from G.P. Gause, 1934)

Gause discovered that when *P. aurelia* and *Paramecium bursaria* were cultured together, neither species suffered decline to the point of extinction. They coexisted but the population of each levelled at about half what it would have been had they been cultured separately. Gause soon realised why *P. aurelia* had not eliminated *P. bursaria* or vice versa. *P. aurelia* tended to feed in the top half of the tube whereas *P. bursaria* had a tendency to feed near the bottom of the tube. Although there was some competition in the overlap region near the middle of the tube, the two species of *Paramecia* were largely not in competition because their feeding behaviour was somewhat different. There were in other words, **niche differences** between them.

Competitive exclusion along the rocky seashore

It is one thing to demonstrate the principle of competitive exclusion under laboratory conditions, quite another to do the same under field conditions. For a start, unlike in a test-tube, organisms are free to leave a natural habitat and we can, therefore, never be sure whether what we are seeing is a consequence of competitive exclusion or caused by some other environmental factor. This is why there are very few unambiguous examples of competitive exclusion that have been experimentally demonstrated under field conditions. One of the best is the work of Joseph Connell, who, in 1961, studied the distribution of two species of barnacles, *Chthamalus stellatus* and *Balanus balanoides*, along the coast of Scotland.

Balanus *versus* Chthamalus

Two species of barnacles frequently occur together on the rocky shores in the intertidal zone along the British coastline. Adult *Chthamalus* generally occupy a zone higher up the shore whereas adult *Balanus* occupy a belt lower down the shore. The rocks colonised by *Balanus*, being closer to the low tide mark, are submerged under water by the incoming tide for a longer period of time each day, which means that barnacles colonising this zone of the rocky shore have more time to feed. Both species have young stages that look like tiny crabs or lobsters that swim about as

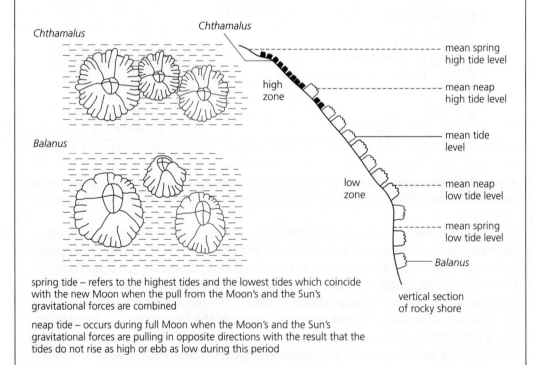

spring tide – refers to the highest tides and the lowest tides which coincide with the new Moon when the pull from the Moon's and the Sun's gravitational forces are combined

vertical section of rocky shore

neap tide – occurs during full Moon when the Moon's and the Sun's gravitational forces are pulling in opposite directions with the result that the tides do not rise as high or ebb as low during this period

Figure 5.11 *Chthamalus* occupies the high zone of the rocky shore, *Balanus* occupies the low zone

members of the zooplankton. As they grow older, the larval forms fix themselves on to the surface of a rock where they will remain attached for the rest of their lives.

In an attempt to try to understand why the two species of barnacles were distributed in the way they were, Joseph Connell cleared experimental patches of rock in the intertidal zone of all barnacles. By holding a sheet of plate glass in a fixed position over the experimental patches, he was able to map the colonisation of the bare patches of rock. In this way, he was able to show that the free-swimming planktonic larvae of both species of barnacles were perfectly capable and did in fact attach themselves on to bare rock at any point in the intertidal zone. Having attached themselves, they then developed into sessile adult forms. However, in the lower intertidal zone, the faster growing *Balanus* individuals crowded out any *Chthamalus* individuals that settled there by quite simply growing over and crushing them. Only by keeping some sites free of *Balanus* were *Chthamalus* able to thrive in the lower intertidal zone. Furthermore, the few *Chthamalus* individuals that survived a year's crowding by *Balanus* in the lower zone were much smaller than the ones that grew up in *Balanus*-free areas. Connell was thus able to demonstrate that *Chthamalus* was capable of growing in the lower intertidal zone but was excluded from this zone by competition with *Balanus*.

Balanus, however, is not as resistant to desiccation as *Chthamalus* and it cannot tolerate long periods of exposure to air and the drying action of the Sun. Since the upper shore zone is left uncovered by the tides for long periods each day, *Balanus* is excluded from this zone by physical desiccation. *Chthamalus* can therefore settle in the upper zone free from competition by *Balanus*.

Mutualism

The types of interspecific interactions that have been considered so far have all been **negative interactions** in the sense that an increase in the population of one species has had the effect of decreasing the population growth rate of another species. For example, competition between the members of two different populations has resulted in both species being harmed by the presence of the other. In predation, one species benefits but the other is harmed.

Positive interactions, that is, those where an increase in the population of one species, increases the population growth rate of another species, are also common and important. The term **mutualism** is used to refer to associations of organisms belonging to two different species in which each species helps the other to survive. The pollination of flowers by insects, the dispersal of seeds and fruits by animals, the cellulose-digesting bacteria in the rumen of cows and the nitrogen-fixing bacteria in the root nodules of leguminous plants, are just a few well-known examples. Less well known but ecologically very important is the mutualistic relationship between forest trees and fungi.

Mycorrhiza – a symbiosis

Many forest and fruit trees of agricultural importance benefit by forming symbiotic relationships with soil fungi. (The term **symbiosis** is used to refer to a close relationship between two different types of organisms and it includes mutualism and parasitism.) The fungus lives intimately with the roots of the trees, sometimes forming a dense sheath of threads or hyphae around the root with some of the fungal hyphae penetrating into the root between the root cells and with others penetrating into the root cells themselves. The association is known as a **mycorrhiza**. There is experimental evidence which suggests that trees that grow in soils poor in phosphorus benefit from a mycorrhiza. This is probably because the thread-like body of the fungus serves as an extension of the root system of the plant. By exploring beyond the root surface, the fungus is able to convert environmental phosphate into a soluble form for transport back to the root. The mycorrhizas may also transport water collected from beyond the reach of the root system and this could be critically important in arid regions. Most trees are so dependent on the fungi that they fare poorly when the soil is lacking in fungi. There is also recent evidence which suggests that the mycorrhizas mount a kind of guard, protecting the roots from attack by pathogenic fungi and small parasitic soil nematodes. Precisely how they do this is still not clear.

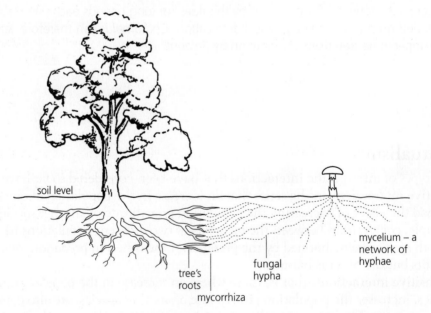

Figure 5.12 Mycorrhiza – an intimate association between the hyphae of fungi and the tree's roots benefits both

The intimate association is not without benefit to the mycorrhizal fungi. Botanists have recently shown that trees move sugars into the surroundings of the fungi, for them to absorb.

What effect does mutualism have on communities in an ecosystem? There are unfortunately not many well-documented studies but the widely accepted view is that it should have an enriching and stabilising effect. Enriching because if one partner of a pair of mutualistic organisms invades or colonises a new habitat, the other partner is also likely to be present. The gains in diversity or species richness, when it does happen, tend to occur not singly but in pairs.

As for the stabilising effect, consider for example the plant-pollinator system. If there are more flowers, there will be more food for pollinating insects and this will in turn lead to a more efficient pollination and so on. This type of density-dependent self-regulatory system in which one population supports another population should lead to greater community stability because of its buffering effect on each other's population growth.

Parasitism

Parasitism is an intimate association between organisms of different species in which the larger of the two, known as the **host**, is a source of food, developmental stimuli and a habitat for the smaller, known as the **parasite**. Put another way, the parasite is at some stage in its life cycle metabolically dependent on the host, whereas the host organism can do quite well without the parasite.

Most parasites lead a highly specialised type of existence. Internal parasites, for example, live in moist unchanging conditions of total darkness and have no use for eyes and other sense organs because their environment is singularly lacking in external stimuli. They consequently lack sense organs of the type found in their free-living relatives and have degenerate nervous systems. They may also have poor locomotory capabilities and, because their food can be absorbed directly through their external surface, they have poorly developed digestive tracts. These losses are often compensated for by the following:

- the possession of elaborate organs of attachment such as hooks, suckers or claws
- well-developed reproductive organs often with an asexual multiplicative phase at some stage within their life cycle
- the use of an intermediate vector such as a biting insect to carry the parasite from a weakened or incapacitated host to another susceptible one.

The tapeworm

The adult pork tapeworm (*Taenia solium*) is an internal parasite which inhabits the human intestine and which can grow to between 2 to 7 metres in length. It has a flattened body and it lacks a mouth or digestive tract. Its food comes to it predigested and it feeds by quite simply absorbing a proportion of the host organism's products of digestion, namely sugars and amino acids, which it takes in directly through its external body surface.

At one end the tapeworm has a small knob-like head called a **scolex** which is equipped with a crown of large hooks alternating with small hooks and there are, in addition, four prominent suckers. These structures firmly anchor the scolex to the host's intestinal wall, thus preventing the parasite from being ejected by peristaltic contractions of the intestinal wall. Behind the scolex is a narrow neck-like region which is continually forming new segment-like parts of the tapeworm's body. Each segment-like part called a **proglottid** is packed with the tapeworm's reproductive organs and not much else. The hindmost proglottids, which are the oldest, are filled with eggs. These ripe proglottids are continually detaching themselves from the tapeworm and are shed to the exterior together with the host's faeces.

The eggs, as many as 850 000 per proglottid, are released by the rupture of the proglottid wall. In parts of the world lacking modern sanitation, the eggs are dispersed on the ground and are eventually swallowed by pigs. The tiny parasites that emerge from the eggs bore their way through the pig's gut wall and enter the blood stream. The tiny parasites are then carried to the muscles where they grow to the size of a pea to become what are known as **bladder worms**. At this stage, the scolex, which is recognisable by its crown of hooks, is completely invaginated (turned inside out – as happens when we quickly remove a rubber glove from the hand) inside the bladder-like structure.

Humans become infected when undercooked pork infested with bladder worms is eaten. Once inside the human intestine, the bladder worms, in response to a specific stimulus, become evaginated (the opposite of invaginated). The scolex attaches to the intestinal wall, new proglottids form and, even though the piece of pork may have been infested with several bladder worms, only one tapeworm develops to maturity.

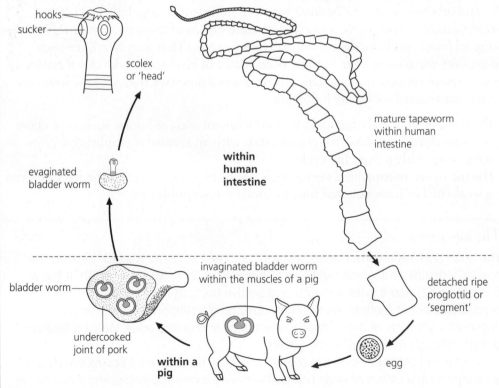

Figure 5.13 The life cycle of a tapeworm

The liver fluke

The liver fluke (*Fasciola hepatica*) is an internal parasite of sheep, cattle, horses, goats, deer and humans. It is brownish in colour and can grow to about 3 cm long and about 1.3 cm wide. It is broad and flat and somewhat pointed at its front and rear ends. It has two suckers, one at the anterior end which surrounds the mouth and another in the middle on its lower surface. It uses its suckers for attachment and locomotion, moving by looping, using its suckers alternately.

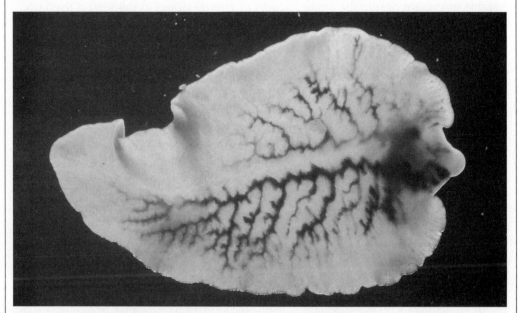

Figure 5.14 Sheep liver fluke – stained to show its much-branched intestine

Liver flukes inhabit the bile duct. They feed on a diet of blood which is sucked from blood vessels in the duct wall. Its mouth leads into a muscular pharynx and then into a branching digestive tract. It is not an obligatory protein feeder as it can absorb sugars and amino acids directly through its body wall when these are available. The rest of its body consists mostly of reproductive organs.

Adult liver flukes lay their eggs into the bile duct. Each fully grown adult can lay up to 3500 eggs per day. The eggs are carried by bile juice into the intestine and are eventually passed out to the exterior together with the host organism's faeces. If the weather is warm and the ground is damp, a lid on the eggs opens to allow a ciliated larva to crawl out. After swimming around in water for a chance encounter with a snail, the larva bores its way into the muscular foot of the snail. Within the body of the snail, the parasite passes through a series of asexual multiplicative stages. The larvae then work their way out of the body of the snail to encyst on a wet blade of grass.

Vertebrate hosts become infected by ingesting the encysted larvae either together with a blade of grass or in drinking water. Within the intestine, the juvenile parasite migrates through the gut wall to take up residence within the bile duct. The entire life cycle takes about 5 months to complete.

Dodder – a plant parasite

Dodder, the common name for *Cuscuta*, is a plant parasite of a variety of flowering plants including clover, nettle, gorse and heather. A member of the Morning Glory family, it is a leafless plant with reddish, thread-like twining stems. It bears spherical clusters of pinkish-white flowers each with a bell-shaped, five-lobed corolla tube. (The corolla is the collective term for the petals of a flower.)

A dodder plant begins life as a seed on the ground. As if aware that it must find a suitable host plant before the limited supply of energy stored in the seed is used up, the germinating seedling produces only a short stump-like root and instead channels its energy into producing a rapidly elongating, slender, leafless stem. The stem grows horizontally over the ground and reaches out for a suitable host plant by describing a circular path (not unlike the second hand of a clock) as it elongates. If it is fortunate enough to make contact with the living stem of a suitable host plant, it then coils tightly around it, rarely making more than three turns in the process. In response to specific chemicals on the host plant, the parasite is stimulated to produce root-like suckers called **haustoria** at points of closest contact with the host plant. Moving through and between the cells of the host plant, the developing haustorium establishes close connections with the host plant's xylem and phloem vessels. Having plumbed itself into the host plant's vascular tissues, the parasite then proceeds to take the easy route to life by taking for itself water and nutrients provided by the host plant.

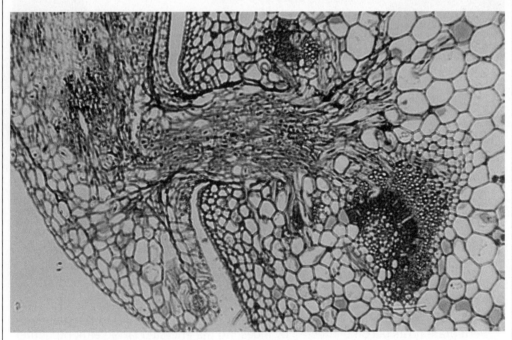

Figure 5.15 Dodder, a parasitic plant, plumbs its sucking root into the vascular tissues of the host plant

Ecologists take a broad view on parasitism. They regard parasites as essentially another type of predator – one that consumes its prey often from within. There are, of course, fundamental differences between predators and parasites. Carnivorous predators, for a start, are generally larger than their prey and are capable of overpowering and killing them and then eating them up within a short period of time. Parasites, on the other hand, being much smaller than their host, extract only relatively small quantities of nutrients from their host and consequently do not usually do much harm to their hosts. Parasites are also often totally dependent on just one type of host whereas predators usually consume a variety of prey. To a parasite, its host is not only a source of food but the host organism can also provide shelter and serve as a moist incubator for itself and its young and in some cases act as a vehicle for transporting the parasite and its offspring to other potential hosts. Little wonder therefore that many parasites have evolved to do little damage to their hosts, for to do harm would be to destroy their food source and their cosy habitat.

Ecologists are unconcerned with such differences of 'fine detail'. They take the broad view that anything that has been said about predators, such as density-dependent regulatory controls which predators may exert over the size of their prey populations, applies equally to parasites and their hosts.

Questions

4 Explain how the introduction of an alien species could speed up the extinction rate amongst indigenous species.
5 Distinguish between the following:
  a intraspecific and interspecific competition
  b parasitism and mutualism
  c density-dependent and density-independent factors.
6 Explain why mutualistic associations between organisms are of fairly common occurrence in nature. Describe a *named* example of mutualism and state the benefits to each of the partners.

Examination questions

1 Two species may interact in a number of ways. These interactions may be beneficial, harmful or have no effect on the individuals involved.
  a Complete the table to show the likely consequence of the interaction for the two individuals involved. Use + for a beneficial effect, − for a harmful effect and 0 for one where there is no effect on the individual concerned. Explain the effects. (4)

Type of interaction	Effect on individual of species A	Effect on individual of species B	Explanation
Predation	+	−	Species A kills and eats species B
Parasitism			
Mutualism			

b Explain why intraspecific competition may be described as a density-dependent factor affecting population growth.   (2)

c Give **one** example of a density-independent factor and describe how it may affect population size in a named organism   (2)

(total = 8)

NEAB, June 1995

2 Graphs A and B below represent two predator–prey relationships. The two curves in Graph A show the annual fluctuations in two populations of mites, one of which preys upon the other. The two curves in Graph B show the *attack success rate* of a hawk (the predator) upon a flock of pigeons and the *median reaction distance* of the pigeon flock. Study the graphs, then answer the questions which follow.

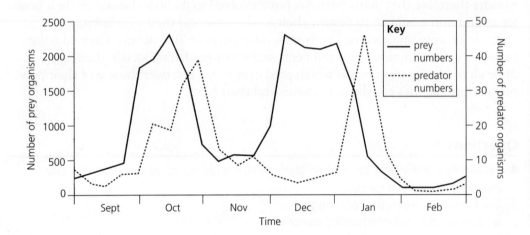

Graph A Fluctuations in populations of two mites, one of which preys upon the other, with time

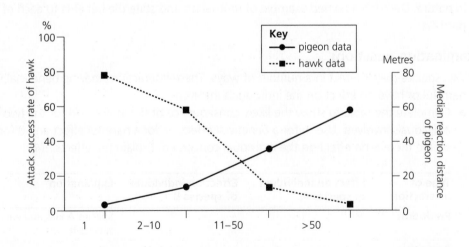

Graph B Relationships between the hunting success rate of a hawk and its prey, a flock of pigeons

Note:
Attack success rate is a measure of the number of successful captures of the prey by the predator during the observed period.
Median reaction distance is an indication of the efficiency of visual detection of the prey by the predator.

a i) Give **three** different ways by which the predator numbers can be increased.   (3)

   ii) Explain why the **predator** curve of Graph A is out of phase with the **prey** curve.   (3)

b i) What is the relationship between the number of pigeons in the flock and the median reaction distance of the pigeons?   (1)

   ii) Suggest **two** possible reasons for this relationship.   (2)

   iii) What is the percentage chance of survival of a solitary pigeon in the above situation?   (1)

   iv) Suggest a possible disadvantage to the pigeons of having large flock sizes.   (1)

(total = 11)

UODLE, March 1996

3 Use the information in the passage below to answer the questions which follow.

Squirrel dynamics

Our native red squirrel *Sciurus vulgaris* is no longer as familiar as it was a century ago. The grey squirrel *Sciurus carolinensis*, a North American species, which was released here for ornamental purposes, is now extremely common. Sixty years ago biologists realised that the decline of the red squirrel and the expansion of the grey squirrel population were somehow connected.

The grey squirrel is something of a specialist, feeding especially on large seeds that are abundant in autumn in broad-leaved woodlands.

One suggestion for the relative success of the grey squirrel in Britain was that it was able to out-compete the red squirrel. The popular view was that the larger grey squirrels (weighing about 550 g) were attacking the red squirrels (weighing about 300 g). In fact neither species takes much notice of the other, and the historical evidence is at variance with the idea that greys drive out reds.

Grey squirrels spread slowly and wherever they had been established for more than 15 years the reds were usually missing. Detailed studies have shown that in some areas the two species have coexisted for 16 years or more but in other areas the reds had disappeared before the greys arrived.

Another suggestion is that grey squirrels carry a disease to which they are resistant but to which the reds succumb. However, it is considered that a disease would spread rapidly and not explain the 15 year takeover period.

Red squirrel populations living in conifer forests often survive long after they have disappeared from the surrounding countryside. Comparisons of the two species suggest ways in which their ecologies differ so that red squirrels might do better in coniferous woodland and grey squirrels better in deciduous woods. For instance, reds spend much more time in the canopy and less time on the ground than greys, this matches the fact that they are lighter, more nimble and put on less fat for the winter. Most conifers take two years to ripen their cones, so there are always cones available in the canopy for a squirrel which is light and nimble enough to get to them. Broad-leaved trees shed their seeds in autumn so that acorns, chestnuts and beechnuts have to be collected from the ground. Both squirrels can produce two litters a year; a female grey squirrel, which has the ability to exploit the rich autumn seed crop, will be better placed to produce a strong litter of early young.

Grey squirrels have a further advantage which has probably been decisive. They can digest acorns more efficiently than red squirrels who do eat acorns but cannot digest them properly, and given a pure acorn diet they lose weight. Conservationists have bemoaned the extensive use of alien conifers by commercial forestry and have asked for more native conifers and broad-leaved trees to be planted. This is just what grey squirrels prefer. Serious consideration is now being given to felling oaks in areas which are red squirrel strongholds to remove the grey advantage. Where screens of deciduous trees are needed small-seeded species should be used.

It may be possible to exploit the weight difference between the species to design a food hopper which allows red squirrels to feed on peanuts and hazelnuts but not grey squirrels. Alternatively, the hopper could dispense poison bait but only to animals weighing over 400 g so that it selectively poisons grey squirrels. There may be red squirrels that have evolved mechanisms for digesting acorns or genetic engineering could be used to give red squirrels the relevant genes from grey squirrels.

Adapted from: D.W. Yalden, Squirrel Dynamics. *Biological Sciences Review*, Vol. 6 No. 2.

a Give **three** pieces of evidence to suggest that grey squirrels have not **actively** displaced the native red ones.   (3)
b Why is it unlikely that disease is responsible for the decline of the red squirrels?   (1)
c i) Give **two** reasons why red squirrels are better adapted than grey squirrels to living in coniferous woodland.   (2)
   ii) Give **two** reasons why grey squirrels are better adapted than red squirrels to living in deciduous woodland.   (2)
d Give **three** ways in which the red squirrel might be encouraged and be given a selective advantage over the grey squirrel.   (3)   (total = 11)

UODLE, June 1995

Communities and succession

If a plot of bare agricultural land is abandoned to nature, common weeds would usually be the first to invade the site. They would then be followed by perennial grasses and tall herbs and after many years of being left unattended, the land would have the appearance of a shrubby meadow. In due time, a forest of trees dominated, in lowland areas, by oak would grow on the abandoned site. This directional process of community change over time at a site is known as **ecological succession**. The entire range of communities that succeed one another at a site is known as a **sere**. Seres are classified into a number of types depending on environmental conditions. Those that start in freshwater are known as **hydroseres**; very dry places give rise to **xeroseres** and seres that develop on bare rock are known as **lithoseres**.

The first organisms to invade and develop a new site are known as **pioneer species**. Starting with the pioneer community, each more or less distinct community in a succession, which together makes up a sere, is known as a **seral stage**. The final mature community which becomes established and which perpetuates itself indefinitely undergoing little further change is known as a **climax community**.

Although animal communities do undergo parallel changes in an ecological succession, the focus is generally on the more obvious changes in the plant communities mainly because the vast majority of animals are small, inconspicuous, mobile and often well camouflaged.

During an ecological succession, there is generally an increase in the:

- height and biomass of the plants
- structural complexity of the plant community
- growth rate or productivity of the vegetation, and
- number of species occupying the site.

Starting with a few pioneer species, the site may eventually, if it is located in the tropics, be occupied by a rain forest community consisting of many thousands of different species. However, towards the later stages of a succession, a slight decline in species richness may sometimes be observed. In forest communities, for example, the dominant trees, by cutting off light to ground-cover plants, may exert an inhibitory effect on their growth.

Figure 6.1 A rain forest is an example of a climax community. It is the final stage in succession

Types of succession

Ecologists recognise two main types of succession:

1 **Primary succession**, which occurs on newly formed habitats that have not previously supported a community. The succession that develops on newly formed volcanic islands, bare rocks exposed by an avalanche, sand dunes, ponds and lakes are examples.
2 **Secondary succession**, which occurs on sites that have previously supported a community of some sort. The sequence of communities that invade and replace one another following abandonment of farm land, leading eventually to the establishment of a forest community, is an example. Another is the gradual re-emergence of a community resembling the previous one following destruction by fire.

Examples of primary succession

Succession on bare rock

Consider what happens when a retreating glacier creates a new habitat consisting of bare rocks. The first organisms to colonise such harsh terrain, perhaps only briefly at first, when the rocks are wet with rain, are likely to be **lichens** carried there as spores in the wind. Lichens are a symbiotic partnership between an alga and a fungus. They can commonly be found growing like crusts on the surface of rocks, walls and on the barks of trees (in unpolluted habitats). They are well suited for colonising exposed bare rock surfaces because the hyphae of the fungus can penetrate tiny cracks to absorb inorganic nutrients. The fungal hyphae can also cling firmly to the rock and act as a cradle to provide shelter and support for the alga, which, unlike its fungal partner, is capable of making organic food molecules from simple inorganic raw materials by photosynthesis. Lichens release acids which corrode the rocks, thus creating tiny crevices that trap dust and other debris. In this way, they make the rock face less inhospitable for other species that arrive later.

Figure 6.2 Lichens are often the first organisms to colonise bare rock

Mosses are usually the next to colonise the rocky habitat. They have spores which are easily carried by the wind. Mosses have unicellular root-like hairs called *rhizoids* which enable them to cling to tiny crevices. The moss plants tend also to grow in tight clumps which trap water, dust particles and their own dead remains, thus helping to create a thin veneer of soil. Plants, such as **clover**, which are capable of nitrogen fixation, can flourish on the thin layer of still nutrient-poor soil. Their decomposing remains enrich the soil with nitrates thus making it more fertile. Drought-resistant **ferns** may be the next to invade the habitat. In time, **grasses** may appear and, because they are taller than the mosses, they can, by a process of competitive exclusion, suppress the mosses while at the same time trapping more dust and debris. Their dead, decomposing remains will also add to the organic content of an ever deepening layer of soil. As the soil layer builds up, tall herbaceous plants and **shrubs** such as buddleia (*Buddleia* sp.) with deeper rooting systems can become established. The shrubs will eventually give way to trees and in a time scale of perhaps a thousand years, what was once a habitat consisting of pristine rocks becomes covered in a layer of soil deep enough to support a forest community dominated by **trees** such as oak.

Succession in a pond

A pond or lake originates as clear water, which to start with is low in mineral nutrients. Sediments and dissolved minerals are carried into the pond from the surrounding land by drainage and runoff rain water, thereby enriching the pond with mineral nutrients. In time, **plankton** and other pioneer species, carried there by the wind, will colonise the pond. At the water's edge, **submerged aquatic plants** take root in the soft mud, their distribution into the deeper parts being restricted by light penetration into the water. These submerged plants may also be affected in their distribution by **free-floating plants** above them, especially types such as duckweed (*Lemna* sp.) that grow densely and are thus capable of cutting off light to the submerged plants below them.

Succession in a pond occurs because sediments and the partly decomposed dead remains of plants settle to the bottom, gradually making the pond shallower. Silt, carried there by surface runoff will accumulate near the margins of the pond, trapped there by submerged plants rooted to the mud below. As the sediments accumulate and the soft mud rises, the changing environmental conditions favour the growth of **rooted floating plants** such as water lilies (e.g. *Nuphar* sp.) along the margins of the pond. These rooted floating plants can anchor themselves to the mud and extend their leaves to the surface to receive the full intensity of light. Their broad floating leaves can cut off light to the submerged plants and, by a process of competitive exclusion, they can gradually take over territory once occupied by the submerged plants. The submerged plants have, in their turn, encroached further into the pond to take advantage of shallower conditions there, as the pond gradually fills up with silt and dead plant and animal matter. In time, where once rooted floating plants grew, the rising mud creates conditions which are shallow enough for **emergent plants** such as bulrushes and reeds to grow. These emergent plants may, to start with, grow between the rooted floating plants but, by propagating vegetatively and

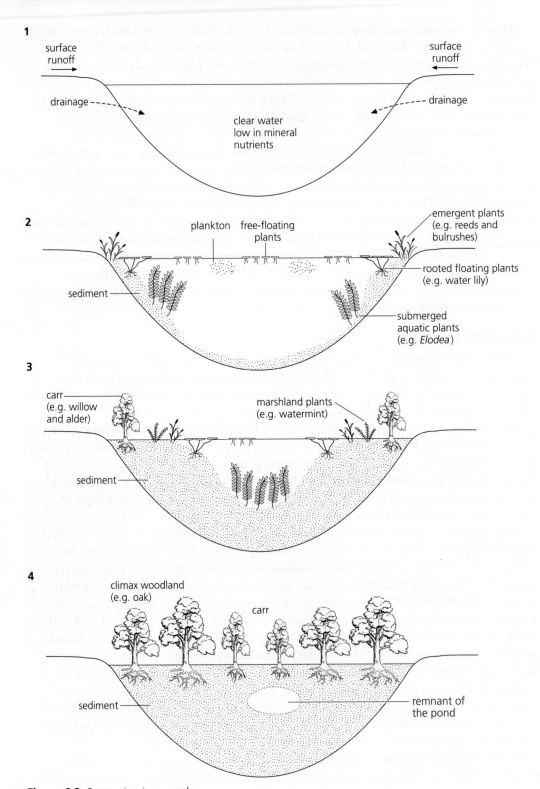

1

surface runoff →

← surface runoff

drainage - - - →

← - - - drainage

clear water low in mineral nutrients

2

plankton   free-floating plants

emergent plants (e.g. reeds and bulrushes)

sediment

rooted floating plants (e.g. water lily)

submerged aquatic plants (e.g. *Elodea*)

3

carr (e.g. willow and alder)

marshland plants (e.g. watermint)

sediment

4

climax woodland (e.g. oak)

carr

sediment

remnant of the pond

Figure 6.3 Succession in a pond

growing very closely together, they will eventually displace the rooted floating plants. Their tight formation allows sediments to accumulate rapidly and to consolidate to form land which is dry enough for **marshland plants** and **wetland trees** such as willow and alder to become established. Alder possesses nitrogen-fixing root nodules and is often one of the first trees to become established on land which may from time to time be submerged under flood water. The shrubby woodland formed by the wetland trees is known as **carr**. In time, the pond contracts even further and eventually disappears completely so that what was once a pond is now woodland dominated by **deep-rooted trees** such as oak.

Zonation

A visit to a natural pond reveals plants growing in more or less distinct (but seldom clear-cut) zones near its margins, with the floating plants furthest out in deep water and the bulrushes and reeds nearest its landward border. Each of these zones represents a different seral stage in the process of succession in the pond. If the process of succession has been going long enough, wetland trees may also be present on land adjacent to the pond. The term **zonation** is used to refer to the spatial distribution of organisms in bands or zones in accordance with variations in the physical environment, such as the depth of the water, degree of light penetration, nature of the substratum, and so on.

Secondary succession

Compared with primary successions, which, at least in their early stages, proceed very slowly, secondary successions occur at a much faster pace and are characterised initially by rapid turnover of typically opportunistic species that move in to exploit what is already a hospitable environment. Among the first to invade a bare plot of land abandoned by farmers are wind-dispersed common garden **weeds**. These plants are typically annuals and short-lived perennials. They grow quickly, gaining early advantage from the relative absence of competition for light and nutrients. The annual weeds, however, lack methods of vegetative propagation and are gradually crowded out by **tall perennials** such as the rosebay willow-herb (*Epilobium angustifolium*) and various types of **grasses**, both of which are capable of very vigorous vegetative

Figure 6.4 Rosebay willow-herb – a tall herbaceous perennial which commonly establishes itself 3 to 6 years after land has been left abandoned

growth. Some common garden escapes such as lupins (*Lupinus nootkatensis*) may also invade the abandoned plot of land. After 10 years, the site has the appearance of a grassy meadow with scattered clumps of tall herbs. Butterflies, bees and other insects will be attracted to the flowering plants and in time birds and mammals will follow as the food chains and food webs gradually rebuild themselves. In time, small woody plants collectively known as **shrubs** would establish themselves, the final stage consisting of a climax community dominated by **woodland trees** arriving perhaps about 40 to 60 years after the site was first left vacant by humans.

a

b

c

Figure 6.5 Secondary succession on urban waste ground. (a) Relatively bare urban waste ground; (b) 4 years later the vegetation on the waste ground consists mainly of tall herbaceous plants including a few garden escapes (lupins); (c) 40 years later, a climax community consisting of woodland trees has established

Why does succession occur?

Three hypotheses have been put forward to explain the mechanism underlying the replacement of one species by another.

Facilitation hypothesis

According to the **facilitation hypothesis**, succession occurs because earlier species modify the environment in such a way as to make it less favourable for themselves and more suitable for other species that arrive later. These later arrivals, being better suited to the altered conditions, grow more vigorously and, by competitive exclusion, displace the earlier species. In other words, succession occurs because of the effects of species on their local environment. Having established themselves, the later arrivals continue to modify their local environment and, in so doing, promote further succession.

Tolerance hypothesis

The **tolerance hypothesis** states that later arrivals have a lower tolerance level for resources. By reducing the available resources to below the level needed to sustain those that arrived earlier, the later arrivals are thus able to displace them. For example, the saplings of oak are shade tolerant and are able to grow in the shade of shrubs and other sun-loving plants. In time, the oak saplings will grow into young trees tall enough to overshadow the shorter plants and thus displace them.

Inhibition hypothesis

Many types of fungi can prevent other microorganisms from invading their space by secreting chemicals known as antibiotics. There is also some evidence which suggests that several types of parasites can delay (but not prevent) the entry of saprobionts into recently dead tissues. (Saprobionts are microorganisms, mainly bacteria and fungi, that feed by secreting enzymes on to dead matter.) This type of behaviour, where organisms resist invasion of their space, has prompted ecologists to put forward the **inhibition hypothesis** as a mechanism for the replacement of one species by another. According to this hypothesis, all species will resist invasion by competitors and are displaced only as a result of death or damage by factors other than competition. Succession, to put it succinctly, proceeds in the direction of longer-lived species.

Consider again succession on an abandoned plot of agricultural land. The pioneer plant species are adapted for colonisation because they devote much of their energy to seed production and divert only a relatively small proportion for body growth. They are consequently small in size and live relatively short lives. On bare ground, smallness is not a disadvantage. Having occupied the space, they would resist displacement by others that arrive later. However, most pioneer species do not live beyond one season and, when one of them dies, the vacant **niche space** or gap in the habitat becomes available for occupation by others. Any seedling which happens by chance to be present at that moment in time can take over the available space and if several are present, the best adapted among them, that is, the one that grows most rapidly, will take over the available space. Once established, it will grow to tower over any would-be rivals and hold on to its niche space until it dies. The result is a community which, in species composition, is randomly mixed but whose community structure gradually changes from small, short-lived, wind-dispersed species which are poor competitors, to taller, animal-dispersed species which have longer generation times (live longer) and produce few but large seeds.

The general view among ecologists is that succession, in all probability, involves all three mechanisms with the facilitation model playing a key role during the early stages of a primary succession.

Species richness and succession

The term **species richness** implies a wealth of species and it may be defined as the number of species in a given area. As a general rule, species richness tends to increase during succession but there is usually a slight decrease in the number of plant species towards the later stages of succession. Why does species richness increase and then decline slightly?

Consider succession on volcanic rock. The initial species richness is zero because freshly cooled volcanic rock is totally abiotic. During the early stages of succession, only a few specialised types of plants, which are capable of withstanding exposed conditions and which possess roots that can cling to cracks and crevices in the rocks, are able to establish themselves. Later, as a layer of soil forms and conditions have become less harsh, a greater number of less specialised invading species are able to establish themselves. They in their turn, by their effects on the environment, can be viewed as creating an increasing number and range of niche spaces suitable for occupation by others. These niche spaces may differ from one another in a variety of ways. In some places, the soil could be shallower; at other places it could be drier, more alkaline, better drained, shaded over, richer in nitrogen and so on. Some invading species will undoubtedly be better suited to one set of environmental conditions as compared with another.

The plants themselves, by their elaborate architecture, could also create a variety of different niche spaces for the animals that live within their canopy. These niche spaces may differ from one another in humidity, temperature, wind speed, protection from predators and so on. They can also differ as potential sources of food and nesting sites. The leaf-litter zone at ground level is another microhabitat which supports a rich variety of invertebrate animals especially those that are not well adapted to resist desiccation. According to the principle of competitive exclusion (see Chapter 5), two species cannot occupy the same niche in direct competition with each other in a stable community. The 'winner' eliminates the 'loser' from the site. This type of replacement of one species by another may not in itself result in an increase in species richness. However, if some invading species were to establish populations in niche spaces not previously occupied (and thus avoid direct competition with other species), the overall result should be an increase in species richness.

When the soil becomes deep enough to support the growth of trees, many shrubs and ground-cover, sun-loving plants would inevitably be shaded out of existence and plant diversity should decline to some extent. By suppressing the growth of tree saplings, grazing animals, such as rabbits and deer, can therefore play an important role in helping to maintain a high level of species richness within the community.

Figure 6.6 Grazing animals such as rabbits, by suppressing the growth of tree saplings, can help to maintain species richness within a community

Climax community

Succession comes to an end with the establishment of a mature, relatively stable community known as the climax. On clay soils in lowland areas of western and central Europe, the climax community is typically a mixed oak forest but on high ground, where the underlying soil is chalky and well drained, the dominant trees are generally beech.

Climax communities are more stable than the seral stages that preceded them. Changes will undoubtedly continue to occur. When one individual dies, another (not necessarily of the same species) takes its place so that the species composition of the community may from time to time change but the overall structure of the forest, its mixture of dominant trees, its understorey of shrubs, herbs and its community of leaf-litter zone organisms, will remain relatively stable year after year.

Climax communities are also adapted to an efficient rate of utilisation of their environmental resources. The rate of nutrient cycling is at its maximum level. Raw materials such as water, carbon dioxide and minerals are efficiently taken up by the plant community and returned to the environment through the processes of respiration and decomposition by the producer, consumer and decomposer communities.

The rate of energy intake by photosynthesis is balanced by the rate of energy loss by respiration so that the biomass of the climax community is held more or less constant and at a maximum level.

Deflected succession (plagioclimax)

Repeated disturbances such as grazing by cattle or sheep, floods, fire or human activity can act as **arresting factors** to halt or set back the process of succession. A succession which is held in check for prolonged periods is said to have reached a **subclimax** stage. For example, heather moorlands are common in upland parts of the British Isles which were once woodland. Heavy grazing and frequent accidental or deliberate fires keep the community at a subclimax stage. Such a stable plant community which is maintained by persistent human interference or by the activities of domestic animals is known as **plagioclimax** (Greek word *plagios* meaning '*oblique*' or '*deflected*'). If the arresting factors of grazing and burning are removed, the heather-dominated plagioclimax vegetation would soon be invaded by birch and pine and a woodland climax community would eventually be re-established.

Questions

1 Define the terms
   a ecological succession
   b climax community
   c deflected succession.
2 Explain how ecological succession can lead to
   a changes in species richness
   b the establishment of a forest and
   c greater stability within the ecosystem.
3 Describe the roles of
   a fungi and
   b leguminous plants in promoting primary succession on bare rock.

Biomes

Communities that extend over large geographical areas are known as **biomes**. Examples include tropical rain forests, deserts and coral reefs.

Tropical rain forests

Tropical rain forests extend like a broad but discontinuous belt of luxuriant vegetation between the Tropics of Cancer and Capricorn, 23.5° latitude North and South of the equator. They cover the low-lying areas of South and Central America, Africa, South East Asia and North Australia. The climate in these regions is hot and moist with temperatures ranging from 24 to 28 °C throughout the year and with rainfall often in excess of 2000 mm per year.

The tropical rain forests cover less than 2% of the Earth's surface but they contain an estimated five million plant and animal species (40 to 50% of the world's total). A single hectare of Peruvian rain forest was recently recorded to contain nearly 300 different species of tree – eight times as many as in the whole of the United Kingdom. Another study in Equador came up with a figure of 50 000 to 60 000 ent species of insects and spiders within a single hectare of Amazonian rain three times as many as the whole of the United Kingdom.

Although tropical rain forest trees shed their leaves, different species do so at different times with some continually growing new leaves to replace those that have been shed. The effect is a forest which is evergreen in appearance throughout the year. There is no single dominant tree species in a tropical rain forest and, although the forest is made up of many different tree species, the trees share many features in common. These include:

- tallness – most tropical rain forest trees grow to 30 to 50 metres in height
- straight trunks stabilised by buttress roots that spread sideways rather than downwards
- shallow root systems that are adapted to rapidly absorb minerals released by decomposition on the forest floor
- smooth, whitish green barks
- few low branches
- branching near the top end of the trunk to produce a wide umbrella-shaped crown high above the ground
- leaves that are typically oblong in shape with thick waxy cuticles (to reduce water losses by transpiration) and generally dark green in colour (indicating good light-absorbing capabilities).

Figure 6.7 Tropical rain forest trees are tall, with straight trunks and few low branches

Figure 6.8 The trunks of tropical rain forest trees are supported by buttress roots that spread sideways rather than downwards

Tropical rain forests are also characterised by the presence of many different species of woody climbing plants known as **lianas**. These plants start life on the forest floor, growing upwards by twining around the trunks of trees or by holding on to other plants by means of hooks or coiling organs called **tendrils**. Not having to support their own body weight, lianas can channel much of their energy into their climbing habit and thus grow quickly in length to reach the uppermost levels of the forest canopy. Acting like tough ropes, they form a tangle of loops and coils that entwine adjacent trees together. Some species of lianas conserve energy while growing in the darker understorey of the forest by producing small leaves. On reaching the canopy, they then produce larger, differently shaped leaves to take full advantage of the available sunlight.

Another feature of tropical rain forests is the presence of vast numbers of **epiphytes** growing among the canopy. These are green plants that grow on the trunks and branches of trees rather than in the soil. They are not parasitic and manufacture their own food by photosynthesis. Their aerial roots enable them to absorb rain and runoff water. They get their mineral nutrients by absorbing minerals released by decomposition of leaves and other organic debris that fall on them from the canopy of the forest. Epiphytes merely use the trunks and branches of trees as high platforms to gain a favourable place in the sun for themselves. Orchids and ferns are among the most common epiphytes in tropical rain forests.

Only as little as 2% of the sunlight which falls on the tropical rain forest canopy reaches the forest floor. The dimly lit forest floor is consequently sparsely populated by herbaceous plants and is generally bare except for a few mosses, ferns and saplings. The conditions at ground level are warm and moist – ideal for a rapid rate of decomposition, which explains why there is only a thin layer of leaf-litter, consisting mostly of freshly fallen leaves, on the forest floor.

Most of the tropical rain forest animals live within the canopy with relatively few moving between the forest floor and the canopy. This is not surprising since the bulk of the available food is in the canopy layer. A rich variety of insects including beetles, stick insects, caterpillars, plant bugs (hemiptera), mites, ticks and mosquitoes use the forest canopy as a habitat. However, because of the absence of low branches, the cryptic coloration of many

Figure 6.9 Epiphytes – plants that use the trunks and branches of trees as high platforms in the sun

of the insects, their small size or slow movements, the rain forest often seems surprisingly lacking in animal life to the casual visitor. Some biting insects, such as mosquitoes that normally stay within the canopy feeding on forest mammals and birds, may make their presence felt by descending to the forest floor to feed on humans when their natural habitat is disturbed by the felling of trees for timber. Ants are another group of insects that can reveal their presence by biting. Most ants are omnivorous and play an important role in stripping the flesh from small mammals and birds that lie dead on the forest floor.

Many mammals and birds use the rain forest canopy as a habitat. Prominent among them are monkeys, gibbons, sloths, squirrels, shrews, marsupials and birds of paradise. Some, like elephants, tigers, tapirs, wild boars and mouse deer, are confined to the forest floor.

Deserts

Deserts are arid areas in which the vegetation is either absent or very sparse and rainfall is less than 250 mm per year. They make up about 20% of the Earth's land surface and include the vast Sahara Desert in North Africa, the smaller Namib Desert of coastal south-west Africa, the Kalahari of southern Africa, the Atacama Desert of Peru and Chile, the deserts of central Asia (Takla Makan and Gobi) and the deserts of south-western United States and Australia. These regions have clear cloudless skies for most of the year, intense solar radiation, dry air and warm temperatures.

Desert surfaces may be of different types. They may consist of smooth baked clay, if the desert was once a lake that dried up, or of pebbles and bare rock, if the topsoil has been blown away by the wind. The popular view of deserts consisting of drifting sand dunes is generally true only of some parts of most deserts. Only 10% of the Sahara, for example, is covered by sheets of loose sand.

Desert plants

The natural vegetation in deserts is generally short and thinly scattered over the ground, with large patches of bare ground between individual plants. Desert plants can broadly be subdivided into three types:

1 rain-dependent annuals
2 succulent perennials
3 spiny shrubs.

Rain-dependent annuals

The bulk of the climax vegetation in many deserts consists not of perennials but of annuals. These are small herbaceous plants that are adapted to make the most of the desert's brief rainy season. They survive the long dry season as dormant seeds and, at the start of the wet season, the seeds promptly germinate in response to the arrival of the first significant shower of rain. The seedlings that emerge sprout roots that grow just below the soil surface to soak up the rain water. They have stems that are slender and leaves that are thin and which display none of the usual drought-resistant (xerophytic) characteristics of plants adapted to life in dry habitats such as thick waxy cuticles, reduced leaf size, and so on. These herbaceous plants are essentially opportunistic species and are not unlike annuals of wetter habitats.

Shortly after germination, they rush into blossom. The delicate flowers then give way to vast quantities of seeds which are quickly scattered. The seeds are highly drought-resistant and can live on the arid soil for years. With their life cycles completed in just a few weeks, the rain-dependent annuals wither and die as the soil dries out.

Succulent perennials

Succulent perennials, such as **cacti**, are not the most numerous but certainly the most conspicuous and best known desert plants. Cacti are native to the deserts of North and South America where they occur in greatest number and diversity. They exhibit many xerophytic features. These include:

- thick fleshy stems that store water
- fluted or grooved stems that allow for expansion or contraction of the stem depending on the amount of water stored in the fleshy tissues
- leaves modified into spines to reduce water losses by transpiration and to ward off browsing animals
- few stomata, often located in grooves to reduce water losses by transpiration
- thick waxy cuticles or a covering of hairs to reduce water losses by transpiration
- extensive, shallow root systems for rapid absorption of rain water before it evaporates or drains through the porous soil.

Figure 6.10 A cactus plant – a native of the Arizona Desert

In African deserts, where cacti are absent, there are strikingly similar succulents among members of the spurge family (Euphorbiaceae).

Spiny shrubs

These are woody perennials with long tap roots that can reach underground sources of water for a considerable period into the dry season. Some shrubs shed their leaves and are leafless for most of the dry season. Others have very small, narrow leaves which are retained throughout the dry season. Many have leaves that are modified into spines or thorns.

Desert animals

Most small desert animals avoid the intense heat of the midday sun by hiding inactively in burrows dug into the ground. Some, like the kangaroo rat (*Dipodomys*), seal the entrances to their burrows with soil, thus creating conditions within their burrows which are not only cooler but also more humid than the conditions outside. Larger desert animals such as the ostrich avoid the midday heat by seeking the shade of a large tree.

The largest of the desert animals, the camel, is well adapted for life in hot arid deserts.

- It has a thick insulating layer of hair on its back to help reduce heat gains from the midday sun.
- It stores large amounts of fat in its hump which, when broken down to release energy, produce metabolic water that enables the camel to survive a long desert journey until it gets the next opportunity to drink.
- Camels can tolerate dehydration amounting to a water loss of 40% of their total body water.
- A thirsty camel can drink 100 dm^3 of water in 10 minutes.
- To conserve water, the camel excretes concentrated urine and dry faeces.
- To reduce water losses by sweating, the camel allows its body temperature to drop to 33.9 °C at night while it sleeps with its bare belly in contact with the cold ground. As the Sun rises and its body gradually warms up, the camel delays the start of sweating until its body temperature rises to 40.5 °C, which is 3.6 °C higher than when humans start to sweat.

Other desert adaptations include:

- bushy eyebrows and long eye lashes to stop sand from getting into its eyes
- nostrils that can close during a sand storm
- feet with soft cushions that spread out to stop the camel from sinking into loose sand
- lips covered with thick coarse hairs to protect them when eating the spiny desert shrubs.

Figure 6.11 A camel is a well-adapted member of the desert community of plants and animals

Coral reefs

Coral reefs are ridges of limestone built up from the sea floor mainly from the hard, calcareous external skeletons of billions of tiny marine animals called **coral polyps** and the cement-like crustiness of **coralline algae**. Coral reefs cover 0.1% of the Earth's surface and, with few exceptions, are located in tropical shallow waters between latitudes 30° North and South of the equator. Their nooks and crannies provide shelter for myriads of other marine organisms including gastropod molluscs, sponges, spiny lobsters, sea urchins, starfish, squids, sea cucumbers and a whole variety of often brightly coloured and exotic-looking fish. Coral reefs rank among the most biologically productive of all marine ecosystems and are estimated to harbour a total of about 950 000 species – about 8 to 9% of the world's total.

Reef-building corals grow best in water which is:

- clear
- of normal salinity
- not too rough
- well aerated
- rich in plankton
- not colder than 16 °C or warmer than 29 °C.

Figure 6.12 Coral reefs rank among the most biologically productive of all marine ecosystems

Coral polyps

Most coral polyps are colonial organisms. The individual polyps in a colony are connected to neighbouring polyps by tubular extensions of the gut cavity. Each individual coral polyp looks not unlike a tiny version of its close relative, the sea anemone. It has a body which is built essentially like a digestive sac. There is a mouth at the top end surrounded by one or more rings of tentacles. The tentacles are equipped with sting cells. To feed, the polyp uses its sting cells to paralyse very small animals in the seawater. The prey are then pulled into the mouth by the tentacles.

Figure 6.13 Each coral polyp is not unlike a tiny version of its close relative the sea anemone

Coral polyps are protected by a hard external skeleton composed of calcium carbonate. The mineral is deposited in a cup-shaped form with the polyp inside the cup. When living polyps die, their hard skeletons remain and are used as solid bases by new polyps so that, over time, layer upon layer of stony material accumulates to become massive coral reefs hundreds of kilometres long.

The splendid colours which we associate with healthy, live coral are caused by microscopic symbiotic algae called **zooxanthellae** which live within the transparent cells of the polyps. These algae are essential for the existence of coral reefs in two important ways. First, the zooxanthellae export to their hosts much of the organic compounds they produce by photosynthesis, thus nourishing the corals and helping them to grow. Second, by photosynthesis, they accelerate the growth of the coral skeleton by speeding up the rate of deposition of calcium carbonate. Precisely what the link is between the photosynthetic activities of the zooxanthellae and the growth of the coral skeleton is still not clear.

For the zooxanthellae, the main benefits of living inside the polyp cells come from the fact that warm tropical reef waters contain extremely low concentrations of phosphates whereas concentrations are a thousand times higher within the cytoplasm of the host cells. Nutrient concentrations are also relatively stable within the cytoplasm of their hosts whereas outside, nutrient levels can fluctuate widely and supplies can be quite unpredictable.

Coralline algae

Coralline algae are hard, lime-encrusted red seaweeds. They form cement-like crusts over rocks and reefs and are found growing particularly well in places where currents are strong and where waves beat powerfully against the reef. Their crustiness is caused by calcite crystals (a form of calcium carbonate) which are laid down in a regular pattern within their cell walls.

Coralline algae are vital to the formation of durable coral reefs. By taking the full brunt of powerful wave action, they act as the reef's first line of defence against storms that tend to damage the reef.

Questions

4 List the main features of a hot desert ecosystem. Describe the adaptations of desert plants and a *named* desert animal to life in a desert.
5 Compare a tropical rain forest with a hot desert explaining
   a how each habitat gains or loses water
   b how the plants in each habitat are adapted to water availability and
   c the factors that affect the availability of water to organisms that live in the habitat.

Examination questions

1 Following the colonisation of a bare habitat by plants a succession occurs. During succession the number of species present changes as shown in the graph below.

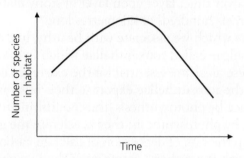

a Suggest why the number of species changes during succession. (2)

b i) Indicate on the graph using the letter **X** where species which are poor competitors are most likely to occur, giving a reason for your answer. (2)

ii) Indicate on the graph using the letter **Y** where species which have long generation times are most likely to occur, giving a reason for your answer. (2)

c Explain how the stability of an ecosystem increases during succession. (2)

d Explain what is meant by the term *deflected succession*. (2) (total = 10)

UCLES, Nov 1996

2 a List **three** principal features of coral reef biomes. (3)

The figure shows a vertical section through a typical coral reef.

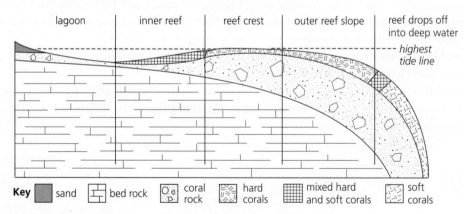

b With reference to the figure:

i) describe the distribution of corals over the reef (3)

ii) suggest reasons for the distribution you have described in i). (3)

c Suggest how each of the following limiting factors affects the survival of the coral.

i) Plankton supply (1)

ii) Oxygen availability (1)

Many human activities are responsible for the damage and destruction of coral reefs.

d Outline **two** such activities which damage or destroy coral reefs. (4) (total = 15)

UCLES, June 1997

The human impact on the environment

World human population growth

The Ancient Romans and the Chinese were known to have kept records of their respective populations for tax purposes. Based on such records, historians put the world human population in the year AD 400 at about 100 million. It was still under 500 million by the year 1650. By the early 1930s, it had exceeded 2000 million and 45 years later, by the mid 1970s, the world human population had nearly doubled to 4000 million. It was 5300 million in 1990 and projections from the United Nations and the World Bank suggest that it will double again to over 9000 million by the middle of the 21st century. A graph of the world human population plotted against time, shows a steeply rising **J-shaped growth curve**. This rapid increase in the world's population is sometimes referred to as the **population explosion**.

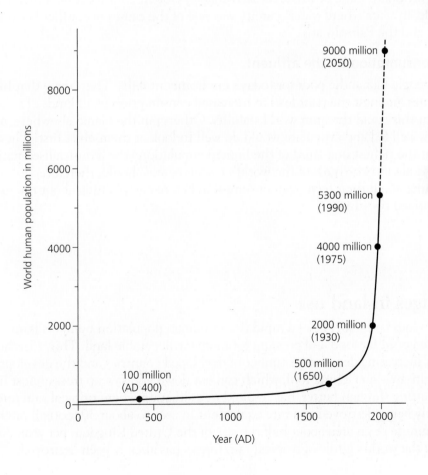

Figure 7.1 J-shaped world human population growth curve

Environmental damage and conflict

What effect will this unprecedented increase in humanity have on the environment? Can the growing human population feed itself?

Expert opinion is divided broadly into two camps. The optimists, who are mainly economists and biotechnologists, believe that improved methods of agriculture together with technological innovation can be relied upon to produce enough food and maintain a high enough standard of living for the human race, even if the world human population grows to much larger than the projected 10 000 million. The pessimists on the other hand, who are mainly environmentalists, take the view that the biosphere is already close to its carrying capacity. They argue that unless there is a slowing down in the rate of human population growth, nature will act to end the human population explosion in very unpleasant ways. They point out that many renewable resources such as freshwater supplies, fish stocks and the atmosphere are already under threat. Some, like the secretary general of the 1996 United Nations Habitat II conference, have gone so far as to suggest quite boldly that the next war would be fought over water. They argue that if one sector of society takes a disproportionate share of whatever is available, violent conflict could erupt as, for example, in Gaza where water scarcity was one of the causes of conflict between the Israelis and the Palestinians.

Overconsumption by the affluent

Some people blame the poor for today's environmental ills. They argue that high birth rates amongst the poor lead to increased consumption of all kinds of resources and that this could threaten world stability. Others put the blame elsewhere, arguing that the well fed and articulate would do well to look at themselves first! They point out that the richest one-third of the human population (the industrialised nations) consume about two-thirds of the world's resources and should, therefore, do something about their own overconsumption before complaining about the needs of the deprived two-thirds.

Changes in land use

One obvious consequence of a rapid rise in human population numbers is an increased need for food and pressure for more fertile, arable land. This, together with an ever increasing demand for timber in developed countries and the development of the chainsaw – a machine tool, which can cut down and saw up trees almost like a knife cutting through butter, has resulted in a situation where tropical rain forests are currently being destroyed at a rate equivalent in area to about 30 football pitches every minute or an area about half the size of the United Kingdom per year. About a third of the world's girdle of tropical rain forests has already been destroyed.

Deforestation

The term **deforestation** is used to refer to the cutting down of forest trees for commercial purposes or to the slash-and-burn methods of clearing forests as a cheap way of creating arable land.

Figure 7.2 Deforestation in South America – not all loggers are as destructive as shown above

The shrinking tropical rain forests

The felling of selected trees need not in itself be very destructive to the environment. However, because of the way tropical rain forest trees are entangled together by the growth of woody vines (see tropical rain forest, page 104), each tree felled for timber brings down with it many smaller trees around it. Added to this is the use of heavy machinery to drag out the fallen logs. Observers estimate that if loggers extract 10% of the timber in an area, they typically leave behind a trail of destruction amounting to 50% of the remaining stock of immature trees, through the careless use of heavy logging equipment.

Threat to biodiversity

An inevitable consequence of the removal of the tree canopy is its impact on wildlife. Because no one knows exactly how many species there are in rain forests, estimates of the effect of deforestation on species diversity vary. In 1974, a gathering of scientists concerned with the problem put the overall extinction rate for all species – plants, animals and microorganisms, at about 100 species a year. Current estimates are much higher. Based on a very conservative figure that there are two million species living in the moist tropical rain forests of the world, ecologists calculate that the overall extinction rate due to deforestation may be as high as between 4000 and 6000 species per year or about one plant or animal species every 2 hours. This is about 10 000 times faster than the natural background rate of extinction (the rate prior to the Industrial Revolution).

Value of maintaining species diversity

- The world will undoubtedly be a much poorer place without its rich variety of jungle plants and animals. It has taken millions of years of evolution for nature to produce them and they could be lost for ever in a matter of decades, if the present rate of deforestation continues.
- About half the drugs in clinical use today are derived from living organisms. Many more await discovery. This immensely rich potential source of new medicines would be lost if the organisms became extinct.
- Tropical rain forest plants are an untapped source of new varieties of crop plants for food and other commercially important substances. For example, the best rubber comes from a tree called *Hevea braziliensis*, which is a native of the Amazonian rain forest.

Other effects of deforestation

Quite apart from the loss of a natural habitat for wildlife, the effects of deforestation on the environment can be quite severe in other ways. These include its impact on the soil, low-lying plains, coral reefs and the climate.

Increased soil erosion and crop failures

Tropical rain forest soils are generally low in mineral content because available mineral nutrients are rapidly absorbed by the plants and incorporated into their tissues. When trees are cut down and the timber is removed, the minerals contained in the timber are exported with the wood, leaving the soil poorer. Removal of the protective tree canopy layer also exposes the soil to the full effects of heavy torrential rains, which can quickly erode the soil and leach out vital mineral nutrients. This is why cutting down trees to grow crops does not usually lead to efficient use of the land. After 2 or 3 years of crop growth, the soil becomes too nutrient poor to support any agricultural activity and disappointing crop failures are consequently quite normal.

Figure 7.3 Removal of the protective tree canopy exposes the soil to erosion from torrential rain storms

Silting and flooding

Rising levels of silt washed down from deforested hill slopes have also been blamed for an increased risk of flooding in the plains below. In 1988, for example, silt deposits carried downstream as a consequence of deforestation, caused the Yangtze River in China to rise 10 metres and to burst its banks. The accompanying floods killed 6000 people, left four million people homeless and destroyed millions of hectares of crops.

Forest fires

Another source of damage comes from forest fires started often deliberately by people, usually of low income, who are hungry for land. Encouraged by local government policies to take advantage of the access roads created by logging companies, the settlers stake for themselves a plot of land close to the road for cultivation or for cattle grazing. Fires are often started as a cheap way of clearing the land for cultivation. High resolution satellite photographs are also pinning the blame for forest fires on large plantation owners in some tropical countries who have been using forest fires to clear land for oil palm cultivation. Palm oil fetches a high price on the commodities market. The fires can sometimes rage uncontrollably for weeks, causing immense damage and wastage to the forest ecosystem and emitting carbon dioxide which can add significantly to the problems associated with global warming (see pages 131–135).

Damage to coral reefs

Most corals are very sensitive to smothering by sediments. These sediments, which are washed into the sea from deforested tracts of land, interfere with the functioning sting cells on the coral polyp's tentacles thus preventing them from feeding. The murky water also stops light from filtering through to the symbiotic microscopic algae that live within the cells of the polyps. Marine scientists in the Philippines estimate that as much as 90% of the archipelago's 34 000 km^2 of coral reefs are dying or showing signs of deterioration as a result of being buried under sediments or from other causes such as the discharge of untreated sewage.

Climate change

Rain forests, by transpiration, recycle a considerable amount of the rain water that falls on them. The water vapour transpired by the trees provides moisture in the air to form clouds that produce rain further downwind. Extensive deforestation can threaten this recycling of coastal rainfall, bringing longer and more frequent periods of drought further inland.

In Africa, for example, 90% of the rain forest that once grew along the West African coastline has disappeared owing to deforestation for timber and for conversion into arable land or as a result of mining for minerals. Although it has not yet happened, there are fears (expressed in a recent report by the Centre for Global Change Science at the Massachusetts Institute of Technology, MIT) that further deforestation in the West African region could result in 'a complete collapse of the West African monsoon'. If the MIT model is correct, it could mean longer and more frequent droughts in vulnerable parts of the African continent and the expansion of the existing deserts. The fact that rainfall since 1970 over the whole of West Africa has been less than before is an ominous sign that the model may indeed be correct. Deforestation in the Amazon basin could, in time, have a similar impact on Brazil.

The destruction of boreal forests

Tropical rain forests are not the only forests that are being destroyed. Near-pristine, ancient coniferous forests that cover Canada, Scandinavia and Russia are being cut down on a vast scale so that the land can be cleared for replanting with commercially useful single varieties of pine and spruce to feed the First World's demand for paper. The timber industry claims that this type of 'clear cutting' mimics the effects of natural forest fires. Finnish timber even carries labels that boast of 'eco-friendly origins' for their wood.

Ecologists, however, argue that natural forest fires always leave some groups of trees undamaged so that during the course of regeneration a whole range of different species becomes re-established. This is not the case with the practice of 'clear cutting' where trees of all ages are totally cut down and then removed. They point out that the practice puts many forest-dwelling species, such as flying squirrels, ospreys, white-backed woodpeckers, mosses, fungi, lichens and a variety of invertebrate species, under the threat of extinction.

The drying up of wetlands

Wetlands are areas of land which are variously covered in shallow open water, being sometimes wet, dry or anywhere in between. Included as wetlands are marshes, mangrove swamps, peatlands, potholes, mudflats and coastal areas including those parts which, at low tide, are covered under water up to 6 metres deep. Wetlands provide a habitat for a rich diversity of birds, mammals, fish, insects, crustacea and molluscs, including many very attractive wetland birds. The blacknecked stork (*Ephippiorhynchus asciaticus*), a large, attractive bird with coral-red legs, which lives on wetlands in India, is just one among many that are on the endangered species list.

Surveys by conservationists in different parts of the world paint a grim picture of the world's wetlands which are disappearing at a rapid rate. Since the days of the early settlers, the United States of America has lost 55% of its wetlands, with the State of California

Figure 7.4 This handsome blacknecked stork, an inhabitant of wetlands in India, is threatened with extinction because its natural habitat is disappearing

heading the list with 91% losses. France has lost 67% of its wetlands, Italy 66% and, in Canada, drainage for agriculture and urban construction such as the building of roads, ports and other amenities has resulted in the loss of about 80% of the marshes along the shores of the Great Lakes and the St Lawrence River.

The threat to the world's wetlands comes mainly from human population growth and the search for more fertile land for farming, as well as pressures for economic advancement especially in association with industrial development, urbanisation and tourism. These pressures may take the form of:

- the building of dams across rivers to divert water for irrigation
- the extraction of ground water
- the erection of barriers as part of drainage schemes to reclaim wetland areas for conversion into arable land for the cultivation of crops such as rice
- the filling up of wetland sites for the construction of industrial sites, or for the construction of various amenities such as seafront entertainment complexes, roads and hotel accommodation for tourists, and so on, and
- the drainage of swamps as a method of controlling malaria and schistosomiasis (a wasting disease caused by parasitic flatworm infestation).

Value of preserving wetlands

Many governments have come to realise that there are economic alternatives to the draining of wetlands for agriculture. One alternative which has been successfully implemented in a number of countries is to put the natural beauty of wetlands to recreational use to earn a living from visiting tourists for licensed hunting and birdwatching. Other reasons why wetlands deserve protection include the fact that they can act like enormous sponges by holding on to water during the rainy season and then releasing the water gradually throughout the rest of the year. Along coastal areas, wetlands can also function as buffers limiting the damaging effects of wave action during stormy weather. For example, in one study of the cost of maintaining sea defences, it was discovered that costs could be reduced twelve fold by quite simply dismantling an existing defence wall and constructing a smaller defence wall 80 metres further inland. This allowed the land in between to revert to a salt marsh, which is what it originally was. Wetlands are also important as traps for sediment that would otherwise be washed out to sea to clog up important shipping channels. By absorbing pollutants, such as nitrates and phosphates, and by acting as natural purifiers of sewage, wetlands have deservedly been described as the 'kidneys of the natural world'.

Desertification

Desertification may be defined as the process of conversion of fertile arid or semi-arid land into desert-like wasteland, largely as a result of adverse human impact. A combination of climate change and land mismanagement can, it is argued, result in vulnerable productive land being converted into desert-like wasteland. The bad practices include:

- **Cultivation on steep slopes and ploughing downhill.** This could lead to soil erosion, as soil made dry and arid by months of drought is simply washed away by the first downpour of rain.
- **Overgrazing.** Grazing too many animals on decreasing areas of pasture could leave the soil unprotected against wind and water erosion. With vegetation regrowth not able to keep pace with cutting by grazing, the exposed topsoil could be blown away by the wind leaving sand and bare rock.
- **Climate change.** Some researchers argue that deserts advance and retreat in accordance with rainfall and that there are few real signs of irreversible

Figure 7.5 Overgrazing – some argue that it is one of the primary causes of desertification

land degradation. They say that desert-like conditions appear during periods of drought and that recovery of apparently irreversibly degraded areas can be quite astonishing following better rainfall. They cite as examples the successive droughts in Ethiopia in the 1980s and how the vegetation burst forth within hours of the return of rainfall. Others hold the view that extensive deforestation, overgrazing and soil erosion could conspire together to turn productive lands into deserts. They further argue that if the accompanying climate change is permanent, the farmers in the drought-stricken areas could be in for a long wait.

Salinisation (or salination)

Salinisation is the build up of salt in the soil, creating problems for agriculture especially on irrigated land in the hot arid and semi-arid regions of the world.

All natural waters, including those that are described as fresh, contain salt. The natural weathering of rocks releases salt which eventually finds its way into streams and rivers and then into the sea. When river water is diverted to irrigate fields that lack proper drainage, the hot weather evaporates the water and the salt is left behind in the soil. As more water evaporates following each watering of the crops, the soil solution becomes increasingly saline and eventually a thick, concrete-like salt crust forms on the surface of the soil making it useless for agriculture. Attempts to wash out the salt from around the roots work only for a few critical weeks. Once the new water has evaporated, the soil is left even more salty for the next growing season. The problem is made worse by deforestation because trees, by transpiring water vapour through their leaves, help to prevent excess ground water (which is rich in salts) from rising close to the soil surface.

Figure 7.6 Salinisation – the scourge of irrigated agriculture. Notice the patches of crust-like salt at the edges of the waterlogged, previously productive land

Salinisation is the scourge of irrigated agriculture in regions of low rainfall. There are today hundreds of thousands of hectares of overirrigated fields in West Pakistan, Egypt, Uzbekistan and Central Africa which have had to be abandoned because of salinisation. What happened in the Sahel, a semi-desert region that separates the Sahara desert from the tropical coastal areas of West Africa, can be taken as a useful example. Encouraged by the availability of cheap credit (provided by international financial institutions) and free land, local 'entrepreneurs' with little knowledge of agriculture began to set up cheap, relatively crude irrigation canals to divert river water on to semi-arid land to claim it for rice or cotton cultivation.

Compared with sorghum or millet – crops that are traditionally cultivated on semi-arid land – rice is much tastier and easier to prepare and consequently more profitable if it can be successfully cultivated. The rice plant most commonly grown in Africa is an upland variety which needs at least 450 millimetres of rainfall per year. The Sahel, with an average rainfall of only 150 millimetres a year, is clearly not suitable for cultivation of the upland variety and the farmers in the Sahel chose instead to cultivate the rice variety commonly grown on flooded fields in Asia. This variety of rice plant needs a water supply that can be accurately regulated and drained. The young seedlings need damp soil but rot in standing water. Once they have grown to about 30 centimetres in height, the plants like to have several centimetres of standing water throughout the period of flowering and ripening.

The potential for rice cultivation in arid lands such as the Sahel is enormous provided the irrigation schemes are properly constructed and managed. Where the irrigation schemes lack proper drainage, however, overirrigation by flooding the land to simulate the flooded rice paddies of Asia may result in one or two satisfactory harvests, but eventually there is disappointment. The irrigation water collects in low-lying desert hollows from where the used water cannot be drained. The stagnant water becomes not only breeding grounds for mosquitoes but it also raises the water table and brings close to the soil surface salty ground water from below. This together with high rates of evaporation soon results in the soil becoming covered in a layer of salt making it useless for crop cultivation.

Importance of adequate drainage

Technical methods for dealing with salinisation are available, and consist essentially of improving the drainage of the land usually by the construction of drainage channels. These should, in arid areas, be at least 2 metres deep so as to prevent salts percolating upwards by capillarity. The drainage channels allow salts to be flushed away from the soil by successive applications of water. The effluents from the drainage network should also be discharged in such a way that they do not create salinisation problems for water users further downstream. This involves discharging the effluents not into the irrigation canal systems of other users further downstream but into the river itself.

Nature has its own desalting process. It consists of the seasonal flooding of the river deltas. The flood waters are very effective in carrying away salt into the oceans. Torrential rains are also important in leaching away salts into rivers.

Monoculture

The term **monoculture** is used to refer to the practice of repeatedly growing the same crop on the same piece of land. The growing of wheat one year and then leaving the land fallow the following year is also regarded as a single-crop or monoculture system. Farmers benefit from a monoculture system in a number of ways:

Figure 7.7 Monoculture – cultivating the same crop on the same plot of land year after year – has its advantages

- investments in specialised expensive machinery can be reduced by having just one type of crop under cultivation
- farmers have the simpler task of having to master just the one technology needed to get into profitable production, including the marketing of the product. Farm management is thus simplified
- if a perennial forage crop is planted, regular reseeding is unnecessary
- the chemical fertiliser programme needed to maintain soil fertility can be more precisely tailored to suit the particular crop, making the work easier
- with higher profits available, the farmer can afford to plant only the very best, disease- and pest-resistant strains
- since different soils exist on the farm, only crops suited for the particular soil can be cultivated. For example, drought-resistant sorghums on dry soils, forage crops on steep hill slopes, and so on.

Although advantageous to the farmer in the short term, monoculture systems are vulnerable to catastrophic decline in the long term. Growing the same crop year after year:

- **Depletes the soil of a specific nutrient.** For example, cereal crops deprive the soil of phosphorus; sugar beet and potato crops take away potassium.
- **May result in greater soil loss by erosion.** Multiple cropping is generally better at protecting the soil by providing greater ground cover. Erosion decreases soil fertility and, no matter how much artificial fertiliser is applied, crop yields are generally lower on eroded soil.
- **Reduces the humus content of the soil.** This is avoided in crop rotation systems by growing a leguminous crop as 'green manure' which is then ploughed into the soil.
- **Exposes the crop plant to increased risk of damage from herbicides.** Soil organic matter is generally a good absorber and inactivator of excess herbicides applied on to the land.
- **Creates conditions that favour the spread of weeds, insect pests and pathogens** associated with a particular crop. When some other crop plant is grown, the pests of the previous crop plant are left to starve.
- **Exposes the farmer to greater risk from economic fluctuations.** With only one crop, the farmer is dependent on just one market and if there is a downturn in that market, the farmer is more at risk from being dragged down with it.

Mining

Mining is the process of extracting minerals and other raw materials such as coal and uranium from the Earth's crust. In **opencast coal mining**, mechanical scrapers are generally used to remove the topsoil followed by the subsoil for transfer by trucks to storage dumps or mounds nearby. The underlying bedrock (known as the overburden) is then removed in successive layers and put on spoil heaps nearby. Finally, when all the unwanted material has been removed and the seam of coal is exposed, machinery in the form of a power shovel is used to dig up the coal and to load it into haulage trucks. Opencast coal mines can generally be worked for up to 12 years, after which the remaining coal is abandoned because it is no longer economical to extract it.

Environmental consequences

Loss of a natural landscape

A direct consequence of opencast mining for minerals or coal is that where there was once the natural beauty of the countryside, there is now a great, gaping hole in the ground with ugly mounds of spoil, some as large as the surrounding hills, dotted around the landscape.

Noise pollution

The early stages of the mining process are also accompanied by a lot of noise from excavators digging into the ground to remove the rocky overburden. If mineral ores are being mined, the process is usually preceded by blasting with dynamite, in which case the noise would be much louder and ground vibrations could damage buildings and other structures nearby.

Dust pollution

A good deal of dust is stirred up at mining sites. The dust in the air in mining towns may sometimes be two to three times higher than recommended limits. Dust from uranium mines is especially hazardous to health since some of it may be radioactive. To protect miners from breathing dust into their lungs, drills used for mining operations are usually fitted with automatic watering down devices to dampen the dust. In coal mining, water is also used to wash the coal as no one likes to buy 'dirty' coal.

Figure 7.8 An opencast copper mine in northern Chile

Contamination of streams and rivers

Water leaching through rocks left over from mining operations may find its way into streams and rivers, turning the river water murky, acid (if the rocks have a high sulphur content) or even orange in colour (if iron compounds are also washed out of the crushed rocks). In one of the worst recent examples of water pollution caused by mining, villagers in Papua New Guinea complained that sediments washed out from a copper and gold mine clogged up the River Ok Tedi making it too shallow for boats to navigate safely, polluted the river with poisonous minerals (cadmium and copper) that killed fish, turtles and crocodiles, and made the water undrinkable.

What are the options?

One approach would be to accept the environmental damage caused by the mining industry on the grounds that it would be too expensive to do anything about it. Another would be to insist on sufficient remedial work to reclaim the land after the mining operation is completed. Holes should be filled in; spoil heaps will need to be levelled off and covered in a layer of soil and then regrassed. A third approach is to insist on sufficient preventive measures to ensure that the damage is kept to a bare minimum. The water that drains from mining tailings should, for example, be prevented from leaching into and contaminating local streams and rivers by collecting it in specially constructed ponds and then treated to remove harmful materials such as heavy metals, toxic wastes and radioactive materials. The fourth and undoubtedly the best option from an environmental point of view, would be to choose not to mine in that area at all. This could be justified on the grounds that the site is one of exceptional beauty or of considerable ecological interest, for example, a habitat for endangered species.

Quarrying

Quarrying is the process of extraction of stone or rock from the Earth's crust for building or road construction. It leaves gaping holes or ugly scars on the sides of hills and it stirs up a great deal of dust. The continual movement of heavy vehicles can also degrade the environment and drive wild animals away from their natural habitat. In India, for example, the movement of excavators accompanying the search for marble has driven away tigers from their natural habitat and put them at risk.

Questions

1 Define **desertification**. Suggest three possible causes and explain how each of them could accelerate the process of desertification.
2 **a** What is meant by salinisation?
   b Describe the essential climatic conditions that promote salinisation.
   c Explain the effects that salinisation has on crop plants.
   d Describe how salinisation may be avoided.
3 For any *named* commercial crop plant, discuss the pros and cons of monoculture.
4 Outline the main causes of a worldwide decline in wildlife habitats and biodiversity.
5 Put forward arguments in favour of and against mining and quarrying.

Pollution

Pollution may be defined as the presence in the environment of substances or energy in quantities that endanger human health, harm living organisms, diminish the amenity value of the environment or interfere with the natural functioning of ecosystems. Pollution is often caused by human action, although natural phenomena such as volcanic eruptions can also act as a source of pollution. Common examples of environmental pollutants include sulphur dioxide, carbon monoxide, nitrogen oxides, smoke, sewage, chemical fertilisers, pesticides, herbicides, oil spills, radioactive wastes, noise and heat.

There are many forms of pollution. These may be broadly classified under the headings: **atmospheric**, **water**, **radioactive** and **thermal** pollution.

Atmospheric pollution

Air pollution results largely from emissions of gases from three principal sources. These are from:

1 the combustion of fossil fuels
2 the activities of microorganisms in association with natural environments modified as a result of agriculture, and
3 gases, with no natural analogues, that are released into the atmosphere by industry.

Major air pollutants include sulphur dioxide, carbon monoxide, nitrogen oxides, methane, ozone, chloroflurocarbons (CFCs), pesticides and particulates (smoke).

Sulphur dioxide is the most harmful air pollutant. It is released whenever fossil fuels containing sulphur impurities are burnt. It is a colourless gas which is irritating to the eyes. It attacks steel, weakens bridges and it is also blamed for being mainly responsible for the decay of national monuments. It dissolves in water to form sulphurous acid (H_2SO_3) and is mainly responsible for what is commonly known as **acid rain**.

Figure 7.9 Smoking factory chimneys – a major source of atmospheric pollution

Acid rain

Acid rain is the popular name for a variety of processes which all involve the deposition on the Earth's surface of acidic materials in the form of rain, snow, dry particles (e.g. soot, fly ash, partly burnt coal) and gases. Rain water is naturally slightly acidic because carbon dioxide dissolves in water to form a weak acid called carbonic acid. Analysis of gases preserved in ice sheets in Greenland suggests that the rain water that fell prior to the Industrial Revolution had a pH ranging from 6 to 7.6. The rain that falls on Central Europe today is a lot more acidic, with an average pH of 4.1. The main cause of acid rain is atmospheric pollution from emissions of sulphur dioxide (SO_2), nitric oxide (NO) and nitrogen dioxide (NO_2) principally from power station chimneys, motor vehicle exhausts and boilers in factories and ships.

Atmospheric chemistry

Some of the sulphur dioxide in the atmosphere comes from natural sources such as rotting vegetation and volcanic activity. The rest (about 85% over Europe) comes from the burning of fossil fuels containing sulphur impurities. Ships, for example, normally burn cheap, polluting oil, typically containing 2.6% sulphur. When sulphur dioxide meets highly reactive chemical agents called free radicals in the atmosphere, it is oxidised to sulphur trioxide (SO_3). The sulphur trioxide, which is a gas, then combines with water to form sulphuric acid (H_2SO_4). The conversion of sulphur trioxide into sulphuric acid happens very fast in water droplets in the atmosphere.

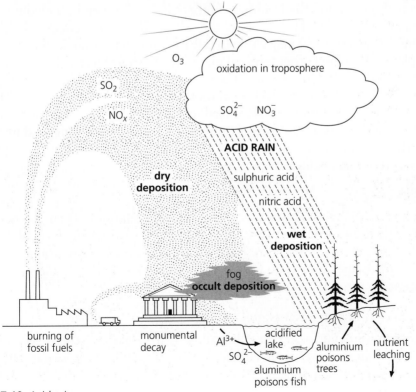

Figure 7.10 Acid rain

$$SO_2 + \tfrac{1}{2}O_2 \longrightarrow SO_3$$
$$SO_3 + H_2O \longrightarrow H_2SO_4$$

The cloud droplets containing sulphuric acid may then fall as acid rain hundreds of kilometres from the source of pollution.

The nitrogen oxides (collectively termed NO_x) in the atmosphere come predominantly from motor vehicle exhausts. Within the cylinders of the internal combustion engine and under high pressure and temperature, nitrogen reacts with oxygen to form oxides of nitrogen. In the atmosphere, nitric oxide rapidly oxidises to nitrogen dioxide which then changes to nitric acid (HNO_3).

Defoliation of trees

Acid rain has been blamed for the drastic decline of forests in many parts of eastern United States and Europe. A European study carried out in 1986 classified 20% of the trees in Germany and 29% in the Netherlands to be moderately or severely defoliated. One hypothesis which attempts to explain the demise of the trees is that acid rain falling on the soil releases potentially toxic substances such as aluminium from soil minerals. All soils contain large quantities of aluminium. The aluminium in the soil is, however, normally in an insoluble form. Acids promote detachment of aluminium from its soil mineral compound, allowing aluminium ions to compete with calcium ions for binding sites on the surface of young roots. The effect is to block the uptake of calcium ions by plants.

Acid rain also promotes the leaching of other vital soil minerals, including magnesium and potassium. The acidity of the soil has the further effect of killing soil microorganisms which play a major role in releasing minerals from dead tissues for re-use by plants. Trees and other forms of plant life are thus starved of vital minerals. Weakened by starvation, the trees lose their leaves or needles and their ability to photosynthesise. This leads to a decline in root growth and the ability of the affected plants to take up mineral nutrients. Reduced to a starving, defenceless state, the trees succumb to attack by disease-causing organisms, such as parasitic fungi and insects, which are the actual cause of their death. Drought or frost damage could also push the trees into terminal decline.

Indicator species

Some species have a low tolerance for environmental pollutants. Their absence or presence can therefore provide a useful indication as to whether the level of pollution has exceeded a certain threshold. Such species are known as **indicator species**. Certain species of lichens, for example, are very sensitive to sulphur dioxide and can therefore act as indicators of atmospheric pollution.

Acidification of freshwater rivers and lakes

Acidified runoff water and acid rain falling directly into lakes have also been blamed for the disappearance of fish, particularly trout and salmon from thousands of lakes and rivers in southern Scandinavia. A characteristic feature of acidified lakes is the slow rate of decomposition of organic matter. This is because bacteria, which are nature's most efficient decomposers, function poorly in acid conditions. The result is an altered ecosystem consisting of crystal clear water hosting a luxuriant growth of green algae but a much reduced range of living species. Fish die in acidified lakes mainly from poisoning by aluminium. The aluminium interferes with gill function by causing the surfaces of the gills to be covered in thick mucus, thus reducing their ability to take up oxygen.

Acidification of lakes can be countered by adding powdered limestone to the water and to catchment areas. Liming raises the pH of the water and it also precipitates the aluminium. Liming the catchment areas is more expensive because catchments require up to 100 times as much lime as lake water. However, a single well-targeted application at the water's source can remain effective for up to 10 years.

Figure 7.11 Monitoring the acidity of lakes. Sodium carbonate and sodium chloride are added to reduce the acidity

Building stone decay

Acid rain falling on buildings continuously and progressively dissolves and etches building stones causing them to decay. At sites close to the sources of pollution, the most damaging form of acid rain consists of dry deposition of soot, fly ash and partly burnt particles of oil and sulphur. In dry weather, these particles accumulate on the surfaces of stonework to be mobilised into a strong acid solution in wet weather. Acids can also be deposited on stonework as a film of moisture from fog, mist or dew. This type of acid rain is known as 'occult deposition' and its acid content can be 20 times more concentrated than the more widely understood form of acid rain.

Figure 7.12 Neutralising acidified waters by adding pulverised lime

Measures for curbing acid rain

The most direct way of reducing air pollutants responsible for acid rain is to burn less fossil fuels. One way of achieving this would be to expand public mass transport systems such as the railways (see Chapter 8, integrated public transport system, pages 164–165). Another would be to develop 'lean-burn' fuel-efficient engines that consume less fuel.

Cleaning up the flue-gas

The key to curbing acid rain lies in reducing sulphur dioxide emissions, two-thirds of which come from fossil-fuelled power stations, especially those burning pulverised coal. One method consists of fitting **flue-gas desulphurisation equipment,** commonly known as 'wet scrubbers', to power stations. The sulphur dioxide in the flue-gas is removed by spraying wet limestone (calcium carbonate) into the hot exhaust gases. The limestone reacts with sulphur dioxide to form calcium sulphate (gypsum), an inert substance. As much as 90% of the sulphur dioxide in exhaust gases can be taken out in this way.

Wet scrubbing systems are, however, expensive to install on existing plants. They require large amounts of water for their operation and they create huge quantities of sludge waste which needs to be put in holding ponds and landfills before it can be sold as building material. A cheaper alternative, especially for power plants nearing the end of their natural lives, is to burn **less-sulphurous fuels** such as natural gas.

Emissions of oxides of nitrogen (NO_x) from power stations can be reduced in one of three ways:

1 The use of **low-NO_x burners**. These burners are designed to allow the flame to burn at lower temperatures so that less nitrogen in the air is oxidised.
2 The installation of **selective catalytic reduction equipment** between the boiler and the chimney stack. The catalyst, which is an alloy of the platinum group metals, promotes the breakdown of oxides of nitrogen to nitrogen and oxygen.
3 The **spraying of a fine mist of urea solution** (concentrated urine) into the furnace. The urea reacts with nitrogen oxide in the flame to form nitrogen.

$$2CO(NH_2)_2 + 4NO + O_2 \longrightarrow 4N_2 + 2CO_2 + 4H_2O$$
urea

The urea injection method is by far the cheapest method because the required equipment is small and its running cost is low.

Catalytic converters for motor vehicles

Since 1993 it has been compulsory in Britain for new cars to be fitted with **catalytic converters**. A catalytic converter is essentially a sophisticated filter. It contains a thin coating of platinum and rhodium on a solid honeycomb support made of metal or ceramic. The tiny pores of the honeycomb provide a large surface area for the catalyst to convert i) the oxides of nitrogen in the car's exhaust emissions to nitrogen and ii) carbon monoxide to carbon dioxide. As much as 80% of the oxides of nitrogen from motor vehicle exhausts can be taken out in this way.

Global warming

The level of carbon dioxide in the air is rising. Analysis of air trapped in ice extracted from ice sheets in Greenland suggests that the level of carbon dioxide in the atmosphere during the Ice Ages that ended 18 000 years ago, was about 200 parts per million (ppm). From an estimated 270 ppm at the start of the Industrial Revolution in the mid 1850s, the carbon dioxide level in the atmosphere has risen 15% to 310 ppm by the mid 1950s. Since then it has been rising even faster, reaching 355 ppm in 1995, a further 16% increase in a matter of 40 years. The additional carbon dioxide released into the atmosphere by the burning of fossil fuels and by deforestation is clearly not being matched by corresponding carbon dioxide absorbing processes, such as additional photosynthesis and diffusion into the oceans (see Chapter 3, the carbon cycle, pages 21–26). Furthermore, carbon dioxide levels in the atmosphere have never ever been quite as high as they are now.

The greenhouse effect

Carbon dioxide is not in itself a dangerous gas but there is concern that the vast quantities of carbon dioxide released into the air by the burning of fossil fuels may, in the longterm, have a deleterious effect on the climate. The fact is that carbon dioxide is an important **heat-trapping gas**.

All hot objects radiate heat energy and the Earth is no exception. The Earth is warmed by energy from the Sun. The Sun's energy comes mainly in the form of shortwave radiation in the visible band of the spectrum. The warming effect of the Sun's rays is responsible for giving the Earth its average surface temperature of about 15 °C. Since the Earth's surface is cooler than the Sun's, the Earth radiates heat energy of a much longer wavelength than the Sun. Unlike the Sun's shortwave radiation, which penetrates the Earth's atmosphere without absorption, the Earth's

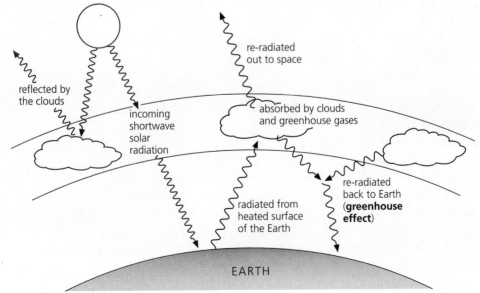

Figure 7.13 The greenhouse effect

longer wavelength infrared radiation penetrates the Earth's atmosphere with greater difficulty and some of it is absorbed by certain gases in the atmosphere to be re-radiated back to the surface of the Earth. Since these heat-trapping gases act in much the same way as glass over a greenhouse, the gases are known as **greenhouse gases** and the warming effect that accompanies re-radiation is known as the **greenhouse effect**.

In itself, the greenhouse effect is no bad thing. Due to the insulating effect of the heat-trapping gases, our planet's surface stays comfortably warm – in fact, 33 °C warmer than it otherwise would be. Without the greenhouse effect, our oceans would remain permanently frozen. The Moon, for example, lacks an atmosphere and its sunlit surface rises to 100 °C and then falls to −150 °C at night.

The other greenhouse gases

Methane is another important greenhouse gas. It is produced by anaerobic bacteria living in bogs, swamps, paddy fields, the gut of cattle and putrefying municipal waste tips. Concentrations of methane in the atmosphere are rising at the rate of 0.6% per year. India, with its millions of cattle and swathes of paddy fields, is believed to be the world's most important contributor of atmospheric methane. The rich nations with their 'mountains' of putricible solid wastes are also significant emitters of this greenhouse gas. The concentration of methane in the atmosphere is small when compared with carbon dioxide (1.7 ppm as compared with 355 ppm). However, molecule for molecule, methane is 20 times more effective as a heat-trapping gas than carbon dioxide and its contribution to the greenhouse effect is therefore quite significant.

Figure 7.14 Methane, released into the atmosphere by anaerobic bacteria living in the gut of herbivores and in swamps, bogs and paddy fields, is another important greenhouse gas

There are four other important heat-trapping gases. These are **chloroflurocarbons (CFCs)**, **nitrous oxide (N_2O)**, **ozone** and **water vapour**. CFCs are used in refrigerators and as propellants in aerosols. With minor exceptions, there is, since January 1995, a general ban on the manufacture of CFCs in the industrialised countries of the world. Nitrous oxide has been accumulating in the atmosphere through the widespread use of nitrogen-based fertilisers.

$$C_6H_{12}O_6 + 6KNO_3 \xrightarrow[\text{denitrifying bacteria}]{\text{denitrification by}} 6CO_2 + 3H_2O + 6KOH + 3N_2O$$

Oxides of nitrogen are also present in motor vehicle exhaust emissions (see atmospheric chemistry, pages 127–128). Ozone is another important heat-trapping gas. Low-level ozone is produced in chemical reactions in the atmosphere involving nitrogen oxides, atmospheric oxygen and ultraviolet light (see low-level ozone, page 137). Water vapour is another heat-trapping gas. It is a strong absorber of infrared radiation.

Effects of global warming

How quickly will the world become warmer? Computer projections predict that average global temperatures will rise by about 2 °C within the next 50 years. What would happen as the world warms up?

Faster rate of decomposition

It is impossible to be certain but one likely outcome from a rise in global temperatures would probably be a speeding up of the rate of decomposition of organic matter which would not be matched by a corresponding increase in the rate of photosynthesis. This is because the rate of decomposition is catalysed by enzymes which are very sensitive to changes in temperature, whereas the rate of photosynthesis is dependent on a number of factors other than temperature including, for example, the availability of nutrients and the intensity of light.

An increase in the rate of decomposition would result in more carbon dioxide and methane being released into the atmosphere, thus speeding up the global warming process.

Rise in sea levels

Another consequence of global warming is a rise in sea levels. The rise would partly be caused by expansion of water as it warms up and partly by the melting of the ice caps. The rate of rise is expected to be 1 to 2 cm per year.

Figure 7.15 Global warming could put polar bears under threat of extinction as their habitat shrinks northwards

Some species would inevitably become extinct as they are left stranded in their shrinking habitats. Animals like polar bears and walruses could come under threat of extinction as they are pushed northwards by the shrinking tundra.

Another group of animals that may be threatened by rising sea levels is corals. These cnidarians grow actively near the surface of the water and may not be able to grow fast enough to keep pace with the rising water level.

The inhabitants of some island states such as the Marshall Islands in the Pacific may find their homes submerged under the sea and be forced to evacuate.

Ground-water supplies in some coastal areas may become contaminated with seawater and become worthless for drinking or for agriculture.

Sexual imbalance among reptiles

The sex of many species of reptiles is determined by the temperature at which their eggs are incubated. Global warming could lead to sexual imbalance and extinction of many reptilian species.

Decline in the numbers of frogs and other amphibians

The warmer winters may cause hibernating animals such as frogs to burn up more of their fat stores thus leaving them less fit and less able to reproduce when spring arrives.

Northward migration of the treeline

A 1 °C rise in temperature is equivalent to shifting the latitudes on either side of the equator by 100 to 150 kilometres. This could result in the treeline moving northwards but probably only slowly because forests require stable conditions, rich soils and centuries to develop. Wind-dispersed trees will probably spread fastest.

Ferocious storms and protracted droughts

Global warming would also probably be accompanied by increased rainfall due to a higher rate of evaporation of water. Climatologists expect storms to be more ferocious and protracted droughts to be experienced in many of the important food-growing areas further inland.

Landslips and a threat to water supplies in some areas

The sudden downpours may trigger landslips, contaminating rivers with runoff making it harder for water companies to collect enough to meet supplies.

Freezing winters in Europe

Europe is on the same latitude as Canada but enjoys much milder winters because of the warming effects of the Gulf Stream – a broad drift of warm water, originating in the Gulf of Mexico. Being warmer, the waters of the Gulf Stream are less dense and float on top of the colder Atlantic waters as the Gulf Stream drifts northwards. On reaching the north Atlantic, the Gulf Stream warms the air over Europe, becoming itself colder and therefore denser as it starts to sink. Having lost water by evaporation along its journey, it has also become more saline and less buoyant; which is another reason why it sinks when it arrives off the coast of east Greenland. It is this huge body of cold, salty, sinking water which, acting like a **gigantic plunger**, provides the driving force for the ocean currents of the Atlantic. It pushes the cold deep waters of the Atlantic southwards towards the Antarctic and pulls the warm surface waters of the Gulf Stream northwards towards Europe.

Man-made global warming could turn off the Gulf Stream and plunge winter temperatures in Britain and Western Europe to Arctic levels. The few degrees rise in temperature from global warming would cause the polar ice caps to melt. If large quantities of fresh water from melting ice were to dilute the saline north Atlantic water, it would make the water less dense. Instead of sinking, the north Atlantic water would stay afloat bringing the Gulf Stream to a halt. Instead of bringing warmth to Europe, winter temperatures could plummet, falling by as much as 10 °C. This could have a devastating effect on agriculture in western Europe leading to widespread starvation.

Ozone depletion

Ozone is a highly reactive molecule made up of three atoms of oxygen (O_3). It is one of the more noxious pollutants when present in the air at low altitude but its presence in the upper atmosphere is beneficial because it acts as a shield, blocking out much of the harmful incoming solar ultraviolet (UV) radiation from reaching the ground.

Atmospheric ozone

A beneficial layer of ozone exists high up in the stratosphere, 15 to 35 kilometres above the ground. It is formed by the action of ultraviolet radiation on oxygen. The dioxygen molecule splits into two highly reactive oxygen atoms. These oxygen atoms then react with other unsplit oxygen molecules to create ozone.

$$O_2 \xrightarrow[\text{radiation}]{\text{UV}} O + O$$
$$O + O_2 \longrightarrow O_3$$

When sunlight passes through the ozone layer in the stratosphere, much of the Sun's UV radiation is absorbed and humans and other organisms are thus protected from its harmful effects.

Fears of a human threat to the ozone layer were first voiced in the early 1970s when it was thought that the Concorde would be one of many supersonic aircraft that would one day fill the skies. It was argued that oxides of nitrogen (NO_x) emitted by the jet aircraft could catalyse the destruction of the protective ozone layer in the stratosphere by means of a catalytic cycle of reactions in which nitric oxide reacts with ozone and is reformed at the end of each cycle. In this way, nitric oxide, behaving like a catalyst, is re-used again and again to destroy more and more ozone molecules. Atoms of chlorine could also act in the same way, as shown below:

$$X + O_3 \longrightarrow XO + O_2$$
$$XO + O \longrightarrow X + O_2$$
$$\textbf{net result: } O_3 + O \longrightarrow 2O_2$$

where X is the catalyst which could either be nitric oxide (NO), an atom of chlorine (Cl) or a few other types of molecules:

1 With nitric oxide as the catalyst:

$$NO + O_3 \longrightarrow NO_2 + O_2$$
$$NO_2 + O \longrightarrow NO + O_2$$

2 With a chlorine atom as the catalyst:

$$Cl + O_3 \longrightarrow ClO + O_2$$
$$ClO + O \longrightarrow Cl + O_2$$

CFCs

The catalysts for the destruction of the ozone layer in the stratosphere are all breakdown products of gases that have drifted upwards, in many cases from man-made sources. Prominent among them are substances called **chlorofluorocarbons (CFCs)**. These compounds, as their name implies, contain chlorine. Because they are very inert substances (which is why they were used in refrigeration and aerosol cans), they can, when released into the environment, reach the stratosphere without breakdown. They are broken down naturally only when they have risen above the ozone layer and are eventually shattered by the Sun's UV radiation to become very reactive **free radicals**. (Free radicals are atoms or molecules with one or more unpaired electrons.)

$$CFCl_3 \xrightarrow{\text{UV radiation}} CFCl_2 + Cl$$

When the reaction products sink into the ozone layer, the chlorine atoms react with ozone molecules bringing about their destruction.

The so-called 'ozone-friendly' substitutes for CFCs are the **hydrofluorocarbons (HFCs)** and **hydrochlorofluorocarbons (HCFCs)**. These substitutes have at least one hydrogen atom in their molecular structure which can easily be displaced by reactive chemicals in the atmosphere known as hydroxyl free radicals. This makes HFCs and HCFCs much less stable as compared with CFCs. They will therefore break down well before the stratosphere and cause no harm to the ozone layer.

Emissions from jumbo jets

Emissions from civil aircraft are another major source of destruction of the ozone layer. This is especially true of the present generation of jumbo jets which

Figure 7.16 Concorde and the present generation of jumbo jets that fly high in the stratosphere, leave a trail of sulphuric acid droplets that act as nuclei for chlorine and other pollutants to settle and destroy ozone

fly ever higher to take advantage of lower fuel costs that come from cruising in the thin air of the stratosphere. Because aircraft fuel contains trace impurities including sulphur, aircraft exhaust emissions contain sulphur trioxide, which readily reacts with water vapour to form in the wake of the aircraft a fog consisting of tiny particles of sulphuric acid. Due to a dearth of particles in the stratospheric air, the presence of these particles of sulphuric acid provides the surface on which chlorine pollutants can settle to destroy ozone.

Harmful effects of ozone depletion

It is difficult to be sure what biological effects depletion of the ozone layer will have on humans and living organisms. What we do know is that high levels of UV radiation can cause skin cancers, eye cataracts and immune deficiencies in humans. Quantitative estimates, however, vary widely. One study makes the prediction that a 2 to 3% reduction in stratospheric ozone cover would lead to 800 000 avoidable deaths from suppressed immune systems and 40 million extra cases of skin cancer among the present inhabitants of the Earth.

Another suggestion is that a thinning of the ozone layer at high latitudes will result in plankton, which are sensitive to UV light, being killed and this will in turn result in less carbon dioxide being absorbed from the atmosphere for photosynthesis, thus making the problems of global warming even greater.

Low-level ozone

In the lower atmosphere, ozone is formed when ultraviolet light decomposes nitrogen dioxide to nitric oxide and atomic oxygen. The highly reactive oxygen atom then combines with an oxygen molecule to form ozone.

$$NO_2 \xrightarrow{\text{UV radiation}} NO + O$$
$$O + O_2 \longrightarrow O_3$$

Since there are no direct sources of ozone in the environment, ozone is known as a **secondary pollutant**.

Harmful effects

Ozone has two unpaired electrons and is consequently a powerful oxidising agent. Ground-level ozone:

- weakens the body's immune defence system probably by overwhelming the body's natural antioxidant defence mechanisms
- irritates the lungs, which can lead to symptoms such as coughing, breathing difficulties and inflammation of the airways

Figure 7.17 Motor vehicle exhausts release nitrogen oxides, which, in the presence of ultraviolet light, react with oxygen to produce low-level ozone

- irritates the eyes
- can be damaging to the DNA in mammalian cells. German scientists are recommending its reclassification as a 'suspected carcinogen' (cancer-causing substance)
- has been blamed for what is known as 'dieback' in beech trees in which the foliage density of the crown of the trees falls, often by as much as 60 to 80%
- harms crop plants especially wheat, barley, spinach, peas, beans and radishes. Crop yields are lower in areas affected by ozone pollution.

Plugging the ozone hole

Policy makers at government and industrial levels have several options. They can:

- **Ban the use of CFCs in refrigerators and aerosols.** 150 governments have already signed the 1987 Montreal Protocol curbing the use of ozone-destroying chemicals.
- **Produce jet aircraft fuel with a lower sulphur content and redesign aircraft engines to emit less sulphur trioxide.** This is probably the best option for the aircraft industry because other options such as making aircraft fly lower will only add to air pollution problems closer to ground.
- **Reduce vehicle use.** Since motor vehicle exhaust emissions are important sources of nitrogen oxides in the air, curbing motor vehicle use would certainly help to reduce ground-level ozone (see Chapter 8, integrated public transport system, pages 164–165).
- **Develop less polluting propulsion systems.** The development of a popular, practical electric car would certainly be an important step forward.

Figure 7.18 Greenpeace staging a protest against the use of CFCs in 1990

Particulate (smoke) pollution

Smoke consists of fine solid particles suspended in a gas. Those (of an older generation) who were around at the time of the infamous London smog of December 1952, may recall how dense the smog was. It was reported that people in cinemas could not see the screen, while some others walking alongside the River Thames fell into it because they could not see where the river was.

The smog was caused by a combination of very cold conditions and smoke pollution. To keep warm, most houses kept fires burning using coal as the major fuel. In the cold London air, water vapour condensed around the smoke particles to form a thick yellow smog that persisted for 4 days. Many elderly people were reported to have died from respiratory ailments in ambulances on their way to hospital. Others were left wheezing on trolleys in hospital corridors because every available bed had been taken up. The **Clean Air Act** of 1956 followed and smokeless zones were created, in which only smoke-free fuels were allowed to be burnt.

Dangers of particulate pollution

Recent research in the United States has shown that particulate air pollution is still a major threat to health, but the culprit nowadays is not the heavy, black soot particles of the 1950s but **fine particulates** – clusters of much smaller particles, known as **PM10s**, because each particle is less than 10 micrometres in diameter. PM10s are emitted into the air mostly from exhaust pipes of cars, lorries and buses, especially those burning diesel fuel. They are more dangerous than the large soot particles for two reasons. First, their small size allows them to penetrate deeper into the lungs and, second, the PM10s may be coated with a nitrated polycyclic aromatic hydrocarbon called

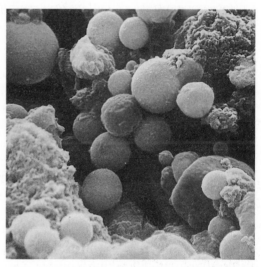

Figure 7.19 Electronmicrograph of fine particulates collected from urban air

3-nitrobenzanthrone, a byproduct of burnt diesel fuel. This substance has recently been shown to be strongly carcinogenic. Bus and cab drivers have double the national average of lung cancer probably because of increased exposure to this carcinogen.

In a recent report on the dangers of airborne particulate pollution, a panel of experts from the World Health Organisation warned that, out of a sample of one million individuals, 1400 extra asthmatics would be forced to reach out for their asthma inhalers, six more than usual will be admitted to hospital for respiratory complaints and four more than usual will die, if they are exposed to more than 50 micrograms of PM10s per cubic metre of air over a 3 day period. In most British cities the PM10 level rises above 50 micrograms per cubic metre for up to 40 days per year.

What can be done?

- Governments could impose tighter limits on exhaust emissions.
- Local authorities could be empowered to divert traffic away from air pollution black spots.
- The type of vehicle, the volume of traffic using certain routes and the speed limit could be controlled.
- Working hours could be staggered to ease air pollution problems during peak periods.

Heavy metal pollution

Another class of environmental pollutants are heavy metals such as lead, mercury, cadmium, copper, zinc, and chromium. Some of these metals are essential for health in trace concentrations but are toxic in higher concentrations.

Lead

Lead interferes with the brain's neuronal connections (the so called 'wiring circuits'), which explains why children with 'above average' levels of lead in their blood have lower IQs and a reduced ability to concentrate as compared with a control group.

Lead (in the form of tetraethyl lead) is used as a fuel additive in petrol to prevent engine 'knock', a metallic sound which is a sign of poor combustion. It is emitted into the air in motor vehicle exhausts. Other sources of lead pollution include dust from lead-smelting works, battery-breaking yards, flaking lead paint, lead water pipes, lead roofing materials and vegetables contaminated by lead in polluted air. The use of unleaded petrol, leadless paint and copper or plastic pipes has helped to reduce the input of lead into the environment.

Mercury

Mercury is another highly toxic heavy metal. It can cause mental retardation, loss of control of motor nerves (uncontrollable shaking) and spontaneous abortion.

Mercury vapour is released into the air when discarded mercury batteries are burnt together with household rubbish in municipal incinerators. The local crematorium is another, possibly

Figure 7.20 Vaporising the mercury out of the amalgam to obtain pure gold

significant, source of mercury pollution. A team of Swiss researchers made the interesting discovery that when a human corpse is cremated, it releases, on average, about 1 gram of mercury vapours into the air. The toxic vapours were presumably released by evaporation of the amalgam fillings in the corpse's teeth. The Swiss workers showed in their calculations that, working at full capacity, a modern city crematorium could release enough mercury vapours to have a 'significant impact' on the environment. They proposed the fitting of activated charcoal filters in crematorium chimneys to cut out this source of air pollution.

In Brazil, Venezuela, the Philippines and Indonesia, mercury is used to precipitate out dissolved gold from the watery sediments of gold mines. The mercury reacts with the gold to form an amalgam. The gold–mercury amalgam is then heated in a pan over an open fire to vaporise the mercury leaving a nugget of pure gold. The wind disperses the mercury vapour far and wide. Much of it is washed out of the atmosphere by the rain. From the soil, the mercury, which is now in the form of methyl mercury, is leached into rivers and then carried into lakes. Edible carnivorous fish in lakes 200 kilometres from gold mines have been reported to have as much as 2 to 3 micrograms (μg) of mercury per gram wet weight in their body tissues. The World Health Organisation's recommendation is that anything above 0.2 to 0.3 μg of mercury per gram wet weight is unfit for human consumption.

Other heavy metals

The main sources of the other heavy metal pollutants are known. Large concentrations of chromium in effluents can generally be traced to leather tanneries or manufacturers of dyes. Cadmium and nickel come mainly from factories producing long-life batteries. These and other industries are required by law to recover metallic ions from industrial effluents before the waste water leaves the factory. This is usually done by ion exchange, a process that simply swaps undesirable ions for less troublesome ones.

Some nickel, zinc and chromium in sewage effluents result from corrosion of pipes and household appliances and these are much harder to keep under control.

Pesticides

Pesticides are chemical substances that kill pests. They can be subdivided into three groups: **herbicides, fungicides** and **insecticides**. Herbicides are weed-killers and they account for the bulk of pesticide sales in the developed nations of the world. Fungicides, as their name implies, kill fungi and insecticides kill insects. Of the three types of pesticides, there is more controversy surrounding the use of insecticides than herbicides or fungicides because insecticides are generally more toxic to humans and to wildlife.

Insecticides are sold under many different brand names but they can broadly be subdivided into four main groups: **organochlorine, organophosphate, carbamate** and **pyrethroid**.

Organochlorine insecticides

DDT (dichlorodiphenyltrichloroethane) was the first widely used synthetic chemical pesticide. It is an organochlorine insecticide – it has a chemical structure consisting of chlorine atoms attached to hydrocarbon rings. Other common organochlorine insecticides include dieldrin and toxaphene.

The organochlorine insecticides are chemically stable, which means that they will persist in the environment and retain their potency for many years. This was at first thought to be a bonus but, as it turned out, it in fact was a fatal flaw (see 'bioaccumulation' below). Organochlorines enter the body of insects through the waxy cuticle of the insect or through its gut lining. They kill insects by interfering with the conduction of nerve impulses along nerve axons.

Effect on wildlife

The organochlorines were at first thought to be harmless to warm-blooded animals. Then, in the late 1950s and early 1960s people in England began to notice an increase in the numbers of dead wood pigeons, pheasants and foxes. Furthermore, the populations of birds of prey, such as sparrowhawks and peregrine falcons, had mysteriously plummeted. Similar happenings were reported in the north-eastern United States where ospreys and bald eagles were becoming extinct. Comparisons of the eggs of the surviving birds of prey with eggs in

Figure 7.21 Why did ecologists notice a dramatic drop in the numbers of birds of prey in the early 1960s?

museum collections, showed that the threatened birds were laying eggs with much thinner eggshells than usual. As well as dying from a suspected environmental poison, the surviving birds of prey were not reproducing properly because they were laying thin-shelled eggs that cracked easily.

By the early 1970s, researchers in Britain and the United States had established a connection between the thinness of the eggshells and the concentration of DDE residues (a breakdown product of DDT) within the eggs.

Bioaccumulation

When herbivores consume vegetation containing organochlorine residues, the pesticide, which is strongly lipophilic (very soluble in fats and much less soluble in water) tends to accumulate in the body's fatty tissues. The body's fat stores, being water insoluble, are less accessible to the blood and, consequently, any pesticides dissolved in fat are not readily excreted through the kidneys but tend instead to be passed through the food chain. Continuous ingestion of chemically stable lipophilic pesticides (or other toxic chemicals with similar properties) leads to a gradual build up in the level of the toxic substance in the body, a process known as **bioaccumulation**. A top predator may, by this process of bioaccumulation, amass

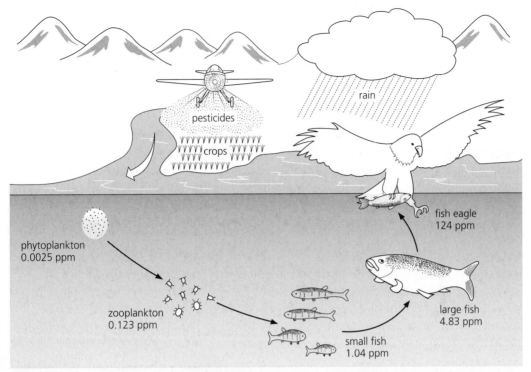

Figure 7.22 Bioaccumulation (the figures are parts per million of pesticide in terms of whole organisms)

toxic chemicals in its body tissues to a level which is a million times higher than in the environment. This is not surprising since predators feed on herbivores that have already concentrated the substance by feeding on large quantities of vegetation. Months later, during winter for example, or when the animal's fat stores are mobilised to provide energy for migration, the pesticides are released into the blood to exert their toxic effects on the tissues of the body.

Thinning of eggshells

DDT does not harm the nervous system of warm-blooded animals. One theory on how it acts to decimate the natural populations of the birds of prey is that its breakdown product, DDE (which also accumulates in the fatty tissues of animals) acts by inhibiting a receptor for the hormone progesterone within the shell gland. The effect is to lower the rate at which calcium is deposited into egg shells shortly before the eggs are laid. The result is eggs which crack easily because their shells are too thin.

Not long after the environmental problems caused by organochlorine insecticides were recognised, a ban was imposed on the use of DDT and other organochlorine pesticides in the developed nations of the world. The developing countries, however, have had more than their fair share of pests including malaria-transmitting mosquitoes and they have consequently continued to use DDT, dieldrin and toxaphene because these insecticides are effective, cheap and relatively safe to use.

Non-persistent pesticides

The withdrawal of the organochlorine insecticides from the market paved the way for farmers in the developed nations to switch to the use of **non-persistent pesticides**. These pesticides are biodegradable and they break down quickly into harmless substances when exposed to the sun and rain. The organophosphates (e.g. parathion and malathion), the carbamates (e.g. aldicarb) and the pyrethroids (e.g. permethrin) are all non-persistent insecticides.

Organophosphate insecticides work by interfering with nerve synapse function. The pesticide binds on to an enzyme called acetylcholinesterase, preventing it from breaking down acetylcholine, a substance which stimulates nerve fibres to activate muscle fibres into action. With acetylcholinesterase inactivated, acetylcholine builds up in nerve junctions stimulating the nerve to fire nerve impulses continuously. The effect is to cause the muscle to twitch, a typical symptom of organophosphate pesticide poisoning.

Organophosphate insecticides have earned for themselves a bad reputation. They are, to start with, much more toxic to mammals than the organochlorine insecticides. According to figures published by the World Health Organisation, it takes 113 milligrams of DDT per kilogram body weight to have a 50% chance of killing a rat. The same result can be achieved with only 3.6 milligrams of parathion per kilogram body weight.

Figure 7.23 Campaigners against the use of pesticides

Birth defects

One organophosphate insecticide called trichlorphon, which is widely used to control parasites on farmed fish, is suspected to be the most likely cause of a spate of birth defects in a Hungarian village between 1989 and 1990. The problem arose when a new director was appointed to a local fish farm. He introduced a fast method of treating fish. Instead of diluting the pesticide before use, he ordered that the fish should be taken out of the water, dipped into neat insecticide and returned to the pond. Levels of trichlorphon in these fish were 1000 times higher than the maximum permitted for consumption. The result was high rates of birth abnormalities in babies whose mothers ate the fish during pregnancy. Some babies were born with lung, heart or intestinal abnormalities and there were several with Down's syndrome.

In Britain, trichlorphon is widely used as a spray on hedges to kill caterpillars and on some fruits and salad vegetables.

Gulf War syndrome

Organophosphate insecticides are the principal suspects for Gulf War syndrome. Symptoms of the condition include difficulties in reasoning, depression, dizziness, disorientation, insomnia, impotence and slurred speech. Many of the sufferers were those who stood on nighttime watch while mists of organophosphate insecticide sprays hovered in the air over their tents. Some were involved in actually carrying out the spraying without wearing protective clothing. There were reports that even the tented canteen areas where the soldiers ate were heavily doused in organophosphate pesticides.

Carried by the wind from the tropics

Inuits have for centuries enjoyed eating seal meat, but their favourite is a slice of fried *murtuk*, the skin and surface fat of the beluga whale. There are recent reports, however, that one in six of these inhabitants of Greenland have potentially harmful levels of mercury, toxaphene and other persistent pesticides including DDT in their blood. Breastfeeding Inuit women have five times the level of pesticides in their milk compared with women living in the lower latitudes. There are reports of school-age children, exposed to the pollutants when in the womb, having short attention spans, learning difficulties, poor memory and lower than the general average IQ.

There are no polluting chemical factories in the Arctic region and the Canadians have banned the use of organochlorine pesticides for over two decades. So where did the pollutants come from? One theory is that volatile pollutants have vaporised from soils as far away as the tropics and have then been carried long distances by the wind to the cold latitudes where, like in a distillation process, they have condensed out in the cold Arctic air as toxic snow and rain. The pesticides have then bioaccumulated in the body fat of animals reaching their highest concentrations on top carnivores such as the beluga whales. Mercury, which probably also originated in the tropics, accumulates in the liver. Analysis of liver tissue of Arctic seals shows that the levels of mercury are 20 to 200 times above WHO guidelines for safe human consumption. Computer models of the atmosphere suggest that highly volatile chemicals can be carried from the tropics to the Arctic in as little as 5 days.

Carbamates and pyrethroids

Like the organophosphate insecticides, carbamates work by acting on nerve synapses but they are generally not as toxic to humans. Pyrethroids are less toxic to mammals than the carbamates but they are lethal to fish and their use near streams, rivers and lakes needs to be strictly controlled. Precisely how pyrethroids work to kill insects is not known.

Questions

6 Describe the effects of acid rain on
   a organisms and
   b the environment.
7 What is the greenhouse effect? Describe the impact of human activities on the greenhouse effect. Explain why reducing carbon dioxide emissions is generally considered to be the key to keeping global warming under control.
8 What is meant by the term **bioaccumulation**? Explain why top predators are more likely to suffer from the toxic effects of persistent pesticides, such as DDT, as compared with organisms lower down the food chain. Explain why some countries, such as Sweden, have banned the use of all forms of chemical pesticides.

Water pollution

Anyone who has idly looked down on to the ground below from an aeroplane flying fairly low over southern England on a bright summer's day, would probably have noticed that there are many ponds and waterways that look 'pea soup' green in colour. These unattractive 'pea soup' ponds and rivers are examples of **eutrophication**, one of the commonest forms of a worldwide water pollution problem. Other types of water pollution include **organic (sewage) pollution, heavy metal pollution** and **oil pollution**.

Eutrophication

Derived from the Greek word *eutrophos* meaning 'well-nourished', the term 'eutrophication' reflects very well the cause of this environmental problem. It is essentially caused by water which is too rich in mineral nutrients. Supplied with an abundance of nutrients, microscopic green algae feed and multiply very rapidly to form dense populations that turn the water green and turbid, not unlike pea soup! One common type of green alga, known as the blanket weed (*Cladophora*), grows to form long filamentous strands that look like ugly masses of green hair.

Figure 7.24 A river choked with blanket weed, a filamentous green alga

Pure water in unpolluted streams and lakes is crystal clear and it supports a rich diversity of living organisms. Mineral nutrient levels are low in pure natural fresh water, especially in phosphate and nitrates. There are insufficient minerals in this type of water to support dense populations of microscopic green algae. Competition for vital minerals among plants favours the large longer-lived plant species because they can 'hold on' to their vital minerals for a longer period of time, whereas those with shorter life-spans must release their captured minerals for recycling when they die.

When nutrient levels are too high

When mineral nutrient levels are too high, it is the microscopic algae which gain the upper hand. Their larger surface area to volume ratios allow them to take up minerals from their environment at a faster rate, as compared with the larger bottom-living plants. The result is a population explosion of microscopic algae near the surface layers of the pond or lake where plenty of light is available. Light to the deeper parts is thus blocked off. When the algae die in the autumn, bacteria of decay feed on the organic remains of the plants, multiplying rapidly. The bacteria use up dissolved oxygen needed to sustain fish and other creatures. If the deoxygenation is severe enough, fish and other aquatic animals die and the eutrophicated pond or lake becomes biologically dead, except for the dense blanket of green algae near the surface and thriving populations of anaerobic bacteria feeding on the decomposing vegetation at the bottom.

Eutrophication can therefore be defined as the process by which water becomes excessively enriched with nutrients, thus encouraging rapid growth of algal populations and the killing of other pond-dwelling organisms such as rooted aquatic plants and fish.

Sources of mineral nutrient pollution

High levels of minerals in water, especially phosphates and nitrates, can be traced to two main sources. The first is surface runoff and leaching of chemical fertilisers applied on to agricultural land or suburban lawns. The rain washes these minerals into streams or rivers especially those that run through towns or agricultural land. The second is the discharge of mineral-rich treated sewage effluents into rivers and lakes. There are high levels of phosphates in detergents and they enter the sewage system through kitchen sinks, laundry and dishwashing machines. The nitrates in sewage effluents come mainly from the activities of nitrifying bacteria.

Preventive measures

- Farmers should be encouraged to use less chemical fertilisers.
- Where practicable, organic farming should be encouraged – less nitrate is probably leached out of organic farms as compared with conventional farms.
- The use of low-phosphate detergents should also be encouraged.
- Sewage effluents should be treated to lower their phosphate and nitrate content before discharge into rivers or lakes.

Organic pollution (sewage)

Sewage is the water-borne waste from toilets, bathrooms, kitchen sinks and washing machines, mixed with some industrial effluents and some natural runoff water from the streets. The main components of sewage are human faeces, urine, paper, bits of food, soap, detergents, household chemicals such as bleach and disinfectants, sand, grit and other road debris, some heavy metals, oils and pesticides.

Raw sewage and the environment

If a small quantity of sewage finds its way into a river, aerobic microorganisms of decay (mainly bacteria and fungi) perform the useful function of breaking down the organic matter to carbon dioxide and water. The river is thus said to 'clean itself out'. The problem arises when large quantities of raw sewage are discharged into rivers or lakes. The high organic content of the sewage promotes rapid growth of aerobic bacteria of decay which consume vast quantities of dissolved oxygen. The water soon becomes anaerobic. Fish and other forms of aquatic animal life die from lack of oxygen. Anaerobic bacteria thrive in such conditions, multiplying in great numbers. One type, the sulphate-reducing bacteria, produce hydrogen sulphide gas from sulphates present in the water. The gas has the smell of rotten eggs and it explains why heavily polluted rivers and lakes emit an unpleasant odour.

There are many solid particles in suspension in untreated sewage, which makes the water murky and uninviting. When present in large quantities, the suspended solids reduce light penetration, thus restricting photosynthesis and the production of oxygen by submerged water plants and phytoplankton.

Many types of viruses and other pathogenic microorganisms are present in untreated sewage. These microorganisms can cause intestinal diseases, such as typhoid, cholera and dysentery, if the contaminated water is consumed.

Dumping raw sewage into the sea

More than half of the world's human population live in coastal towns along the sea or in river deltas or along estuaries at the mouth of rivers. Because of the high cost of building sewage treatment plants, most coastal towns (including many in Britain) dispose of the town's raw sewage by pouring it through outfalls that empty directly into the sea. This much cheaper method of sewage disposal is unsatisfactory for a number of reasons.

1 The excessive discharge of sewage raises the levels of phosphates and nitrates in seawater, which can result in eutrophication along coastal waters.
2 The solids in raw sewage float on the surface of the sea forming an unsightly slick which is rich in pathogenic bacteria (e.g. *Salmonella* and the dangerous killer microbe *Escherichia coli* 0157) and viruses (e.g. the hepatitis A virus).
3 Winds and surface currents may carry the sewage inshore, polluting beaches not only with an unpleasant odour but also unsightly muck and pathogenic microorganisms.

After pressure from other European nations, Britain has in recent years agreed to phase out by the end of 1998 its practice of dumping by ship sludge from sewage treatment works into the North Sea. It has also agreed to implement a European Union Urban Waste Water Treatment Directive, which requires, as minimum standards, primary treatment – the removal of lumps – for large discharges of sewage into coastal waters and secondary treatment – the removal of most of the organic matter – for discharges of sewage into estuaries.

The treatment of sewage

The main aim in sewage treatment is to remove or reduce the solids and the organic material so that the water can be safely discharged into rivers, lakes or the sea or re-used, for example, for agriculture. Sewage treatment can be subdivided into two main phases termed **primary** and **secondary**.

Primary treatment
The first phase in the treatment of sewage involves the use of physical means of separating the suspended solids from the waste water. It consists, to start with, of passing the incoming sewage through fixed screens composed of parallel metal bars placed in the waterways. The aim of the screening process is to remove large objects such as rags, sticks, plastic containers and other coarse particles. The screens need cleaning regularly by hand or mechanically. The sewage is then directed into primary

Figure 7.25 A sewage treatment plant

sedimentation tanks where the rate of water flow is considerably reduced to allow grit, sand and other settleable solids to settle to the bottom. The effect is to separate the sewage into solid and aqueous fractions.

Secondary treatment
The aim in secondary treatment is to i) oxidise the organic matter; ii) lower the ammonia/nitrate content; and iii) inactivate the pathogenic microorganisms. Secondary treatment is biological in nature and it involves the use of separate procedures for the treatment of the solid and aqueous fractions after primary treatment.

Treatment of the solid fraction
The solid fraction, which is termed **primary sludge**, is the material at the bottom of the tank. It is removed to another tank called an **aerobic sludge digester** to allow anaerobic bacteria including methanogens to feed on the organic material and to degrade it to methane and carbon dioxide. The methane (biogas) is then used to produce electricity for driving the stirrers and the air pumps in the sewage works.

Treatment of the aqueous fraction

The supernatant or aqueous fraction is subjected to treatment in one of two ways namely, the **trickling filter system** or the **activated-sludge process**. The aim in both these processes is to put the waste water in close contact with as many aerobic bacteria as possible so as to enable them to feed on the organic matter and to oxidise it to carbon dioxide.

The trickling filter system

In the trickling filter system, the liquid fraction from the settling tanks is sprayed over beds of medium-sized rock chippings in a large shallow tank, by means of a rotating distributor. The spraying saturates the liquid with air. Various types of microorganisms form a slimy layer over the surface of the chippings. Bacteria are by far the most important. Others include fungi, algae, ciliates and a variety of other protoctists. As the water trickles over the porous material, the organic matter carried in the water is used as food predominantly by bacteria and fungi and oxidised to carbon dioxide and water by a process of microbial respiration. The carbon dioxide produced, escapes into the air. Since the beds are not submerged, oxygen in the air diffuses into the water relatively easily. About 90% of the soluble organic content of the waste water is removed by this process of aerobic degradation of the organic matter and the water that trickles through is thus considerably purified.

The activated sludge process

In the activated sludge process, the aqueous fraction from the settling tanks is directed to an aeration tank where the waste water is stirred and vigorously aerated by allowing streams of compressed air to bubble through it via thousands of air diffusers. The treatment encourages the growth of aerobic bacteria which feed on the organic matter, oxidising it to carbon dioxide and water.

The activated sludge process is highly efficient and is widely used in cities around the world. Up to 98% of the soluble organic content of the waste water is removed by this process. Its main advantages are:

- its efficiency (up to 98% of the soluble organic content of the liquid can be removed)
- the relatively small size of the treatment plant (made possible by the high concentration of active microorganisms in the aeration tank).

Reducing the phosphate and nitrate content of the effluents

Phosphates can be precipitated out by treatment with alum and lime or iron, a process known as **stripping**. Nitrates can be taken out at the sewage works by passing the effluents through a tank filled with **rotting barley straw**. The straw allows a rich population of denitrifying bacteria to develop. Under anaerobic conditions, these bacteria break down nitrates to nitrogen gas. The hydrolysed barley straw may also release algal inhibitors which help to suppress algal growth.

Oil pollution

Whenever an accident occurs at sea and oil from a tanker is spilt, the oil spreads rapidly forming a slick which may be many kilometres long. If the oil slick is washed on to a shore line, the beach soon becomes covered in a thick, black, tarry mat of oily material. An estimated 300 000 guillemots (sea birds), 4000 sea otters and countless numbers of invertebrates died in the Exxon Valdez spill of March 1989 off the coast of Alaska.

Hosing with detergents

Attempts to clear the beaches by hosing with detergents are never satisfactory. The tide often returns the oil to the seemingly cleaned up beach and, even worse, the detergents kill natural populations of bacteria that feed on hydrocarbons, thus delaying the natural, biological process of recovery of the ecosystem.

Spraying with nitrogen and phosphorus

Laboratory studies show that natural populations of **oil-degrading bacteria** work only at the oil–water interface. Their growth is limited by the availability of nutrients, especially phosphates and nitrates. One technique for speeding up the cleaning of oil spills is to spray oleophilic (oil-loving) compounds of phosphorus and nitrogen that will stick on to the oil-coated rocks and stones, thus encouraging the growth of oil-degrading bacteria where they are most required.

Figure 7.26 In calm weather, oil spills can be contained using floating booms (inflatable ballast tubes)

Another technique consists of containing the spilled oil by surrounding it with floating booms. These are inflatable ballast tubes which can be used to stop the oil a metre above and a metre below from spreading while the slick is still out in the open sea. A mixed culture of oil-degrading bacteria together with appropriate quantities of mineral nutrients could then be sprayed on to the oil. The main disadvantage of this method is that the booms are expensive and they cannot be used in weather conditions that are worse than Force 4 gales (equivalent to winds gusting at 35 kilometres per hour).

Radioactive pollution

In the early hours of Saturday 26 April 1986, a massive explosion ripped open one of four reactors of the Chernobyl nuclear power station in the Ukraine. It was the world's worst nuclear accident. The force of the blast carried pieces of hot radioactive debris high into the air. The wind carried the radioactive cloud across vast areas of Europe, contaminating crops, livestock and land with radioactive fallout.

What is radioactivity?

Radioactivity is the spontaneous restructuring of unstable nuclei of atoms accompanied by the emission of subatomic particles or energy. It is a property of many naturally occurring elements, especially those with heavy atoms such as uranium, radium and thorium. To spontaneously convert from an unstable state to a less energetic but more stable state, the unstable nuclei periodically emit a flash of energy. These emissions may take the form of **alpha (α) particles, beta (β) particles** or **gamma (γ) rays**.

An α particle consists of two protons and two neutrons (the equivalent of the nucleus of a helium atom). The emission of an α particle signals the decay of an unstable parent nucleus as it splits into two daughter nuclei, one (the α particle) much smaller than the other. Alpha particles are emitted at tremendous speeds but soon slow down and generally travel only a few centimetres through the air.

The β particle consists of either a negatively charged electron or an elusive particle called an antineutrino, or their antimatter counterparts. The emission of a β particle signals the transformation of a neutron (electrically neutral nuclear particle) to a proton (positively charged nuclear particle).

Gamma rays are electromagnetic radiation of very short wavelength and they carry away some of the energy from the nuclear reaction. Gamma rays can penetrate deeply into human flesh and destroy cells. Of the three types of radiation, they are by far the most damaging.

Sources of radioactivity

Natural

The soil typically contains three parts (by weight) per million of uranium, ten parts per million of thorium and a number of other naturally radioactive substances. The decay of their unstable nuclei gives rise to what is known as **low-level background radiation**. Natural low-level background radiation can damage DNA and it probably played a significant role in bringing about gene mutations that, over a period of many millions of years, helped to bring about the evolution of new species.

Higher levels of background radiation have been recorded on slag heaps surrounding uranium mines in various parts of the world. These huge piles of waste tailings usually contain small but significant quantities of radioactive materials with active radioactive lives lasting several thousand years. The dust from the unprotected piles of waste can be carried by the wind and if breathed into the lungs, it can lead to lung cancer (see effects of radioactivity, p. 156). For example, more than 5% of the 100 000 individuals who worked at a uranium mine in East Germany, developed Schneeberg lung disease, a type of bronchial cancer.

Figure 7.27 One of several slag heaps of a uranium mine in Germany. They not only look ugly but are a danger to health because they contain significant quantities of radioactive material

Artificial

In addition to radiation from natural sources, there is human-initiated radiation from the production of nuclear weapons and nuclear power. The fuel for nuclear power in conventional nuclear reactors consists initially of a mixture of two naturally occurring isotopes (forms) of uranium: 235 (so called because it has 235 particles in its nucleus) and 238. Uranium 235 is rare and it is highly fissionable (meaning its nucleus will disintegrate easily). Uranium 238, which forms the bulk of the nuclear fuel (96.7%), is much more abundant in nature and it is ordinarily quite stable. When enriched uranium 235 is mixed with uranium 238, neutrons from 235 will strike other uranium nuclei causing them either to split and thus release more nuclear particles or to absorb the neutrons and thus increase in mass. These nuclear reactions result in a variety of products being formed, many of which are themselves radioactive. Of particular interest is a byproduct of nuclear reactors called **plutonium 239**, a radioactive heavy metal not found in nature which is used for making atomic bombs.

Legacy of the Cold War

During the Cold War, the United States defence officials were primarily concerned with keeping ahead in the development of nuclear weapons. Environmental issues such as the safe disposal of radioactive waste took a back seat. Nuclear waste, produced by batteries of plutonium-making nuclear reactors in association with the US nuclear arms development programme, was stored in huge stainless steel tanks, sealed and then, quite indiscriminately, dumped on to a waste site not far from where the nuclear reactors were located. The heat energy emitted by the radioactive material within the tanks kept the toxic liquids boiling and burping for years. Several tanks sprang leaks. Altogether, an estimated 190 000 cubic metres of highly radioactive solid waste and about two billion cubic metres of less radioactive liquid and chemical waste were buried in shallow trenches, stored in tanks or quite literally poured into the ground at the waste site in the south-eastern corner of Washington state, USA. The waste has contaminated ground water in the surrounding area and whether the area can ever be made safe for habitation again remains to be seen. The US government plans to spend $50 billion over the next 75 years to build robots to clear up the mess left behind as a legacy of the nuclear arms race.

The Russians have not acquitted themselves too well either. They recently disclosed that they had dumped 16 nuclear reactors from ships and submarines into the Kara Sea in the Arctic. Over a period of many years, they have also admitted that they poured the equivalent of 20 Chernobyls worth of high-level radioactive waste into lakes and underground formations at a site called Tomsk-7 in Central Siberia. However, much of the radioactive material 'stored' in the Tomsk site was deposited into rock fractures capped by clay – a method of disposal which was considered safe by the US authorities until the late 1950s.

Britain stopped dumping nuclear waste into the Atlantic in 1983 but has not yet signed the relevant international treaty because it wants to keep its options open to scupper its fleet of nuclear-powered submarines.

Figure 7.28 Tanks containing radioactive waste dumped into a shallow trench at a site in Washington state, USA. Many of the tanks, each the size of a small office block, have leaked and contaminated ground water in the surrounding area

Radiation from the disposal of nuclear waste

The nuclear industry produces a variety of wastes which need to be properly disposed of. One of the main difficulties with nuclear waste is that even after a million years, the radioactive material can emit radiation in doses above the level considered safe by today's standards. By that time, of course, much of the radioactive nuclei (known as **radionuclides**) will have decayed and the total amount of radiation emitted will be very much less. To ensure that future generations are not put at a greater health risk than the present generation, the radioactive waste should be disposed of in burial places capable of isolating the material for a million years.

Radiation from nuclear accidents

Large populations can also be exposed to dangerous quantities of radionuclides if there is an accident to a nuclear reactor causing the containing vessel to burst or during the transportation of radioactive materials.

Accidents resulting in the release of radioactive debris

1957: The core of an atomic pile manufacturing plutonium at Windscale in north-west England overheated and part of the reactor caught fire.

1968: A B-52 bomber crashed on to a floating iceberg off Greenland dispersing plutonium into the shallow coastal waters.

1977: A loud explosion at the nuclear plant in Dounreay, Scotland spewed hot radioactive particles on to the surrounding grounds and along Dounreay's beaches.

1979: An accident in the pressurised-water nuclear power station on Three Mile Island in Pennsylvania, USA resulted in radioactive atomic fission products escaping into the environment causing considerable public alarm and mass evacuation of people living in the area.

Figure 7.29 How some of the British press reported the world's worst nuclear accident

1986: One of four nuclear reactors at the nuclear power station at Chernobyl exploded, releasing vast quantities of radioactive material into the atmosphere. The radioactive cloud showered radioactive debris over much of Eastern Europe, Scandinavia and parts of Britain. The World Health Organisation estimates that the Chernobyl nuclear accident released 200 times as much radioactivity as the first atomic bombs dropped on Hiroshima and Nagasaki put together.

Radiation from a nuclear explosion

The direct blast from the detonation of a thermonuclear warhead at ground level would be catastrophic. The heat generated by the nuclear explosion would instantly vaporise the nuclear weapon itself and create a luminous fireball which would provide an intense source of γ radiation. The radiation would heat up the surrounding air which would expand causing the fireball to rise. The updraft would lift large quantities of pulverised soil and other debris, leaving a massive crater in the ground. The huge mushroom cloud consisting of soil, debris and radionuclides may be carried hundreds of kilometres by the wind. As the fireball cools, the radionuclides would condense on the particles of dirt and after a period of time, the contaminated particles would return to the ground as radioactive fallout. The fallout particles would continue to emit harmful γ and β radiation for decades.

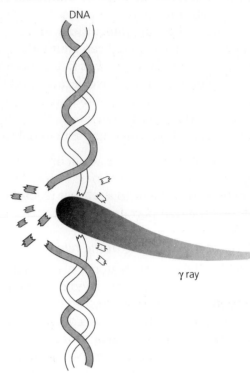

Figure 7.30 A direct hit from a γ ray could shatter a DNA molecule

Effects of radioactivity

Environmental particles contaminated with radionuclides enter the body through two main routes – by ingestion or inhalation. Once inside the body, the radionuclides can continue emitting gamma rays in all directions for years to come. These energetic rays travel in straight lines, penetrating through body tissues easily. They can quite readily rip through one or both strands of DNA molecules that lie in their path. Cells have enzymes that can repair damaged DNA, but errors can occur, strands that mis-match can rejoin and the result is one or more of the many forms of gene mutations such as base substitutions, deletions and so on.

Put simply, high doses of radioactivity can damage DNA, increasing the chances of gene mutations. The result would be an increase in the:

- numbers of aborted pregnancies
- numbers of babies born with birth defects
- incidence of lung cancer, digestive system cancer and thyroid cancer, especially in children
- numbers of individuals with severely impaired immune systems
- rate of gene mutations in plants and animals which may result in organisms genetically quite different from those living today occupying the planet in perhaps 200 years after a nuclear holocaust.

Storage and disposal of radioactive waste

Wastes from the nuclear industry are traditionally classified under three headings – **high**, **intermediate** and **low level**. Spent fuel rods and the most active solidified waste from fuel rod reprocessing plants are classified as high-level waste. The cladding that surrounds the fuel rods, old reactor components, gas filters and other waste from effluent treatment are classified as intermediate-level waste. Anything that is slightly contaminated with radioactive material such as protective clothing, damaged equipment, air filters, ash from burnt low-level waste, rubble and steel work from decommissioned nuclear power plants, are grouped together as low-level waste.

High-level nuclear waste, consisting of spent fuel rods, has been accumulating in water-filled basins at commercial nuclear reactor sites for years as they await a decision for a permanent resting place for them. One of the difficulties is that no one really wants these highly toxic substances buried in their own backyard. Most experts who have studied the problem agree that there are really only two options, i) burial sites deep underground and ii) burial deep within clay-rich mud flats below the oceans.

A burial site below ground

Deep underground disposal is an option which is being considered by many nations with nuclear power plants. The idea is to create a vault consisting of a series of interconnected horizontal tunnels, at a depth of about 1200 metres below ground, for use as a repository. The site chosen should:

- be free from earthquakes
- have a water table which is well below the level of the repository so that it will be unlikely for the water table to rise high enough to flood the repository
- have overlying rocks which are impermeable to water
- be far away from likely human habitation in the future, so that in the event of the ground water being contaminated, the ground water would not be inadvertently used by people sinking wells into it.

High-level waste will generate its own heat from nuclear reactions and needs cooling and shielding during transport. For permanent disposal, the waste should be fixed in molten glass, sealed in thick-walled (25 cm thick) stainless steel canisters and then buried in an underground repository surrounded by a thick layer of compacted clay.

Glass is chosen as a matrix for binding high-level waste because it is very resistant to radiation damage and corrodes very slowly. It also has the additional useful property of binding radionuclides such as uranium. Compacted clay is well suited for use as a packing material because it allows dissolved radionuclides to diffuse through it slowly.

Intermediate- and low-level waste should be packed into stainless steel drums filled with highly alkaline grout, a special kind of cement. The drums should then be buried in an underground repository and the spaces between the drums should also be filled with alkaline grout. The high pH of the alkaline grout is useful because radionuclides are less soluble in alkaline conditions.

Figure 7.31 Protesters opposed to plans to build an underground nuclear waste repository in Britain accuse the nuclear industry of trying to fool the public by slicing up the problem into less easily recognisable 'digestible chunks'

Crucial issues facing planners

- The mere mention of radioactive waste sends shivers of fear through the general public and local opposition to a dump site would be very strong.
- Will water penetrate through rock fractures, dissolve out the radionuclides in thousands of years to come and eventually release the radionuclides into the biosphere to enter food chains and transfer them into people?

Burial in mudflats under the oceans

Beneath the oceans, there is a sedimentary layer of clay-rich mud which has the consistency of peanut butter and which is several hundred metres thick. The mud flats overlie what are geologically stable parts of the Earth's crust, which for tens of millions of years have not been subjected to earthquakes or volcanic eruptions of any kind. Scientists believe that the clay-rich mud flats possess very favourable characteristics for safely isolating radioactive nuclear wastes. The clay binds radionuclides; its natural plasticity enables it to seal up cracks in the mud and it has low water permeability. There are also no organisms living deep in the ooze which are capable of transporting radioactive substances upwards to the ocean floor. The idea is to use standard deep-sea drilling equipment to place, deep in the mud at precisely mapped points, alloyed steel canisters of the waste, immobilised in glass. The technique should not be mistaken for the mere dumping of nuclear waste into the sea or ocean.

Some important points for consideration

- The general public needs to be made aware that deep burial in mud flats is not the same as dumping into the sea.
- Further research is needed to measure the actual rate of diffusion of radionuclides through the mud and what the environmental consequences would be if radionuclides did find their way up to the ocean floor.
- What would the environmental consequences be if a cargo consisting of canisters of the nuclear waste were to fall accidentally to the bottom of the ocean?
- What are the implications of deep burial from the point of view of International Law?

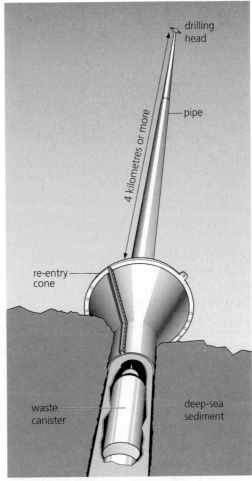

Figure 7.32 Burial of radioactive waste in clay-rich mud beneath the oceans

Thermal pollution

Thermal pollution is the raising of the temperature of a waterway by discharge of heated water from an industrial installation such as nuclear power plants or coal- or gas-fired conventional electricity power generators. If the warmed effluents from such installations are discharged into streams or rivers, they can raise the temperature of the water by 3 to 10 °C.

Heat reduces the solubility of oxygen in water and this can quite readily exacerbate what may already be a precarious situation regarding dissolved oxygen supply to fish and other aquatic organisms, especially if organic effluents are also seeping into the stream or river from old leaky sewers nearby. It could result in the fish being killed and the accelerated growth of algae and other less desirable forms of photosynthetic microorganisms.

Remedy

The warm effluents should be passed through cooling towers before discharge into natural waterways.

Questions

9 Write an essay entitled 'The impact of agricultural practices on the environment'.

10 From the following list of common environmental pollutants:

   a heavy metals, e.g. mercury, b pesticides, c warm water effluents, d radioactive waste and e crude oil,

   choose any three and describe

   i) the source of the pollutant

   ii) its effect on the environment and

   iii) methods of minimising its harmful effects.

11 Nuclear energy is considered a 'clean fuel' and is widely recognised as the fuel that will most probably replace fossil fuels when existing supplies run out. Give three advantages of using nuclear energy and discuss its potential hazards.

Examination questions

1 Read the account below then answer the questions which follow.

Wetlands

Wetlands are temporarily or permanently waterlogged areas bordering aquatic ecosystems. Some may appear unattractive, but support a rich biodiversity and provide data in the form of preserved pollen deposits from which we can learn about past environments. Some permanently waterlogged wetlands have low *productivity*, but where there is wide variation in physical and chemical conditions, such as experienced in estuaries, the adjacent wetlands are the most productive of ecosystems.

   Of all ecosystems, wetlands have suffered the greatest losses and damage as a result of human settlement and changes in land use. Ever increasing demands are being made on water resources; for example, extracting ground water for agriculture has lowered the water table in arid regions such as Saudi Arabia; and the diversion of river water on to farmland for irrigation of cotton in Russia has reduced the Aral Sea to a fraction of its original size. The disappearing Aral Sea and the excessive use of agrochemicals on vast *monocultures* of rice and cotton have resulted in a major environmental disaster and human tragedy.

   In low-lying areas, some coastal wetlands act as natural flood barriers, preventing rising floodwaters from reaching inhabited areas. Other wetlands are used for dumping *treated sewage*, and many areas have become polluted with persistent chemicals and heavy metals, and contaminated with a film of oil. Many flood plains depend for continued productivity on regular flooding. Where this annual flooding has been prevented by damming upland catchment areas, fertility has decreased.

   Peatlands are used as a source of domestic fuel or for horticultural purposes. In addition, many areas are being 'reclaimed' by draining before being planted with coniferous woodland.

From: Biology in Focus, *Biological Conservation*, CUP 1992.

a Explain the meaning of each of the following terms, which are mentioned in the passage.
i) Productivity   (2)
ii) Monoculture   (2)
iii) Treated sewage   (2)
b Give **one** economic reason and **one** environmental reason for conserving wetlands.   (2)   (3)
c Using information in the passage, give **three** ways in which the hydrological (water) cycle has been affected by human activities.   (3)   (total = 14)

UODLE, June 1997

2 One cause of acid rain is the release of sulphur dioxide into the atmosphere.
a Describe the principal way in which sulphur dioxide is released into the atmosphere.   (1)
b Describe **two** specific effects of acid rain on living organisms.   (2)
c The map shows the percentage of trees which have been damaged by acid rain in different European countries.
Suggest an explanation for each of the following:

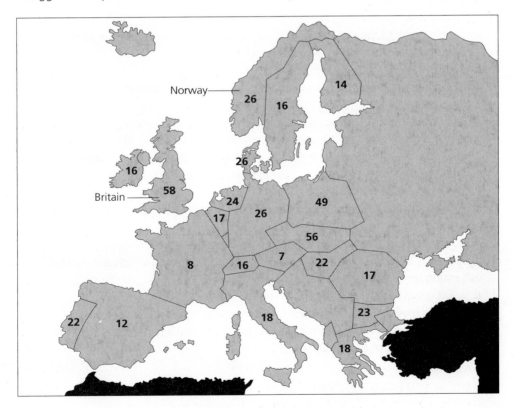

i) the high percentage of damaged trees in Britain   (1)
ii) the fact that Norway has a high percentage of damaged trees even though it is sparsely populated.   (1)   (total = 5)

NEAB, Feb 1996

3 The graph shows changes in the atmospheric carbon dioxide concentrations at Mauna Loa, a site on an island in the middle of the Pacific Ocean, between 1958 and 1988.

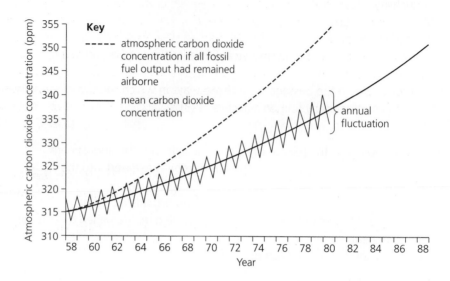

a Suggest why Mauna Loa is regarded as a particularly suitable place to measure concentrations of carbon dioxide. (2)

b With reference to the graph,
   i) Explain why there is an annual fluctuation in the concentration of carbon dioxide. (2)
   ii) Showing your working, calculate the percentage increase in carbon dioxide concentration over the 30 years between 1958 and 1988. (2)
   iii) State the year in which the 1988 mean carbon dioxide concentration would have been reached if all the carbon dioxide from the burning of fossil fuels had remained in the atmosphere. (1)

c Explain why all the carbon dioxide from the burning of fossil fuels does **not** remain in the atmosphere. (2)

Although chlorofluorocarbons (CFCs) are more powerful greenhouse gases than carbon dioxide, it is the increasing concentrations of carbon dioxide which are blamed for enhancing the greenhouse effect.

d i) Explain what is meant by the *greenhouse effect*. (4)
   ii) Explain why carbon dioxide is of more concern than CFCs. (1)
   iii) Suggest **one** other factor in the atmosphere which contributes to the increased concentrations of carbon dioxide. (1)

(total = 15)

UCLES, Nov 1997

Conservation of natural resources

Conservation is the management of human use of the biosphere so that it can continue to yield the greatest sustainable benefits to meet the needs and aspirations of present and future generations. The central purpose in conservation is to ensure that the human species survives by using the natural resources of the biosphere without overexploitation or destruction. Conservation is more than just the passive preservation of nature. It involves taking active steps to counteract or limit the damaging effects of human activities so as to preserve nature in all its diversity and richness for future generations to enjoy.

What are natural resources?

The term natural resource refers to any part of the environment which is of use because it contributes to the production of whatever people require or demand. The most commonly recognised resources are the soil, air, water, minerals, forests, grasslands, arable lands, recreational lands, wildlife habitats, inland waters, fish and other wildlife.

Why is conservation necessary?

Conservation is necessary because the human species occupies a dominant position among living organisms and, as we saw in Chapter 7, humans have shown their capacity to exploit, alter and even harm the environment. Unless humans plan for the future in a responsible way and avoid practices that damage the environment, we may end up squandering away valuable resources which we share with other organisms and which, if properly managed, could still be available for future generations.

Tackling global warming and air pollution

One environmental problem which illustrates the need for agreement at the international level and action at national and local council levels is the threat of impending disaster from global warming and air pollution.

The need for international agreement

International agreement is necessary because air pollutants are often carried by the wind to affect the air quality of another nation. The acid rain that falls on Scandinavian forests, for example, has been blamed on the burning of fossil fuels by coal-fired power stations in Great Britain.

Measures to curb air pollution can be very expensive and the effects of action taken by one nation will benefit all nations, irrespective of whether they themselves took any action or not. Nations that cheat can consequently gain an unfair advantage by being able to manufacture at lower cost. There is also the need to persuade the developing nations to avoid the past mistakes of the developed nations and this may require some 'sugaring of the pill' by way of transfer of technology or technical know how to win cooperation.

Cutting carbon dioxide emissions

In 1995, a United Nations intergovernmental panel of climate scientists meeting in Madrid, arrived at the conclusion that man-made global warming was already underway. Average global temperatures have risen by 0.3 to 0.6 °C this century and, unless urgent action is taken, the world could be 2 °C hotter by the year 2050. A hundred and fifty countries sent delegates to the United Nations Climate Change Convention held at Kyoto in Japan in December 1997 and a legally binding international agreement was reached, aimed at cutting carbon dioxide emissions. The European Union, as a major industrial power, agreed to cut its carbon dioxide emissions to 8% below 1990 levels by the year 2010, provided other industrialised nations also agreed to reduce theirs.

There are various practical measures which can be taken to achieve a reduction in carbon dioxide emissions.

Action at the national level

Investing in an efficient, integrated public transport system

Approximately 30% of the carbon dioxide emissions of the industrialised nations comes from transport and of this, about 75% is from cars, lorries and other road vehicles. Cars alone account for 80% of all vehicle journeys and measures aimed at curbing the use of the private car will undoubtedly reduce carbon dioxide emissions significantly. In addition, there is the extra bonus to be gained from a reduction in carbon monoxide and nitrogen oxides emissions, both of which are greenhouse gases. There will also be benefits to be gained from a reduction in other air pollutants such as sulphur dioxide, which is responsible for acid rain and particulates that damage our health.

Most car owners love their cars for the privacy, freedom and feeling of independence that a car brings. There is also the sheer physical pleasure which driving brings to car owners and the car is widely considered to be a necessity, if for nothing more than to take the groceries home. However, if each car journey takes hours because there is a government policy not to build any more roads and there are repeated traffic jams along the route, most car owners would leave their cars behind and travel by train if that proved to be more convenient. This is where an **integrated public transport system**, involving buses, trains, bicycles and even planes, would come in. Of course, instead of planning for a national road traffic gridlock, there are other ways of persuading car owners to use public transport and leave their cars behind.

Figure 8.1 Too many hours spent in traffic jams may force motorists to look for other means of transport

Action at the municipal/local council level

Investing in a monorail system

Some cities are planning futuristic looking monorails as a system of transport within cities. Unlike conventional trains, monorails can wind round buildings, climb steep hills and are an ideal means of transport within cities. They run on electricity and are much less polluting compared with cars.

Pricing cars off city streets

- **Electronic tolls could be installed at entry points into cities.** By pricing cars off city streets and using the money collected from the tolls, local authorities could invest in improvements in public transport systems. With fewer cars on city streets, more buses could be put on the roads without creating traffic congestion and more people will consequently want to use the service.

Figure 8.2 The monorail – a clean way to travel

- **Increasing the cost of city parking.** This will also have the effect of reducing the numbers of private cars on city streets.
- **Giving city streets over to cyclists and pedestrians.** Not only will this 'at a stroke' reduce carbon dioxide emissions, but it will also clear the city air of harmful pollutants such as ozone and particulates and bring improvements in health to its citizens by promoting a healthier way of living. The provision of loan/hire facilities for bicycles at or near train stations and at entry points into cities will also be helpful.
- **Providing cycle lanes on all new roads.** Most motorists will be more willing to switch to cycling if only they could feel that cycling was safe.

Figure 8.3 More will take to cycling when they can feel that it is safe

Stricter implementation of building regulations

Substantial savings in energy could be achieved by ensuring that buildings are well insulated. This would be reflected not only in lower fuel bills but, ultimately, in less coal, oil or gas being burnt at power stations and, consequently, a cut in carbon dioxide emissions.

Other measures for reducing carbon dioxide emissions

More support for renewable forms of energy

There are renewable sources of energy such as **biofuels** which are much less polluting than fossil fuels. By biofuels ecologists mean fuels based on **biomass** – green plant matter created during photosynthesis. The energy of biofuels is essentially solar energy stored as chemical energy in the organic molecules of plants. This energy can be recovered when plant matter is burnt.

Emissions of carbon dioxide from the burning of biofuels are counterbalanced by absorption for photosynthesis by a new crop of plants so that the overall effect on global warming is zero. Wood fuel (firewood) is a solid biofuel and it is a major source of energy in many parts of the world. **Bioethanol** is biofuel in liquid form.

Solid biofuels (wood fuel)

British farmers are becoming increasingly interested in cultivating fast-growing trees as a source of wood for use as a **solid biofuel**. The two most popular trees are poplar and willow. At the end of the first growing season, the saplings are cut back, a procedure known as **coppicing**. This has the effect of stimulating the plants to produce more shoots. After allowing a further period of three to five years for growth, the shoots are harvested to provide dry wood. This is followed by another period of three to five years for resprouting and growth and then harvesting and so on. In this way, the trees can be repeatedly harvested to provide a sustainable source of energy. When wood fuel is burnt, it generates heat which can be harnessed to produce electricity.

To encourage greater investment in wood fuel production, the Swedish government has adopted a policy of collecting taxes for carbon and sulphur dioxide emissions from the burning of fossil fuels to provide subsidies for solid biofuel production. This has resulted in solid biofuels providing 16% of Sweden's energy requirements. In Britain, solid biofuels account for less than 0.5% of the country's energy requirements. To support this renewable source of energy, the British government has made it obligatory for premium prices to be paid for electricity generated from the burning of biofuels.

Figure 8.4 A fast-growing hybrid willow being grown as a potential source of clean-burning solid biofuel

Bioethanol

In Brazil sugar cane is crushed and the sugary liquid is fermented to yield a liquor which is distilled to produce **bioethanol** (commonly known as alcohol). Brazil today has four million cars running on bioethanol and a further million running on **gasohol**, a mixture of 20% bioethanol and 80% gasoline (petrol). Compared with petrol, bioethanol is a much 'cleaner' fuel. Cars running on bioethanol emit 20–30% less carbon monoxide, 15% less nitrogen oxides, and virtually no sulphur dioxide. In terms of cost, bioethanol costs more to produce than petrol and government subsidies are needed to keep the bioethanol industry in business.

Energy from nuclear power

Advocates of nuclear power point out that it is safe and that it emits no carbon dioxide or sulphur dioxide. Its potential is immense and when all the fossil fuel reserves have been used up, it may yet turn out to be the principal energy source for the future – provided, of course, we come up with a safe way of disposing of nuclear waste.

Reducing deforestation and promoting reforestation

Slash and burn methods have been blamed for many uncontrolled fires that have destroyed large parts of the tropical rain forest. The fires are an important source of carbon dioxide production and the loss of trees makes it harder to balance carbon dioxide output with uptake by plant photosynthesis. Halting deforestation and encouraging reforestation by planting tree saplings wherever appropriate will undoubtedly make a major contribution towards stabilising carbon dioxide levels in the atmosphere and averting the more damaging effects of global warming.

Figure 8.5 Forest fires that rage uncontrollably will only add to the problems of global warming

Action at the individual level

Reducing energy wastage

- We as individuals can make our contribution. If each and every one of us made a regular habit of turning off lights that are not needed, it would all add up to quite substantial savings.
- We could also politely enquire whether our school or the place we work has an energy policy. Have time switches to turn lights and heating on and off at the right time been installed? If not, perhaps a suggestion may be all that is needed.
- We could choose to use only the most energy efficient appliances, motors and lights. The total savings if everyone in Britain did this would add up to an estimated 70% reduction in the amount of electricity we as a nation use.
- We could walk or cycle to school/work and join local conservation organisations.

Addressing the disappearing tropical rain forest problem

Another pressing challenge for the community of nations is the threat of climate change and loss of biodiversity posed by the rapidly shrinking tropical rain forests of the world. International agreement will again be needed because there are conflicts of interest between the advanced nations and the countries of the developing world which will need to be resolved.

Most people would agree that it would be quite unrealistic to expect the developing nations with their impoverished populations to totally give up benefits from the logging of timber. The challenge for the rich nations (whose own forests have largely been destroyed) is to find a way of accommodating the legitimate aspirations for economic advancement of the poor nations while at the same time preventing the tropical rain forests from being massacred.

Sustainable management

One proposal is **sustainable management** – essentially controlled exploitation and replacement by planting tree saplings.

Ecologists who have studied the problem will point out that there are alternatives to destructive logging. If at the start of the logging process the locations of the trees selected for felling are mapped out; vines connected to the trees are cut before the trees are felled; and a route to the selected trees is mapped out so that only 'undesirable' trees are cleared away to create a path for the heavy machinery, the destruction of the forest can be considerably reduced.

Most independent observers, however, hold the view that sustainable management of the rain forest has so far not been a success. Logging companies have, in reality, shown little concern for juvenile plants that lie in their path. From an economic point of view they stand to gain much more by moving in quickly to harvest whatever they can and then proceeding to the next area. Investment in replanting has been negligible because the economic incentives for replanting are not as attractive as the profits that can be made

Figure 8.6 Local people must be allowed to continue to reap the benefits of their own natural resources

from uncontrolled logging. The monitoring of the logging operations has also been somewhat wanting often because of the remoteness of the logged area. The feeling is that unless government officials, conservationists, logging companies, forest dwellers and citizen's action groups put their heads together to devise management plans that work, the rain forests will continue to shrink.

Setting aside preservation areas

Another suggestion is to encourage the poor nations to set aside large areas of the rain forest as **preservation areas**. Parts of the forest in and around concessional areas (where logging is permitted), especially those parts of the forest that are commercially inoperable because the lie of the land is too steep, for example, could be set aside as nature reserves. Whether local logging companies will object to or respect such 'no-go' areas is debatable. Some will also argue that it may be difficult to check whether the harvested timber comes from legal or illegal areas.

Buying up lightly logged land to set aside as preserves

Some observers take the view that forcing logging companies to restore a logged forest by replanting does more harm than good. They suggest that lightly logged land should be purchased cheaply and set aside as preserves to allow nature to re-establish the forest.

Getting pharmaceutical companies to pay for preserving biodiversity

Another idea aims at putting the rain forest's potential as a source of medicine to profitable use. It has been pointed out that there are already 47 major drugs which have originated from tropical plants. They include the anti-malarial drug quinine, the muscle relaxant curare and the pain killer codeine. Researchers estimate that there are probably about 125 000 species of flowering plants in the rain forests of the world. Each of them can, on average, yield six candidate compounds for pharmaceutical screening. Each compound can be tested for 500 types of bioactivity. Since the chance of finding a valuable drug is one in a million, the tropical rain forests could yield a total of 375 valuable drugs. With 47 already discovered, that leaves 328 still to be found. Each drug's value to society is estimated at about US$ 449 million.

If a formula could be worked out to *pay the developing countries just returns* in exchange for preserving the forests from destruction and for organising the parcelling out of plant species for drug companies to screen, the forests may yet be saved from destruction. The deal could be worth many millions of US dollars per year. As an added bonus, the developing countries would also benefit considerably from a transfer of technology, including technological training and jobs for the local inhabitants.

Conservation of fish stocks

In even more urgent need of protection than the tropical rain forests are the world's fish stocks which are being decimated by **overfishing**. After 40 years of steady increases in the tonnage of fish caught in the open seas, the world's fish stocks are dwindling. Canada's once bountiful cod fisheries on its east coast collapsed in 1992. It remained closed for several years and has only recently reopened. The facts are that there are just too many fishing vessels chasing too few fish. Many of these fishing vessels are equipped with sophisticated technology making it easy for them to locate and catch whole schools of fish swimming deep beneath the surface.

One popular fishing technique is **deep water trawling**. It involves dragging a large funnel-shaped net, closed off at the tail end, across the seabed, scraping it for prawns, scallops and fish such as cod, flounder, hake and red snapper. The nets stir up a lot of sediment killing delicate burrowing invertebrates. They can also roll over boulders, exposing animals sheltering underneath and crushing others living attached to the sea floor. This type of 'collateral damage' is causing considerable losses in biodiversity among marine invertebrates.

Compared with tropical rain forests, which can still boast of large tracts of virgin forests totally unspoilt by humans, there are hardly any areas of continental shelf left which have not been damaged by trawling, sometimes as often as six to seven times a year.

Fisheries management

Fish stocks need management to prevent fish populations from collapsing through overfishing. The aim in fisheries management is to ensure that the fish are not taken at a rate which is faster than the rate at which the fish populations can be replaced by reproduction. To achieve such a goal, the following steps will be necessary.

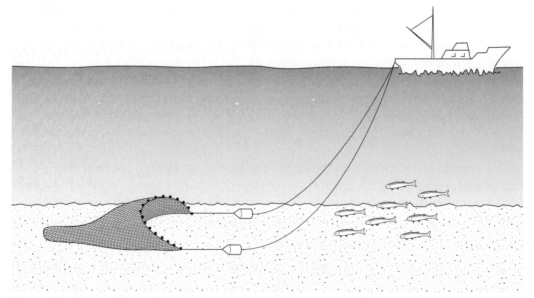

Figure 8.7 Deep water trawling

Investment in fisheries research

Government ministers need sound advice on how to conserve fish stocks. Funds must be made available for marine biologists to do the necessary research to gain a clear understanding of the ecological requirements of fish populations – their breeding habits, spawning areas, how long the young take to reach sexual maturity, what proportion of the adults may be taken without causing permanent damage to the population as a whole, and so on.

Setting enforceable quotas

Based on sound scientific advice, governments will need to pass laws to limit the size of the annual catch. Alternatively, a time limit could be imposed on fishing by the boats. The type of equipment used can also be put under restriction. The aim here is to preserve the ecosystem and to prevent overfishing. There should also be some form of policing to ensure that fishermen are not taking more than their quota. The European Union uses a system of monitoring of fishing boats by satellite.

Prohibition of the use of nets with a smaller mesh size than stipulated

The mesh size of nets used for fishing should also be carefully regulated. Fishing vessels should not be permitted to use nets with a mesh size that is smaller than a stipulated minimum. This is to ensure that juvenile fish can escape, and grow to maturity to replenish the fish stock.

Making it an offence to catch fish smaller than a certain size

This is again aimed at ensuring that there are enough young left to sustain the fish stocks.

Setting aside sanctuaries where fishing is prohibited

Selected areas should be set aside as refuges or sanctuaries where fishing is prohibited. These should include spawning and nursery areas.

The EU's Common Fisheries Policy

The European Union has a Common Fisheries Policy (CFP) which is designed to protect the beleaguered fish stocks in European waters and to prevent overfishing. It embraces all the principles of fisheries management described above. In addition, it aims to cut the fishing effort in EU waters by 30% which would reduce the catch by 20%. The CFP is, quite rightly, hoping to achieve this by focusing on reducing the size of the fishing fleets. It has a restructuring fund which can be used to compensate fishermen for decommissioning their surplus boats.

Figure 8.8 Europe's fishing fleet stays in – too many boats chasing too few fish

Fish stocks in EU waters are, however, continuing to decline for the following reasons:

- The advice given to government ministers may have been based on an overestimation of the size of the existing fish stocks.
- Disgruntled fishermen may have been appeased with quota offers which were too high for the fish populations to sustain.
- The common practice of throwing juvenile fish back into the water may be helping fishermen to keep within their quotas but it may be doing nothing to fish populations because most of the discarded juveniles are too injured to survive.
- A larger mesh size may be needed to allow more of the juvenile fish to escape.
- Fishermen may be taking more than their quota by falsifying their log books.
- Money paid out to fishermen to decommission surplus boats may be finding its way back in the form of improved fishing gear for the remainder of the fleet so that more rather than fewer fish are actually being caught.

Conservation of the African and Asian elephants

When representatives of 103 governments met in Switzerland in October 1989 at a UN Convention on International Trade in Endangered Species (CITES), the world's African elephant population had fallen by 52% to 625 000 in just 10 years. In Kenya alone, the numbers of elephants had dropped from 130 000 in 1973 to only 16 000 in 1989 – an 88% decrease in 15 years. The survival of the world's largest land mammal had become a matter of grave concern and the thought of an African continent totally lacking in elephants was stirring up passions like no other conservation issue could.

The ivory trade

The cause of the problem was illegal hunting of elephants for their tusks. There was at that time a thriving international trade in ivory and organised gangs of **poachers** (local hunters) armed with rifles were slaughtering the elephants to meet an international demand for ivory. Many of the animals were killed in parks and game reserves where hunting was illegal. Poachers could make the equivalent of a year's income by selling just a pair of elephant tusks. The total trade in raw ivory amounted to about a thousand tonnes a year. Exporters would ship the ivory to South Africa, the Middle East, China, Japan, Thailand, Hong Kong, Singapore and Indonesia where there was a demand for carved ivory products. Craftsmen in these countries would use the ivory to make ornaments of various kinds. The largest buyer was Japan because there is a huge demand for personal signature seals made of ivory.

An international ban on the ivory trade

There were cheers all round (or nearly all round because Zimbabwe, Botswana and South Africa argued against it) when CITES banned international trade in elephant products by transferring the African elephant from their Appendix II list (which permits limited trading) to their Appendix I list (which bans all trading). Other endangered animals on the CITES Appendix I list include the tiger (hunted for its skin, bones and certain organs that are used in East Asian medicines), the rhinoceros

Figure 8.9 Killed for its tusks

(hunted for its horns which are used as dagger handles in rich Middle Eastern countries and as tonics and aphrodisiacs in the Far East), the fruit bat (*Pteropus* sp. – a large animal with a wing span of almost a metre which is hunted for its meat) and various species of birds including macaws and parrots.

Listing in Appendix I was, of course, only the first step in halting the wholesale slaughter of the majestic African elephant. Other measures that needed to be taken included:

- imposing an immediate ban on the export or import of ivory
- identifying herds under threat
- building up a well-equipped and effective game ranger force to combat poaching
- encouraging local inhabitants to keep poachers out by paying informants more than the poachers would pay to keep the people quiet
- convincing local inhabitants that they can gain more from tourism than from poaching
- making people who buy ivory goods ashamed of themselves.

After action by CITES, African elephant populations have stabilised at about half a million and in some African countries, it has actually started to increase.

Figure 8.10 Arrested for poaching

The decline of the Asian elephant

Whereas African elephants were killed for their ivory, Asian elephants are under threat for a different reason. Their natural habitats are either vanishing or becoming increasingly fragmented as a direct result of a conflict of interests between the needs of the Asian elephant for refuge and the human need for more cultivated land. Only a few centuries ago, there were millions of Asian elephants roaming the continent of Asia from China in the east to what is today Iran in the west. The existing populations of Asian elephants are now down to a total of about 38 000 of which around 5700 are working animals living in captivity. The ones in the wild live in pockets of forest mainly in India and Burma. Most of these natural habitats are just no longer large enough to sustain viable populations of Asian elephants. The numbers that form breeding populations are becoming so few that there is a danger of inbreeding with a resultant loss of genetic diversity. This leaves the entire isolated population susceptible to being wiped out by a single new strain of disease organism. The outlook for the future of this endangered species looks at best precarious, at worst pretty grim.

Figure 8.11 Asian elephants – losing out to humans

Saving the endangered Asian elephant

To save the Asian elephant:

- the conflict of interest between the elephant and the needs of an expanding human population will need to be resolved
- a 'save the Asian elephant fund' could be set up with the aid of an advertising campaign in the rich developed nations to provide sufficient funds for some of the costly proposals given below
- farmers should be promptly paid full compensation when wild elephants venture out of the forest to raid their crops. This is to ensure that the endangered animals are not harmed in any way by humans
- a vast nature reserve should ideally be set up and restocked with animals transferred from habitats that have become too fragmented. Precisely where would be a matter for international agreement
- 'jungle corridors' could be set up linking fragmented habitats together
- wild elephants from different herds could be captured and then released into a managed conservation park as part of a captive breeding programme to boost their numbers
- a gene bank could be set up to store frozen genetic material of the endangered animals for future use in a programme of breeding by artificial insemination.

Gene banks

Modern technology has progressed to a point where it is now possible to preserve sperm, eggs or even embryos for indefinite periods by freezing in liquid nitrogen at $-196\,°C$. When required, the frozen tissues can be slowly thawed and used for artificial insemination, in vitro fertilisation or embryo implantation. A gene bank containing frozen genetic material of endangered animals would act like a 'frozen zoo' or a form of insurance policy against extinction.

The ideal location for such a gene bank should be in a developed country where power failures are highly unlikely. The chosen country should also be geologically and politically stable and wealthy enough to ensure the long-term security and integrity of the collected genetic material. The United Kingdom would certainly fit the bill nicely.

An obvious advantage of conservation using frozen genetic material is that it is so much easier to carry a flask of frozen sperm as compared with transferring a 3 tonne beast from one location to another for breeding purposes. Furthermore, sperm collected from animals of an earlier generation could be used to produce invigorated offspring for present or even future generations.

Disadvantages include the fact that some animal eggs are difficult to preserve frozen without damage because their yolk tends to freeze, thaw and form crystals at different temperatures from other parts of the egg. It is also sometimes only possible to milk tiny quantities of sperm from endangered animals. Furthermore, some animals have short fertile periods which may be difficult to predict with any accuracy. Lastly, more research will be needed into the techniques of artificial insemination and in vitro fertilisation as the success rates are often quite disappointing.

Figure 8.12 Seeds stored in a cold room at −20°C can remain viable for 15 to 200 years

The shrinking gene pool of agricultural crop plants

Modern farming methods are largely responsible for the disappearance of plant varieties among agricultural plants. Variability is often the last thing farmers have in mind. What they want are crop plants in the field that behave identically in every way. For efficient harvesting and marketing, they would like the plants to grow to the same height, produce fruit at the same time, taste and look the same in the market place and so on. Even food and agriculture regulations favour standardisation. There are, for example EU regulations that prohibit the sale of plant varieties that are not listed in the 'common catalogue'. Many peasant farmers the world over are also contributing to the loss of genetic diversity by growing only 'superior' varieties of crop plants using seeds supplied in bulk by the multinational companies such as ICI and Pioneer. The result is that we have become dependent on just 30 types of crop plants to supply 95% of the human protein and calorie intake.

In a recent report, the UN's Food and Agriculture Organisation warned that a single key mutation in the mildew fungus could wipe out the entire European barley crop because the cultivated barley plant is dependent on just one fungicide and one gene in its fight against the parasitic fungus. It also urged the rich nations to spend more on safeguarding the genetic diversity of the crop plant by offering more help to the 30 or so **seed banks** scattered throughout the world.

Seed banks

Seed banks, also known as gene banks, store large assemblies of seeds of potentially useful wild and crop plants for future use by plant breeders. They are immensely important because the stored genetic material can be used to develop new disease-resistant varieties of plants which could secure our future food supplies.

Figure 8.13 Jackfruits – exotic tropical species of economic importance with recalcitrant seeds

To retain their viability, most seeds that arrive for storage are, to begin with, slowly dried in an environment of low humidity (e.g. a room maintained at 15% relative humidity) until the seed's water content has been reduced to about 5%. They are then cleaned to remove chaff or other bits of material, weighed and then sealed into foil packets lined with plastic. They are then placed in drawers and stored frozen in a cold room maintained at −20 °C. Lowering the moisture content of the seeds before storage is a key step because there is little risk of ice crystals forming and damaging the seed's tissues when the seeds are in a dehydrated condition. The vast majority of seeds will remain viable for between 15 and over 200 years when treated in this way and then stored frozen.

A **germination test** is used to assess the viability of a batch of seeds. If 95 out of 100 seeds germinate, the seeds are said to have a viability of 95%. At well-run seed banks, the seeds are regenerated when their viability falls to 85%. This involves growing the plants and then collecting their seeds as replacement for the earlier batch.

Many tropical plants of economic importance such as mango, coconut, rubber, cocoa and jackfruit have what are known as **recalcitrant seeds** because they lose their viability easily. There is generally so much water in these seeds that it was, until recently, not possible to dry them sufficiently to risk freezing them. However, a technique has been found to get round this problem. Only the embryos of the seeds (which contain much less water) are taken for preservation. These are coated with dimethyl sulphoxide and proline, which protects the embryos against cold injury from atmospheric water. They are then gently blotted to remove excess moisture and carefully dried for an hour before slowly freezing them in stages to −40 °C. They are then subjected to liquid nitrogen treatment for permanent storage at −196 °C. The embryos stored in this way will retain their viability for an indefinite period of time.

Latest estimates are that there are still about a million varieties of agricultural plants scattered in different parts of the world. Their seeds will need to be collected by trained personnel for storage in seed banks before their unique genes are lost forever.

Sites of Special Scientific Interest (SSSIs)

It would indeed be a very drab world if future generations were left only with gene banks to look at. There is undoubtedly a need to conserve wildlife *in situ*, that is, within their own natural habitats. The United Kingdom government under Clement Attlee recognised this in 1949 and introduced a system of designating certain sites noted for their importance by the Nature Conservancy Council as **Sites of Special Scientific Interest (SSSIs)**. There is today a network of 5500 of these sites covering approximately 7.5% of the United Kingdom.

Many conservationists have, however, expressed the view that the SSSI system is ineffectual. While it does prevent the general public from directly damaging a site, there is little, if any, compulsion for the government or anyone else to take positive protective measures because the SSSI system relies on the goodwill of the landowner. Furthermore, existing mining rights have been left intact, and there have been instances in the past when government ministers themselves have played down the importance of SSSIs by giving the go-ahead for motorway construction (as in the case of the Twyford Down SSSI in Hampshire) despite the protests of environmentalists. Conservationists estimate that between 200 and 300 SSSIs are destroyed each year by development schemes such as new road construction or old planning permission and also from pollution, particularly eutrophication (due to bad farm management in adjacent areas). They also point out that there are huge numbers of wildlife, much of it rare and endangered, which get no protection whatsoever because they happen to live outside the SSSIs.

Europe's Habitat Directive

In December 1991, Europe's environment ministers voted in favour of adopting the European Commission's **Habitat Directive**. It aims to protect specific natural habitats such as chalk meadows, limestone pavements, blanket bogs, shingle beaches, saltwater lagoons and oak–hornbeam forests by requiring national governments to empower themselves (mostly through new legislation) to protect sites designated as **Special Areas of Conservation (SACs)**. The directive also requires national governments to revoke old planning permissions, replace voluntary action with compulsion and guarantee positive management of the sites. Conservationists welcome Europe's Habitat Directive because it also makes available a European Union fund for preserving SACs from 'significant deterioration or disturbance'.

Figure 8.14 This site is home to a very rare water snail. The UK government has yet to designate it a Special Area of Conservation. It lies directly in the path of the proposed £100 million Newbury bypass

Conservation's 3Rs – Reduce, Re-use, Recycle

Look into the waste bin (if they have one!) of a poor family in a developing country and you will most probably find nothing much except perhaps a few bits of discarded mouldy vegetables. The poor put everything to good use and throw little away. Dustbins in the rich suburbs of western nations are quite different. They are usually overflowing with discarded packaging, plastic bottles, out of fashion clothes and all kinds of unwanted household items. There is an undoubted link between affluence and wastage.

Twenty million tonnes of household refuse ends up in Britain's dustbins each year. Much of it gets buried in landfill sites which will one day become full. Japan is already running out of space to dump its rubbish and the Japanese government is looking in earnest at conservation's three Rs – **reduce**, **re-use** and **recycle** – to solve its solid waste disposal problems.

Reduce

A change in the affluent society's wasteful lifestyle will certainly go some way towards helping to reduce the amount of waste that we throw out into our bins. If every individual made a conscious effort to treat things with more care and respect and stopped to think before throwing things away simply because they are slightly worn or old, it could all add to quite a considerable reduction in the amount of solid wastes that we generate. Furthermore, if each and every individual refused to succumb to the whims of fashion but chose instead to make personal sacrifices by refraining from buying consumer goods that we do not really need, the manufacturing industries would ultimately be forced to produce less, and this would not be a bad thing if we also took into account the fact that the world's natural resources are limited and rapidly decreasing (in certain key areas). To ensure that future generations can enjoy the same standards of living as we do, the affluent must learn to be less wasteful and to consume less.

Manufacturers could play their part by making a determined effort to reduce the amount of wasteful packaging which makes up about half of the typical contents of a refuse bin in the UK. Governments could also play their part by passing laws that would oblige industry to take more responsibility for the solid wastes that they helped to create.

Figure 8.15 Tackling the household rubbish problem

Re-use

After reduce, re-use is generally considered the next best option. Glass bottles, for example, are a conservationist's favourite because they can be used again and again. If all bottles were standardised for size, they could be gathered and returned to the nearest factory, thus saving on the cost of transport. Advocates of re-use maintain that glass bottles have an average life of 30 to 40 journeys and that even when they are eventually broken, the glass can be recycled. In Germany, where the average individual is in many ways more environmentally aware than in most other countries, more and more consumers are insisting on buying their milk and fruit juices in glass bottles in the firm belief that glass creates less waste.

Another item which can be re-used is discarded clothing. These can be gathered in sacks and given to charities like Oxfam for re-use in developing countries or for making rugs. Care should, however, be taken to ensure that the supply of free used clothes to countries in the developing world does not disrupt local clothing industries.

There are bins on street corners and shops in Germany for old batteries. These are collected and sent to factories where the mercury and cadmium are extracted for re-use to make new batteries.

Recycle

Most German families are also pace setters as far as sorting out their rubbish for recycling is concerned. They will take their used wrapping papers and old newspapers to the paper bank, place unwanted clothing into one plastic bag, put old shoes into another bag, empty plastic and metal containers into a yellow recycle bin, food and other putricible substances into a brown recycle bin and everything else that remains into a black bin for putting into landfills and so on. Recycling has become a way of life for many in the developed nations of the world and for a very good reason.

Unless new sources of raw materials are found or substitutes are developed, certain critical natural resources such as copper, cobalt, nickel and molybdenum will just run out within a decade or two. To conserve natural resources, manufacturing industries will need to produce goods that can eventually be recycled. They should ideally be modelled along the lines of natural ecosystems. In a natural ecosystem, plants synthesise nutrients from raw materials, herbivores feed on plants, carnivores feed on herbivores and their waste products and dead bodies are eventually recycled to provide raw materials for further generations of plants. If manufacturing industries were to be organised to make much greater use of their own reclaimed waste, more of the world's natural resources could be left in the ground for future generations to enjoy.

Recycled plastics

Collected plastics could be sorted by appearance, ground into pellets and then sold to companies that specialise in using reclaimed plastics to produce cheap plastic goods such as picture frames, bicycle decorations, artificial flowers, window frames, and so on. There is a plastic factory in France which makes sweaters from recycled plastic mineral water bottles. The plastic is ground into fine chips, melted, purified and then spun into yarn. The plastic from 27 bottles is needed to make one sweater. The sweaters are 30% wool and 70% polyvinyl chloride (PVC).

Recycled paper

Old newspapers posted into paper banks throughout the UK are collected and transported to a paper mill in Aylesford, Kent for recycling. On arrival, the old newspapers are soaked in water to make pulp, de-inked using soap and solvents, screened and spun to remove staples, glue and dirt and then reformed into paper on a huge machine. The mill is the biggest in Europe and it handles 30 000 truck loads of waste paper per year and turns it into a continuous stream of recycled paper 9 metres wide at a speed of 100 kilometres per hour.

Recycled, organic waste – compost

Organic waste makes up about 40% of household rubbish. If this putricible material, which includes food scraps,

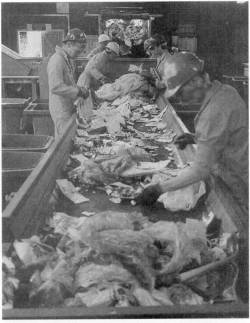

Figure 8.16 Sorting out plastic for recycling

vegetable peelings, cabbage leaves, banana skins and grass cuttings, can be kept separate from non-compostible matter such as light bulbs, old batteries, vacuum cleaner bags, sanitary towels and old shoes (as the Germans do with their yellow, brown and black bins), the organic matter could be recycled into excellent compost. The process involves bacterial decomposition of the organic waste into stable humus which can then be used as a soil conditioner for the growth of plants. There are 150 composting plants in Germany turning out nearly two million tonnes of compost per year. The only snag is that in summer, the brown bins stink and are often teeming with blowfly maggots.

Questions

1 Outline the importance of the conservation of woodlands and forests.
2 Describe four different conservation measures designed to halt the decline in biodiversity.
3 Discuss ways by which the rich industrialised nations could reduce their consumption of natural resources.
4 Name two materials that can be recycled and two that can be re-used. Explain why these materials should be recycled or re-used.

Examination questions

1 a Explain the term *over-exploitation* in regard to a commercially managed ecosystem. (2)
   b The graph overpage shows the relationships between age and various other factors in a wild animal population that is commercially exploited for food.
      i) What is the optimum age when the animals should be caught? (1)
      ii) Over what age range is the rate of increase in biomass greatest? (1)

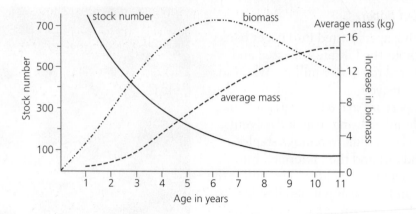

iii) Suggest **one** other piece of data concerning the life history of the animals which would be important in deciding methods of conservation for this ecosystem. (1)

c The three graphs below show the age composition of the animals caught from the wild population (averaged over 5 year periods).

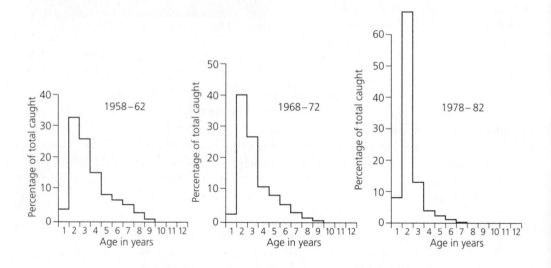

i) Suggest why the age profile of the animals caught has changed from the period 1958–62 to 1978–82. (1)

ii) How might this change in age distribution affect the natural population? Give a reason for your answer. (2)

iii) Suggest **two** ways by which this decline in the age composition of animals caught could be reversed by changes in the way humans manage the population. (2)

(total = 10)

O & C, June 1994

2 Describe **three** ways in which government involvement can help wildlife conservation. (3)

(total = 3)

AEB, Summer 1995

3 The table gives some statistics on the sources of energy in developing countries.

Source of energy	Percentage
Biomass	35
Oil	26
Coal	25
Natural gas	7
Other renewables	6
Nuclear	1

Source: WORLD WATCH INSTITUTE, *State of the World*, 1993 (Earthscan)

a What is meant by *biomass* as used in the table? Give an example. (2)

b Suggest **two** reasons why biomass is less important as an energy source in developed countries. (2)   (total = 4)

AEB, Summer 1995

4 Read the passage about Asian elephants, and then use the information in the passage, together with your own knowledge, to answer the questions which follow.

The future of the Asian elephant is uncertain. There has been a rapid decline in numbers this century and it is estimated that there are now only 50 000 left. The main difficulty for the elephants is one of space; the elephants occupy about 430 000 km^2 of forest of which 130 000 km^2 is in reserves, all of which is in small pockets. There is also conflict with human populations due to crop raiding by solitary bulls and herds of females and juveniles.

The elephants are selective feeders, eating millet, the succulent central shoots of coconut palms, flowering shoots of maize and mangoes and the central pith of banana plants. In one night a single bull might eat 75 kg of food such as millet, but the loss in crop yield is much greater than this. Some of the farmers try to protect their crops without killing the elephants and so receive compensation, but more long-term solutions are being sought to conserve the elephant populations. To achieve this, a detailed study of their behaviour and all aspects of their ecology is necessary.

a i) Explain why there has been a decline in numbers of the Asian elephant. (2)
ii) Why is the distribution of the populations in small pockets an additional problem to the survival of the Asian elephant? (4)

b State **one** reason why the estimate of population size might be unreliable. (1)

c i) Explain why the loss in crop yield caused by crop raiding by elephants is much greater than the amount that they eat. (2)
ii) Suggest **one** way in which farmers might protect their crops without killing elephants. (1)
iii) What aspects of the behaviour and ecology of elephants would need to be known to achieve a long-term solution to the conservation of elephant populations? (3)

The number of African elephants is also declining rapidly.

d i) Outline the main reasons for this decline. (2)
ii) State **one** way in which the decline in numbers of the African elephant is being reduced. (1)   (total = 16)

UCLES, June 1996

Practical ecology

Our understanding and knowledge of ecology come from the study of plants and animals in the field. An ecologist may carry out one of two types of studies: autecology and synecology. Autecology studies an individual species, for example the ecology of limpets on a rocky shore or bluebells in a broad-leaved wood. Synecology studies the whole habitat and all of the organisms found within it, such as the community of animals living in the leaf-litter or the community of a pond.

The keys to successful investigation in practical ecology are to clearly identify the aims and objectives of the study and then to select the most appropriate methods to carry out the study. Practical studies involve taking a range of quantitative and qualitative measurements of the biotic and abiotic factors which could affect the environment.

Measurement of plant populations

Sampling plants is much easier than animals. Plants are generally conspicuous and stationary, which makes identification and sampling straightforward.

Sampling

It is impossible to count every single plant of the same species in a habitat. This would take far too much time and cause damage to the habitat. It is, therefore, necessary to work out how much of the habitat needs to be **sampled**. The study area has to be divided up into small sample areas of equal size. These sample areas have to be selected at random. The data collected from the sample areas can then be used to determine the frequency and distribution of the species across the habitat as a whole.

There are three ways in which sampling can be achieved:

1 **Random sampling.** Samples are taken at randomly selected sample sites throughout the area. Since it is difficult to choose the sampling points without any bias, the preferred method is to use random numbers, either from a table or produced by a computer, to generate coordinates on a grid. The sides of the grid can be marked out on the ground using two measuring tapes.
2 **Systematic sampling.** The samples are taken at regular intervals, ensuring complete coverage of the area. This method is simple to carry out, since it is not necessary to set up a grid with coordinates.
3 **Stratified sampling.** Although samples may be taken at random, there is a chance that all the sample sites will fall in one area or even on the same spot twice. If there are obvious differences in the site, for example two different rock types, then the area can be divided into subsets and samples can be taken from each subset, the number in proportion to the size of the subset. In this way, if one subset covers 20% of the area, 20% of the samples are taken from within it.

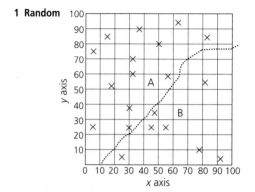

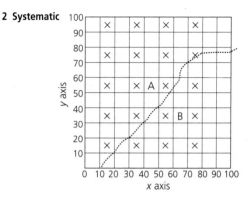

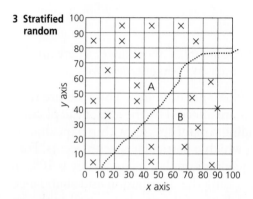

Figure 9.1 Area A (one subset) covers about 60% of the grid therefore gets 12 samples; area B gets 8 samples

The quadrat

The **quadrat** is one of the most useful pieces of equipment in practical ecology. It consists of a four-sided frame of metal or wood. The quadrat is placed over the sample area and all the species of plants enclosed by the sides of the quadrat are either counted or estimates are taken of abundance. Cross wires, or strings, subdivide the frame at, typically, 10 cm intervals, making it easier to estimate abundance. Quadrats vary in size. Large quadrats, which enclose several square metres of vegetation, can be laid out with string and pegs. Small 0.0625 m² quadrats are used for sampling lichens on trees and walls. The most useful size is 0.5 m², enclosing an area of 0.25 m². In general, it is more accurate to use a small quadrat and take many samples than to use a large quadrat and take fewer samples. However, small quadrats may undersample larger species, such as shrubs and trees, and there will be a greater edge effect. For example, the plants at the edge of the quadrat may be partly in and partly outside the quadrat, and a decision has to be made whether to include them or not. Permanent quadrats, made from rope and pegs, can be set up for long-term investigations which measure changes in plant cover over a number of seasons.

It is possible to determine the optimum size of quadrat for a given habitat. First, mark out a tiny quadrat and count the number of species found within it. Then, double the size of the quadrat and record how many new species are recorded. Keep a running total. Continue doubling the size of the quadrat until there is no further increase in the number of species. Once the optimum size has been reached, the extra time and effort put into sampling will be unproductive. The optimum size will vary between habitats, so it is not always safe to assume that a certain size of quadrat will be suitable for all.

It is important to take sufficient samples. Too few samples will yield insufficient information, whereas too many samples wastes time and provides no new information. A similar method to that used to determine quadrat size can be used to determine the optimum number of samples. Using the optimum size of quadrat, count the number of species found in the first quadrat. Place further quadrats and each time record the numbers of any new species. Continue recording until there is no further increase in the number of species. If five quadrats have failed to record any new species, then it is generally safe to assume that no further species will be found.

Measurements of abundance

Quadrats are useful for making quantitative assessments of abundance. There are four measures of abundance: density, frequency, biomass and percentage cover.

1 **Density**. This is the mean number of individuals per unit area. This measure is not suitable for small plants, since the estimates are affected by the size of the plants.
2 **Frequency**. Frequency is the chance of finding a plant species within a quadrat. It is the number, or percentage, of samples in which a particular species occurs. For example, if a species occurs in 2 out of 20 quadrat samples, its frequency is 10%. It is a quick and relatively easy method for assessing the distribution and abundance of a species, but it is affected by the size and shape of the quadrat as well as the size and distribution of the species being investigated. Also, frequency takes no account of density or distribution.
3 **Biomass or yield**. This is a measure of fresh or dry mass of plants at a particular time and in a given area. Since the vegetation has to be sampled, it is a destructive method and requires time and effort to obtain the readings of mass.
4 **Percentage cover**. This is a measure of the amount of cover of a particular species in a quadrat. It avoids the need to count individuals, which can be difficult when assessing clumps of moss or grass, for example. However, there are problems when the vegetation consists of layers which overlap, giving a possible total in excess of 100%.

Abundance scales

The five point **DAFOR scale** is a subjective assessment of abundance in which:

D = Dominant
A = Abundant
F = Frequent
O = Occasional
R = Rare

This is a good method for quickly assessing a large area of vegetation, but it may miss the rarer species and overestimate the more conspicuous species.

It is possible to convert the actual percentage cover reading to a number on a scale, to make comparisons easier. The **Domin scale** is more objective and it ranges from 1 (< 1%) to 10 (almost 100%).

Domin scale

Cover almost 100%	10
Cover 76–99%	9
Cover 51–75%	8
Cover 34–50%	7
Cover 26–33%	6
Cover 11–25%	5
Cover 5–10%	4
Cover 1–4%	3
Cover under 1%	2
Scarce, just 1 or 2 individuals	1
a single individual	+

Point quadrats

An alternative to the **frame quadrat** is the **point quadrat**. This is a free-standing frame with a row of 10 pins, the points of which can be lowered down to touch the ground. The point quadrat is randomly placed using the same methods as described above for the frame quadrat. A record is made of the plant species which are touched when each of the 10 pins is lowered. This gives a number of 'hits'. The figures are used to give an objective assessment of percentage cover.

$$\text{Percentage cover} = \text{hits}/(\text{hits} + \text{misses}) \times 100$$

For example, if the number of samples was 20 then there would be a maximum number of hits and misses of 200. If a species had 30 hits, its percentage cover would be $30/200 \times 100 = 15\%$.

The point quadrat is not without its limitations. In particular, a pin may hit the leaves of more than one species on its way to the ground, giving a total cover value in excess of 100%.

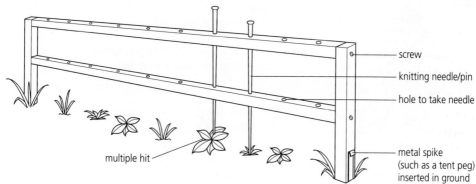

multiple hit

screw

knitting needle/pin

hole to take needle

metal spike
(such as a tent peg)
inserted in ground

Figure 9.2 Point quadrat

Transects

Transects are useful in measuring changes in vegetation across a transition, such as a valley, rock or slope. The samples are taken along the transect.

A **belt transect** is a strip across the study area, typically about 0.5 m wide. Quadrat samples are taken continuously along the line, or at regular intervals such as a metre. The length of the transect, and the number of samples, is determined by the time available for the study. It is useful to take a profile of the transect to indicate change in height along the transect.

A **line transect** is a quicker, though less quantitative, method. A tape is placed along the transect and the plant species touching the line are recorded, either along the entire length, or at regular intervals. This method can be inaccurate, as many species may not touch the line, but it gives a quick impression of the dominant species in the habitat.

Tree girths

The girth of a tree will give a guide to its biomass. This is the circumference of the tree at a height of 1.5 m from the ground. The age of the tree can also be determined from the girth. As a rough estimate, the tree's age is obtained by dividing the girth in metres by 2.

Tree heights

Tree height can be measured using a **clinometer**. This measures the angle of elevation from which the height can be calculated. The clinometer is pointed at the top of the tree. The trigger of the clinometer is then pressed to stop the disc from moving. The angle of elevation is simply read off the clinometer. Two additional measurements are required: the height of the person and his/her distance from the base of the tree. Some simple trigonometry shows that:

$$\text{height } (x) = y \times \tan A° + z$$

therefore, if $y = 50$ m, $z = 1.47$ m and the angle of elevation $A = 20°$, $\tan A° = 0.3640$

$$x = 50 \times 0.364 + 1.47 = 19.67 \text{ m}$$

and the diagram below illustrates this.

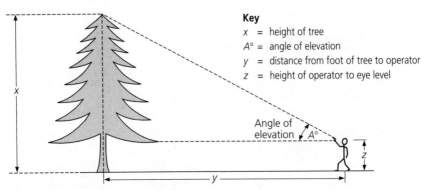

Key
x = height of tree
$A°$ = angle of elevation
y = distance from foot of tree to operator
z = height of operator to eye level

Angle of elevation $A°$

Figure 9.3 Angle of elevation method for determining the height of a tree

Measurement of animal populations

Assessment of animal populations poses far more problems than that of plant populations. Many animals are timid and extremely difficult to locate. Very few are sedentary, so methods of capture have to be employed.

Direct counting

It is sometimes possible to carry out straightforward counts of the animals present, for example, the number of geese in a flock. But surveyors have to be quick and usually they use a method of counting a small sample and multiplying up to give the full number. Sedentary animals, such as limpets and barnacles on a rocky shore, can also be individually counted but, if their numbers run into hundreds or thousands, it is clearly better to sample and extrapolate.

Mark–release–recapture

Since it is usually impossible to count every single individual in a large population, a method of marking the animals can be used. This is particularly useful for active animals, especially winged insects and those which are nocturnal. A large number of the animals are captured and marked with a non-toxic paint. They are then released back into their habitat where they mix with the rest of the population. After one or two days, a second capture exercise, identical to the first, is carried out. A record is made of the total number of animals captured and the number of animals that are marked. The population can then be estimated using the **Lincoln index**.

$$\text{Lincoln index:} \quad \frac{\text{number marked in second sample}}{\text{total caught in second sample}} = \frac{\text{number marked in whole population}}{\text{size of whole population}}$$

Example

Estimating the population size of woodlice living in a log pile. First, 100 individuals were captured, marked on their back with non-toxic white paint, and returned to the log pile. A day later, a sample of 120 animals were caught, of which 20 were marked.
Using the Lincoln index formula:

$$20/120 = 100/x$$

where x = population estimate, so simple re-arrangement shows that:

$$\text{population estimate} = 120 \times 100/20 = 600$$

This procedure can be repeated several times to get a more accurate estimate, using marks of different colours or by placing the marks on different parts of the body. It is important that the manner of marking does not affect the behaviour of the animals or make them more obvious to predators. The method of capture should not cause the animal any undue stress which might make it more vulnerable. Ideally, there should be no migration of animals into and out of the population, and sufficient time must elapse between samples to allow the marked animals to mix with the rest.

Sampling methods

There are a number of different methods of sampling animals in their habitat.

Sweep nets

Nets are ideal for capturing small invertebrates. A **sweep net** is used to sample insects from vegetation. As the net is swept through the vegetation, animals are dislodged and are caught up by the net. Most animals are collected, although insects at the top of the plants may fly away as the net approaches.

Beating tray

Animals on trees and shrubs can be sampled by hitting a branch sharply with a stick and catching the dislodged animals on a **beating tray** or sheet held immediately below the branch. The tray or sheet should be white, so that it is easy to spot the animals. The animals are then collected with a **pooter**. Suction is applied to the mouth piece of the pooter, causing the small insect to be drawn up into the specimen tube. A piece of gauze across the end of the mouth piece prevents the insect from being swallowed!

Pitfall traps

A **pitfall trap** consists of a container made from glass, plastic or metal, which is sunk into the ground with its top level with the soil surface. The trap may be covered by a small stone to keep out rain and predatory birds. Bait, such as meat, fish or fruit, is placed in the trap. Active animals, such as beetles, woodlice and spiders, fall into the trap and are unable to escape. This method cannot be used to estimate population size, but it can be used for comparative purposes. It is possible to investigate the effect of bait, temperature, humidity, habitat and seasonal variation using these traps.

Mammal traps

Small mammals, such as voles and mice, are nocturnal and they may be present in great numbers in a habitat. They can be captured using specially designed **Longworth small mammal traps** baited with grain. This trap is made of metal and consists of two parts: a tunnel with a trap door, which is tripped by a small wire, and a nest box. The nest box is filled with bedding, so that the mammals do not die of cold, and is tilted so that water drains out of the nesting area. The trap is baited and set in the evening. The position of the trap is clearly marked with a stick, so that it can be found again. It is left undisturbed overnight and opened up the following morning. If sufficient traps are put out, it is possible to determine the number of species in the habitat and their range. By marking each animal caught, and repeating trapping over several nights, it is possible to carry out population estimates. In the UK, it is illegal to trap shrews, so the pressure required to trip the wire is set above that applied by a shrew so that they cannot be caught inadvertently.

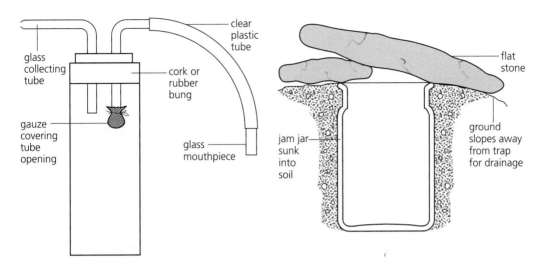

Figure 9.4 The pooter: a useful device for sucking up small insects

Figure 9.5 A pitfall trap

Figure 9.6 Longworth small mammal trap

Tullgren and Baermann funnels

The **Tullgren funnel** is designed to remove small invertebrates from samples of soil and leaf-litter. The soil sample is placed in the funnel, which is supported in an upright position, and a light bulb is placed immediately above it. The invertebrate animals move away from the heat and light given off by the light bulb and fall into the collecting container.

The **Baermann funnel** is very similar to the Tullgren funnel and is used to extract the invertebrates that are found in soil water, such as nematodes. The sample is suspended in water, and the heat and light cause the invertebrates to move from the sample and down the funnel.

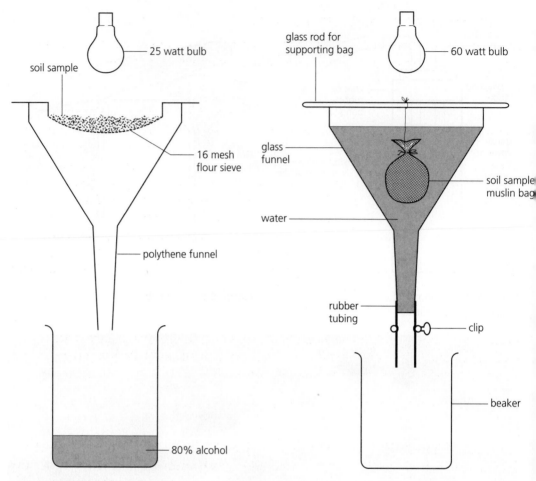

Figure 9.7 Home-made Tullgren funnel   **Figure 9.8** Baermann funnel

Sampling aquatic organisms

Aquatic animals are sampled using nets. Nets can be used to sample free-swimming invertebrates at different levels in the pond or from the marginal weeds. The animals are washed out on to collecting trays where they are identified and counted. Plankton can be collected using nets with an extremely fine mesh.

Benthic invertebrates in the still water of ponds and lakes can be sampled using a **dredge net**. This is a net with a D-shaped frame and steel supports. The net is coarse and the leading edge reinforced. It is towed over the mud at the bottom of a pond dislodging the animals.

Kick sampling

Kick sampling is used to sample benthic invertebrates in moving water. The net is held downstream of the area to be sampled. Then the area in front of the net is disturbed by three or four kicks from the collector's feet. The dislodged animals are carried into the net by the current.

Measurement of abiotic factors

Many abiotic factors can now be recorded using electronic equipment. Quite often, the data can be logged and passed directly into a computer for analysis.

Light

Light is one of the easiest abiotic factors to measure. However, its intensity can fluctuate widely, such as when clouds pass across the Sun or between day and night and even between the seasons. A single measurement is therefore meaningless, so a series of readings need to be obtained over a period of time. Modern **light meters** record the amount of light that falls upon the sensor. The readings are given in arbitrary units, although this is not a problem if the readings are used comparatively. However, if necessary, a light meter can be calibrated to obtain a reading in lux.

In a woodland habitat, it is useful to measure the amount of light penetrating through the canopy layer. This can be achieved by measuring the amount of light falling on ground outside the wood or in a glade and comparing this with the amount of light that reaches the ground under the canopy.

Temperature

Electronic thermometers are most useful in recording temperature, since older mercury thermometers can be difficult to read and break easily. Probes can be attached to monitor soil and water temperatures.

Water factors

pH

A battery operated **pH meter** can give a quick and accurate estimate of water pH. The more expensive models have an electrode which needs to be calibrated prior to use in the field. Alternatively, an estimate of pH can be obtained using universal indicator paper.

Oxygen content

The amount of oxygen in the water is expressed either as $mg\,l^{-1}$ or as a percentage of air saturation. The amount of oxygen dissolved in water varies with temperature; oxygen solubility decreases as temperature rises. Electronic **oxygen meters** give an estimate of dissolved oxygen in the water. The sensor has a thin plastic membrane covering the cathode and its porosity varies with temperature. The meter needs to be calibrated, just prior to use, at the same temperature as the water sample. The easiest way is to take a 100% reading using a saturated water sample, which can be easily produced by shaking a sample of water in a half-filled container for 30 seconds.

Biochemical oxygen demand (BOD)

Oxygen depletion can occur in water contaminated with organic matter, such as sewage and slurry. During the decomposition of the organic matter, the bacteria respire and use up the oxygen. This causes oxygen depletion, which adversely affects other organisms.

The amount of organic matter in the water can be estimated by measuring the **Biochemical Oxygen Demand (BOD)**. The test estimates the amount of oxygen used up by the bacteria and other microorganisms in a sample of water. First, the oxygen content of the sample is measured. The sample is sealed and kept in the dark at 20 °C for 5 days and the oxygen content measured again. The difference between the two measurements is the BOD in milligrams per dm^3 of water. The larger the difference, the greater the number of microorganisms in the water.

An alternative method is the **methylene blue test**. A sample of water is poured slowly into a 250 cm^3 flask and 1 cm^3 of 0.1% methylene blue is added. More water is added to fill the flask completely and then it is sealed. The methylene blue is mixed in by gently inverting the flask. The flask is incubated at 20 °C and the time taken for the water to turn clear is noted. This is useful for comparing the bacterial content of different water samples taken from different sites or at different times.

Use of indicator species

The presence of certain animal species in water can indicate whether the water is polluted or clean. In freshwater, the presence of caddis fly and stone fly larvae, freshwater shrimp, freshwater mussels and limpets is an indication that the water is unpolluted and has a high percentage of dissolved oxygen. Water polluted by organic discharge will be populated by species more tolerant to low oxygen levels, such as blood worms, sludge worms and rat-tailed maggots.

Nitrate and phosphate content

Nitrates and phosphates are essential for plant growth and the amount dissolved in water will affect primary productivity. A sudden increase in nitrate and phosphate levels, caused perhaps by sewage or slurry pollution, can cause **eutrophication**, create a high BOD and lead to loss of aquatic diversity. The levels of nitrate and phosphate in the water can be estimated using **water test kits**. These use a method based on adding chemicals to a sample of water and matching the colour change to a chart.

Water current

The speed at which water moving in a stream or river can be measured using a **flow meter.** This device uses a propeller and revolution counter directly to measure the velocity of the water in metres per second. The operator stands downstream of the flow meter and immerses it vertically into the water. The moving water causes the propellers to turn and the rate of flow is indicated on a calibrated gauge, similar to a speedometer. The flow meter can be immersed to different depths to monitor the current at each level.

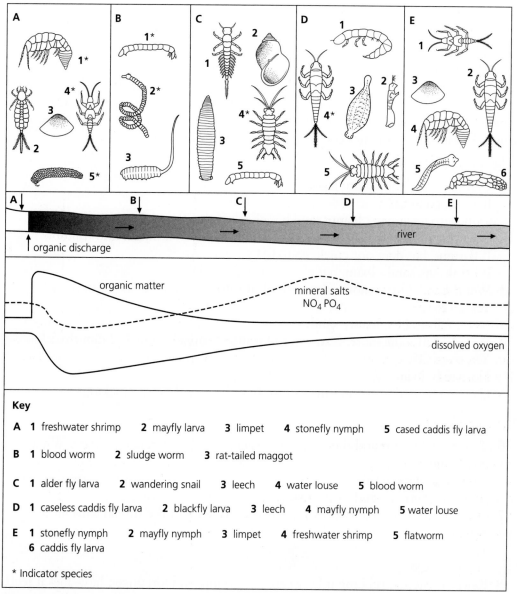

Figure 9.9 Indicator species

Edaphic factors

Soil auger

Soil augers are used to remove small soil samples from specific depths without having to disturb the soil by digging a hole. There are two types of auger. The **cylinder auger** resembles a large apple corer. It has a sharp lower edge and is used to obtain shallow samples. The **corkscrew auger** is used to obtain deep samples. Both types of auger are driven into the soil with a twisting action. Once the auger has reached the desired depth, it is pulled out and the soil sample removed, from either the core or the thread.

Soil texture

The texture of soil is affected by the amount of sand, silt and clay it contains. Soil texture can be quickly assessed by feel. A sample of soil is held in the hand and wetted until it glistens. Soils which feel rough, rasping or gritty contain a high proportion of sand, whereas silty soils feel smooth, soft and silky, and soils which feel fine and sticky contain clay. A mostly sandy soil cannot be formed into a shape, whereas a moist clay soil is easily rolled into thin sausages which can be bent into rings. A loam will form sausages, but these will split when bent.

The dirty hands test

1　Can you roll the soil into a good ball?
　　If easily, go to Q2.
　　Only with great care, **loamy** sand but check with Q2 and 3.
2　What happens when you squeeze the ball between your finger and thumb?
　　It flattens, but does not crack, go to Q3.
　　It breaks up, **sandy loam**, but check with Q3 and 4.
3　Wet the soil a little more. Can you roll it into a sausage about 5 mm thick?
　　Yes, go to Q4.
　　No, it falls to bits, **loamy sand**.
4　Wet the soil some more. Can you roll it into a thread about 1–2 mm thick?
　　Yes, go to Q5.
　　No, **sandy loam**.
5　Can you bend the thread into a horseshoe shape without it cracking?
　　Yes, go to Q7.
　　No, go to Q6.
6　Wet the soil again and then rub it between your thumb and forefinger. What does it feel like?
　　Smooth and pasty, **silty loam**.
　　Rough and gritty, **sandy silty loam**.
7　Can you make a small ring by joining the two ends of the thread without it cracking?
　　Yes, go to Q9.
　　No, go to Q8.
8　Rewetting it and rubbing it between your thumb and forefinger, how does it feel?
　　Very gritty, **sandy clay loam**.
　　Fairly rough, **clay loam**.
　　Heavy and doughy, **silty clay loam**.
9　Roll it again, but do not wet it again and then try and polish the surface with your thumb.
　　Yes – it will take a high polish fairly smoothly, go to Q10.
　　Yes – it will take a polish but there are particles visible, **sandy clay.**
　　No, go back to Q8.
10　Wet the soil again and try to stick your fingers together.
　　It sticks them together very strongly, **clay**.
　　They stick but not very firmly, **silty clay**.

Soil pH

Soil pH can be measured simply by using a pH meter which gives the reading
dial. More accurate measurements can be made using universal indicator solution. A
small soil sample is placed in a small tube into which a small volume of barium
sulphate is added. This flocculates the clay, making it easier to monitor the colour
changes. The tube is topped up with distilled water and shaken well. A few drops of
indicator solution are added and the tube is placed against a white piece of paper so
that the colour can be compared with a chart.

Water content

The water content of soil is determined by measuring the mass of fresh soil and
comparing it with that of the soil when completely dry. First, a crucible is weighed
and a known volume of soil placed inside it. The mass of the crucible and soil sample
is obtained. The crucible and sample are then placed in an oven at 110 °C
overnight. This temperature drives off the water, but does not burn off the organic
matter. The crucible and soil are reweighed and the difference in mass calculated.
The percentage of water in the soil is calculated by:

$$\text{water percentage} = \text{weight loss/weight of fresh soil} \times 100$$

Species diversity

Species diversity is a measure of the number of different species present, rather than
the abundance of each species.

Simple diversity index

The easiest method is to collect a sample of approximately 200 specimens and
examine each in turn. The specimen does not have to be identified, just given a
letter or number. When you examine each one you score it as to whether it is the
same or a different species to the previous specimen. The index of diversity is
calculated by dividing the number of differences by the number of organisms.

Worked example
Five different species were found – A, B, C, D, E in the following order:

A B B C .C D E E E E E A A A C C D E D E A A A C C D D D E E
+ + + + + + + + + + + + + +

The + indicates that the species was different to the previous specimen.

$$\text{Diversity index} = 15/30 = 0.5$$

Simpson's diversity index

The Simpson's diversity index is commonly used to assess plant diversity. All the plants within the sample area are identified and counted. The diversity is calculated as follows:

$$D = \frac{N(N - 1)}{\Sigma n(n - 1)}$$

(where D = diversity index; N = total number of plants; n = number of individuals per species; Σ = sum of).

Recording and presentation of data

Once the data have been collected, they have to be recorded and presented in suitable form in a practical report.

Tables

The easiest way to present data is often to produce a table. This consists of columns which display the numerical values of the variables. Each column is headed with the physical quantity and units, these being separated by a solidus, for example 'Time/min' rather than 'Time (minutes)'. When there is more than one column in a table, the first column should be used for the **independent variable** and subsequent columns for the **dependent variables**.

Graphs

There are a number of different graphs which can be produced, but it is important to use an appropriate type for the data being presented.

Line graphs

Line graphs are a quick and easy way of showing the relationship between two variables, such as light level against time. When plotting the data, the dependent variable should be plotted on the vertical or y axis and the independent variable on the horizontal or x axis. Time is normally plotted on the x axis. The graph should be given an informative title and both axes must be clearly labelled with title and units. The scale gives an immediate visual impression. It should not be too cramped, ideally occupying at least half of the graph paper used. The scale should be easy to use and interpret. The points of the graph are normally joined with a straight line. This is because you do not know how the values vary between the recorded points. If there is more than one line, then each should be labelled to show what each one represents.

Bar charts

Bar charts are used when one or more of the variables is not numerical. For example, with different types of insect, types of vegetable, or blood groups. The bars are of equal width and they do not touch. When the bars are vertical, the chart is sometimes called a **column chart**. Bar or column charts can be used to plot frequency distribution with discrete data, such as the number of eggs found in the nest of a blackbird.

A **histogram** is a special form of bar chart, and is used to plot frequency distribution with continuous data. It would be used, for example, to show the variability of wing length in a fruit fly. The bars are drawn in ascending or descending order and they should touch.

Pie charts

Pie charts are circular graphs and do not have x and y axes. They are used to plot proportional data, such as the proportion of different insects found in leaf-litter. The circle represents the whole and is divided into sectors, each of which is proportional to the size of the sample. The sample values are converted to percentage figures and the size of the sector is determined by calculating the angle which will correspond to the percentage. For example, a percentage value of 25% would be represented by a sector with an angle of 90 degrees. The chart is normally drawn with the sectors in rank order, starting at the 12 o'clock position and moving in a clockwise direction. The different sectors can be shaded or coloured and should be labelled. Comparisons between two pie charts can be made if the area of the circle is proportional to the size of the sample.

Transparency overlays

Overlays are useful to show changes in data over a common set of data. For example, the profile of a shoreline can be drawn on the base graph and then a series of transparent overlays could be used to show the different species and their distribution on the shore.

Pyramid of numbers and biomass

Pyramids are used to show data from successive **trophic levels** (producers, primary consumers, and so on). To produce a **pyramid of numbers**, all the organisms found in a specific area (for example, within a 0.5 m quadrat) are sorted into their trophic level and the total numbers in each level recorded. The numbers present in each trophic level are represented on the graph paper by a horizontal bar. The bar for producers is at the bottom, with the bar for primary consumers on top of that, and so on. The bars are of the same depth, and the length is proportional to the sample size. The bars are normally aligned so that the final pyramid is symmetrical. In a **pyramid of biomass**, the organisms found in each trophic level are weighed and expressed on the graph paper as g/m^2.

Statistical analysis

It is often difficult to see relationships between sets of data without carrying out further analysis. When designing a practical investigation it is important to consider if the data are to be analysed statistically and, if so, what type of technique is to be used. This determines the type and manner in which the data are collected.

Null hypothesis

In order to use a statistical method to test for an effect, it is necessary to make a hypothesis. This is just an idea and the aim of the investigation is to produce evidence that will prove or disprove the hypothesis. Often it is difficult actually to prove a hypothesis, but it is much easier to find evidence that will disprove it. Therefore, it is usual to make a **negative, or null, hypothesis**. For example, there is no difference in the number of oak trees found in two different woods. If, once the data are analysed, the null hypothesis is no longer acceptable, then there must be a difference. The null hypothesis has to be rejected.

Chi-squared

Chi-squared is a statistic which is used to test an association between two sets of measurements collected in different places (frequency data). The data must be grouped into classes, for example colour, size, sex, and the total number of observations must exceed 20.

Chi-squared (χ^2) is a significance test. It tells us whether a relationship is significant or not, and it is based on probability or chance. In order for the relationship to be significant the chances of the results being due to chance must be low. The acceptable level is 5% significance. This means that the results being due to chance occurs only 5 times in every 100. It is also possible to use higher significance levels, such as 1% or 0.1%.

The null hypothesis states that there is no relationship and that differences are due to chance. The data are tabulated in the following manner:

Groups	Observed frequency (O)	Expected frequency (E)	$(O - E)^2/E$

$$\chi^2 = \frac{\Sigma(O - E)^2}{E} \quad (\text{where } \Sigma = \text{sum of})$$

The value of E is calculated by dividing the total number of observations by the number of groups. The **degrees of freedom** are calculated by subtracting 1 from the number of groups, that is $n-1$. A significance level is selected and the χ^2 value is read from a table using the degrees of freedom. The null hypothesis can be rejected if the calculated χ^2 is greater than the critical value.

Worked example
Counts were made of the number of flat periwinkles *Littorina littoralis*, present on four species of seaweed in an area of 20 m² of rocky shore. One hundred periwinkles were sampled.

The null hypothesis states that there is no difference in the numbers of periwinkles on the different seaweeds, their distribution is random.

Groups	Observed frequency (O)	Expected frequency (E)	$(O - E)^2/E$
Spiral wrack	5	25	400/25* = 16
Bladder wrack	40	25	225/25 = 9
Egg wrack	45	25	400/25 = 16
Serrated wrack	10	25	225/25* = 9

*Ignore the negative sign

If the periwinkles were randomly distributed we would expect to find 25 periwinkles on each of the seaweeds.

$$\chi^2 = \Sigma(O - E)^2/E \quad \text{(where } \Sigma = \text{sum of)}$$
$$= 50$$

Degrees of freedom $(n-1) = 3$

From the table the critical value of χ^2 at the 5% level is 7.82. The calculated value of 50 exceeds this value, so the null hypothesis can be rejected. The periwinkles are not randomly distributed. Instead they show a preference for a certain seaweed over another.

The *t*-test

A *t*-test is carried out to measure the degree of overlap between two sets of data by comparing the two **means**. The data must be normally distributed around the means for this test to be valid.

When there is a large difference between the means of the two samples and the data are clustered tightly around these means, the value of t will be large. If the difference between the two means is small and the data are widely spread, the value of t will be small. So, the larger the value of t, the more certain we are that the two sets of data are different. The value of t is compared against a table of critical values, usually at the 5% significance level. This means that there is 1 in 20 chance of obtaining a value of t equal to the critical value purely owing to random variation. If the value of t is greater than the critical value, then there is a significant difference between the two sets of data.

Worked example
It was noticed that ivy leaves growing in a brightly lit position were narrower than those growing in a shady position. Twenty-three leaves from each plant were sampled and measured across their widest point.

The null hypothesis states that there is no difference in the width of leaves from the two plants.

n (number)	x_1	x_1^2	x_2	x_2^2
1	4.6	21.16	4.5	20.25
2	5.0	25.0	3.1	9.61
3	4.5	20.25	4.1	16.81
4	4.5	19.36	3.1	9.61
5	4.5	20.25	3.1	9.61
6	4.7	22.09	3.3	10.89
7	4.8	23.04	3.5	12.25
8	6.4	40.96	3.5	12.25
9	4.4	19.36	3.8	14.44
10	4.3	18.49	3.0	9.00
11	5.1	26.01	3.6	12.96
12	3.8	14.44	3.8	14.44
13	3.6	12.96	4.5	20.25
14	5.5	30.25	2.8	7.84
15	5.3	28.09	4.2	17.64
16	4.7	22.09	3.9	15.21
17	4.7	22.09	3.4	11.56
18	5.7	32.49	3.6	12.96
19	4.1	16.81	3.6	12.96
20	6.5	42.25	3.7	13.69
21	5.4	29.16	4.1	16.81
22	5.4	29.16	4.4	19.36
23	4.0	16.00	2.8	7.84
Total for each column	Σx_1 111.4	Σx_1^2 551.76	Σx_2 83.4	Σx_2^2 308.24
Calculate mean by dividing by n, where n = 23	$\Sigma x_1/n = \bar{x}_1$ 4.84	$\Sigma x_1^2/n$ 23.99	$\Sigma x_2/n = \bar{x}_2$ 3.63	$\Sigma x_2^2/n$ 13.40
Mean squared	$\bar{x}_1^2$ 23.43	–	$\bar{x}_2^2$ 13.18	–
Calculate the variance $\Sigma x^2/n - \bar{x}^2$	23.99–23.43		13.40–13.18	
	$s_1^2 = 0.56$		$s_2^2 = 0.22$	

To calculate the value of t

$$t = \frac{(\bar{x}_1 - \bar{x}_2)}{\sqrt{\frac{s_1^2}{n_1} + \frac{s_2^2}{n_2}}} = \frac{4.84 - 3.63}{\sqrt{\frac{0.56}{23} + \frac{0.22}{23}}}$$

$$= 6.57 \text{ (highly significant at 0.1\%)}$$

Mann–Whitney U test

This test is used when the data are not normally distributed and the mean is not an appropriate value to use. Instead the **median** (the middle value in the range) value is used. The **Mann–Whitney U test** is a method of comparing the median of two sets of data.

All the data from both samples are arranged in numerical order and ranked, the lowest value with the lowest rank and the highest value the highest rank. Identical values are given the same rank. The next stage is to sum the ranks for each set of data and insert the values into the statistical formula. The smallest U values are obtained when there is no overlap between the two sets of data.

Worked example
A student investigated the number of mayfly nymphs in two different habitats, a shallow pool and a deep pool in the same river. He kick sampled for 1 minute at six randomly selected sites and obtained the results below.

Sample	1	2	3	4	5	6	Median
Shallow	10	9	15	16	21	9	12.5
Deep	2	3	5	12	6	8	5.5

Stage 1: arrange the data in order and then in rank order. The lowest value is given the lowest rank, the highest value the highest rank.

No. in shallow pool						9	9	10		15	16	21
Rank						6.5	6.5	8		10	11	12
No. in deep pool	2	3	5	6	8				12			
Rank	1	2	3	4	5				9			

Stage 2: sum the ranks for each set of data.

$$\Sigma R_1 = 6.5 + 6.5 + 8 + 10 + 11 + 12 = 54$$
$$\Sigma R_2 = 1 + 2 + 3 + 4 + 5 + 9 = 24$$

Stage 3: calculate U_1 and U_2 values using the following formula:

$$U_1 = n_1 \times n_2 + \tfrac{1}{2}n_2(n_2 + 1) - \Sigma R_2$$
$$= 36 + 3 \times 7 - 24 = 33$$
$$U_2 = n_1 \times n_2 + \tfrac{1}{2}n_1(n_1 + 1) - \Sigma R_1$$
$$= 36 + 3 \times 7 - 54 = 3$$

where n_1 and n_2 are the number of samples.

Using the smaller of the two values, in this case U_2 of 3, look up the value in the tables of U statistics. The critical value at 5% is 5. Since the smallest U value is less than that in the table, the difference between the two samples of mayflies was significant at the 5% level.

Suggestions for further reading

1 Ecological projects by Phil Bradfield, *Biological Sciences Review* Vol. 8, No. 5, May 1996.
2 On the rocks by John Crothers, *Biological Sciences Review* Vol. 2, No. 5, May 1990.
3 Investigating woodlands by Gordon Blower, *Biological Sciences Review* Vol. 4, No. 5, May 1992.
4 Ecological Sampling by Gareth Williams, *Biological Sciences Review* Vol. 6, No. 3, January 1994.
5 Biological statistics (part 1) by Wilbert Garvin, *Biological Sciences Review* Vol. 7, No. 4, March 1995.
6 Biological statistics (part 2) by Wilbert Garvin, *Biological Sciences Review* Vol. 9, No. 3, January 1997.
7 Biological statistics (part 3) by Wilbert Garvin, *Biological Sciences Review* Vol. 9, No. 4, March 1997.
8 *Advanced Biology: Principles and Applications Study Guide* by C.J. Clegg with D.G. Mackean, P.H. Openshaw and R.C. Reynolds (1996), John Murray (Publishers) Ltd.
9 *Urban Ecology* by M. Collins (1984), Cambridge University Press.
10 *Techniques and Fieldwork in Ecology* by Gareth Williams (1987), Bell and Hyman.

Examination questions

1 In an investigation to measure the size of a grasshopper population in a field, 30 grasshoppers were captured and marked with a small dot of paint before being released. The next day, 24 grasshoppers were captured using the same technique and of these, 6 were found to be marked with the paint dot.
   a Suggest a suitable technique for capturing grasshoppers. (1)
   b Estimate the size of the grasshopper population in the field. Show your working. (2)
   c Give **three** assumptions which must be made when estimating population size using the capture and recapture method. (3)   (total = 6)
   NEAB, June 1995

2 a Some students wished to compare the distribution of sea bindweed, *Calystegia soldanella*, in two different locations on a sand dune system. Describe how they could carry out such a study. (4)
   b Describe how you could measure accurately **two** abiotic factors which could be influencing the distribution. (6)

C

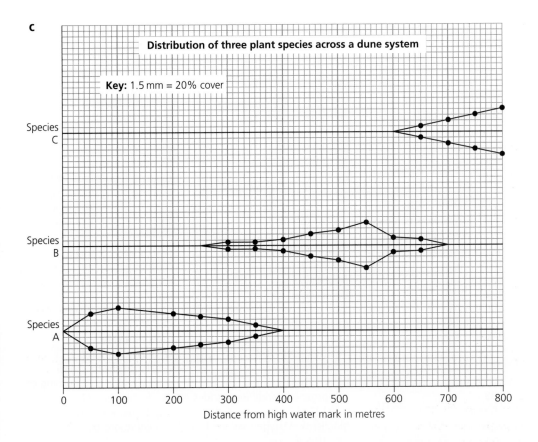

i) A kite diagram of the distribution of three plants across the dune system from a point just above high water mark to a point inland is shown above. Briefly explain how these data would have been obtained. (3)

ii) What feature of plant and animal communities is demonstrated by this diagram? (1)

iii) What is the name given to the stable community of organisms which results at the end of this process? (1)

(total = 15)

UODLE, June 1995

Index

temperate grasslands 4
temperature 43–5
  and biodiversity 45
  frost damage 44
  frost drought 44
  measurement of 193
  summer cold 44–5
  winter warmth 44
tendrils 106
territoriality 82
territory 82
t-test 201–2
thermal pollution 159–60
three Rs of conservation
    179–81
  recycle 180–1
  reduce 179
  re-use 180
thylakoid 46–7
Tilia cordata 44
tolerance hypothesis of
    succession 101
top predators 3
toxaphene 143
transects 188
transparency overlays 199
transpiration 35
treeline, northward migration
    of 134
trees 97
  deep-rooted 99
  defoliation by acid rain 128
  girths 188
  heights 188
  wetland 99
  woodland 100
  see also forests; tropical rain
  forests
trickling filter system 150
trophic levels 14
tropical rain forests 4, 95,
    104–7

felling of 115
payment to preserve
    biodiversity 169
preservation areas 169
preservation of lightly logged
    land 169
sustainable management
    168–9
Tullgren funnel 191, 192
tundra 4
turgor 63
  see also osmosis

universal indicator paper 193
uranium 153
urease 27

vehicle exhaust emissions 137,
    138
  see also carbon dioxide
    emissions

water 38–43
  adaptations for conservation
    42–3
  availability, and distribution of
    terrestrial organisms 42
  conservation 42–3
  current 194
  dipolarity 38–9
  effect of interception 42
  heat capacity 40–1
  ice 39
  latent heat of vaporisation
    41
  liquid 39

mass flow 59
maximum density 40
movements 65–6
pollution 146
solvent properties 41
splitting of 46
structure 39
  see also osmosis
water content of soil 197
water cycle *see* hydrologic cycle
water potential 62
  equation 63–4
water table 35
water test kits 194
water vapour 133
weeds 99, 123
wetlands
  drying up of 119–20
  preservation of 120
  trees 99
wilting 63
wind 54
  carriage of pesticides by 145
winter temperatures, effect of
    global warming 134–5
wood fuel 166
woodland trees 100
woodlouse 10

xeroseres 95

yield 186

zinc pollution 140–1
zonation 99
zooxanthellae 111